ANTHONY B. DAWSON is a member of the Department of English at the University of British Columbia.

The precise relation between the spectator and the work of art was a matter of great interest to late Renaissance and baroque artists, playwrights as well as painters. In Shakespeare's plays the relation between audience and stage life is crucial. The plays constantly remind the audience of the complex fictiveness of their experience yet they also project a reality specifically through illusion. *Indirections* is a study of twelve plays in which Shakespeare sets up situations and relationships between the characters analogous to the relationship established between audience and play.

This book examines the varied uses of illusion, deceit, disguise, and manipulation in the plays, both comedies and tragedies, and traces Shakespeare's use of illusion through his career – from the buoyant optimism of the great comedies and the ambiguity of the middle years to the new richness and power in the romances.

Dawson suggests that the way characters respond to illusory situations sets up a model for the way audiences are meant to respond to the plays themselves. Such action at least initially establishes a basis for the movement of characters from self-delusion to self-knowledge. This process of self-realization enables the characters to distinguish truth from appearance, love from infatuation; and significantly, it is a direct result of involvement with illusion and role-playing. It is as if the characters must arrive, within the movement of the plot, at an understanding of, and response to, the nature of drama itself parallel to the audience's experience of the play as a whole. This subtle interplay between audience and characters, where each in a sense represents the other, depends for its life on the physical and psychic distances created by the theatre.

ANTHONY B. DAWSON

INDIRECTIONS:
Shakespeare and
the Art of Illusion

UNIVERSITY OF TORONTO PRESS
Toronto Buffalo London

© University of Toronto Press 1978
Toronto   Buffalo   London
Printed in Canada

Library of Congress Cataloging in Publication Data

Dawson, Anthony B

Indirections : Shakespeare and the art of illusion.

Includes bibliographical references and index.
1. Shakespeare, William, 1564-1616 – Criticism and
interpretation.   2. Disguise in literature.   I. Title
PR3069.D57D3   822.3'3   78-6016
ISBN 0-8020-5413-7 (Can)

In memory of my father

Your bait of falsehood takes this carp of truth;
And thus do we of wisdom and of reach,
With windlasses and with assays of bias,
By indirections find directions out.

(*Hamlet* II.i.63-6)

Preface

I have called this book *Indirections* for two reasons. The first is that it deals with disguise, trickery, manipulation, and related forms of illusion, and the second is that each chapter represents an 'assay of bias,' an attempt to round upon the central theme from a particular standpoint. I am interested in pursuing and defining a theory which will illuminate Shakespeare's use of illusion and I find that the most effective way of doing so is to examine particular plays on their own terms, though within the context of the function of illusion. The construction of the theory is thus both cumulative and indirect. Each play, each chapter, provides a slightly different perspective and helps complete the theoretical picture.

For reasons explained in the introduction, my focus is on comedy, but not exclusively. Many of the devices and processes I explore are central to tragedy as well, and to most drama, and my book reflects this in the sections on the three tragedies and *Troilus and Cressida*. It is clear that other tragedies (such as *Othello* and *Coriolanus*) could also have been included, but, for reasons of economy, I have chosen to concentrate on three or four, each of which provides a different and interesting angle.

Anyone who writes about Shakespeare is indebted to the many who have done so before him. To single out a few of these may be difficult, but I owe a special debt to Northrop Frye's *A Natural Perspective*, C.L. Barber's *Shakespeare's Festive Comedy*, and, to a lesser extent, Anne Righter's *Shakespeare and the Idea of the Play*. In addition, I would like to acknowledge my deep indebtedness to Professors G.B. Evans of Harvard, and Daniel Seltzer, now of Princeton, and to extend my thanks to other colleagues and friends who have read all or parts of the manuscript, in particular Richard Strier, Peter Pitzele, and Kay Stockholder. Lastly, I would like to thank my students at the University of British Columbia, many of whom have patiently acted as sounding boards, allowing me to exercise my ideas and thereby make them, I hope, more resilient and flexible. Thanks also to Jean Wilson, who edited the manuscript, and to Rosemary Leach, who typed it.

Unless otherwise noted, the text I have used throughout is that of G.L. Kittredge. The section on *King Lear* which forms the first part of Chapter 7 originally appeared in a slightly different form in *Wascana Review* IX 1 (Spring 1974).

This book has been published with the assistance of a grant from the Humanities Research Council of Canada, using funds provided by the Canada Council, and a grant from the Andrew W. Mellon Foundation to the University of Toronto Press.

AD

Contents

Introduction

What happens to the reader of *Don Quixote* when, reading quietly through Part
II of that work, he comes upon a reference to Part I as one of the books the hero
reads and refers to? The reader will necessarily be drawn up short. He will be
amused, certainly, and puzzled, as the book suddenly curls away from him and
back upon itself. His feeling may be similar to that of the viewer who stands long
enough in front of Velasquez's *Las Meninas* to realize that he himself and his reaction to the picture is in some oblique sense the subject of the picture. We view-
ers stand in the exact position of the models for another picture that is being
painted within the picture. Standing to the left of the picture before us, and
looking right into our eyes (and into the eyes of the models for the picture he is
painting), is an artist. The artist is Velasquez himself and in front of him there is
a huge canvas, its back to us, while beside him, in the right foreground, the deni-
zens of the court are arranged carefully around the Infanta Maria. At the far end
of the room there is a mirror, in which is reflected the king and queen, who are
sitting for their portraits and whose position we occupy. The reflection is like a
passage in which our entry into the picture is ironically challenged (*we* should be
reflected) and at the same time subtly identified with that of the noble subjects
of the other, unseen, picture. The viewer is asked to be both subject and artist at
the same time, to enter into the intricacies of the relations in the painting to the
degree that only the artist knows them, and yet to be part of those relations by
occupying the place of the couple being painted within the painting.[1] Our experience and awareness of these complex relations is in large part the subject of the
painting. The reader of *Don Quixote* is involved in a similar experience: he is
suddenly made an accomplice of the author - we can almost see Cervantes wink-
ing at us - while at the same time he must enter into the fiction that, within the
fiction, the fictional Part I actually exists (as, of course, it does exist in 'reality'),
independent of the fictional man who is its hero.

The knottiness of the reflexivity of such works may, in Viola's words, be 'too much for me t'untie,' but the issue it raises should be clear enough. The precise relation between spectator and work of art was a matter of great interest to late Renaissance and baroque artists, in part because the value of the work resided primarily in that relation. Shakespeare, because he is working in the drama, proceeds somewhat differently from novelist or painter, though analogously. For him, too, the relation between audience and stage life is crucial; for him, too, the audience's awareness of the complex fictiveness of their experience is fundamental; but he has the additional advantage of being able to enact, or have his actors enact within the play, the very processes which the play itself sets out to encourage in its audience.

This book examines a number of Shakespeare's plays from the point of view of their reflexivity, that is, their use of self-conscious techniques which radically affect the relation of the audience to the play. It is primarily, then, a study of the varied uses of illusion, deceit, disguise, and manipulation. Since such tricks are generally associated with comedy, the focus is on the comedies, but it is part of my argument that Shakespeare often used such 'comic' devices in tragedy as well, and for similar purposes. I am interested both in characters and in audiences as they become involved in, or respond to, various acts of illusion. Generally, I shall argue, the way characters respond to illusory situations within the reality constructed by the play is a model for the way audiences are meant to respond to the plays themselves. Some characters, the disguisers and manipulators, spend a good deal of time creating scenes for themselves and others to play. Such action, which is remarkably common in Shakespeare's plays, at least initially establishes a basis for the movement of characters from self-delusion to self-knowledge. This learning process leads to a sense of realized identity, enabling the character to distinguish, for example, appearance from truth, infatuation from love; and, more important, it is a direct result of involvement with illusion and role-playing. It is as if the characters must arrive, within the movement of the plot, at an understanding of, and response to, the nature of drama itself. For drama, like the illusions which the characters in these plays face, makes reality intelligible by presenting it to us as an illusion and thereby allowing us to take an ironic, detached attitude towards it. As Shakespeare creates it, the subtle interplay between audience and characters, where each in a sense represents the other, depends for its life on the physical and psychic distances created by the theatre. I am, then, interested in plays as *performed*, though not in particular performances.

The reflexive quality of these plays is their most characteristic feature. For two reasons, disguise is the device most fitted to this effect: first, it is self-consciously artificial – the audience must make a double effort in order to sus-

pend disbelief; second, it involves the actors in games with each other that re-
flect back on the play and the audience's relationship to it. Disguise, not surprisingly, can take many forms. But the usual structure arising out of disguise, and
the reflexivity that often accompanies it, has always been typical more of comedy than of tragedy. This book originally was focussed on a particular function
of disguise – when it is used to manipulate and control comic action and attitude. *As You Like It* provides the paradigm for this type of disguise, where the
illusion is used to draw the characters into a 'pageant' which turns out to be illu-
minative for them, for the manipulative heroine, and for the audience. A similar
process, though somewhat less developed, is at the basis of the comic action of
The Merchant of Venice, while *A Midsummer Night's Dream* and *Twelfth Night*
provide slightly different, but analogous movements.

There is a certain optimism about comic processes implicit in these earlier
plays, a sense of possibility, a naïve faith in the harmlessness of deceit and in the
general validity of theatrical processes both within plays and within theatres. At
a certain point in his career, Shakespeare came to question this faith with a good
deal of bitterness. Perhaps the experience of deceit that he records in the sonnets
had something to do with this change; it certainly led him to probe and mock his
profession and his public self within the context of the sonnets themselves. A
pervasive despair about the *value* of the mask seems to have overcome him. *Hamlet* is a crucial play in this regard. In *Hamlet*, for the first time, the use of disguise becomes primarily negative, both in terms of its consequences, and in
terms of the ambivalence towards deceit and manipulation created by the context in which Hamlet plays out his role.

My analysis of *Hamlet* in Chapter 3 broadens the scope of the study by looking at the political implications of the ideas raised by comic processes. I am thus
interested in *Hamlet* as a cultural product and commentary, and in the hero's
problem both as a struggle for personal identity and a paradigm for such a struggle within a changing culture. The uses of illusion in this are multiple, but instead of turning back on the play's action in a comic way, they tend to assault
the audience by reinforcing the duplicity which surrounds what is being presented on the stage. Hamlet finds that the techniques of comedy are inadequate
to the task of righting his world (though they are perfectly adequate in plays
such as *The Merchant of Venice* and *As You Like It*). Since Shakespeare, as well
as Hamlet, had valued theatrical techniques as a way of confronting and moving
the world, the failure here suggests that the whole dramatic enterprise had
soured for him. This may have resulted, in Shakespeare's own life, in the despair
about his professional identity mentioned above; there is some indication of this
despair in the sonnets. Also, the anger and bitterness which characterize *Troilus
and Cressida*, probably his next play, plus the élitist appeal suggested by its pre-

face and implicit in the highly abstract and intellectual language and theme, all imply a disaffection with his 'public means.' This play, like *Hamlet*, expresses a profound distrust of illusion (everything in the play is split in two), which twists the audience's acceptance into resistance, just as Troilus's belief in an illusion leads him, not to understanding, but into a logical impossibility.

In the so-called 'problem comedies,' *All's Well that Ends Well* and *Measure for Measure*, there is again ambivalence towards the comic processes which Shakespeare had developed earlier, but it takes a different shape. Unlike *Hamlet* or *Troilus and Cressida*, there is an assertion of traditional comic form, but the problem is that the form collides with the subject matter. We have a sense that the main characters in these plays do not learn enough, that they leave the stage without coming to terms with themselves, their evil, or the evil around them. Shakespeare thus seems to be testing the value and limits of the comic shape as he had earlier devised it; and he evidently finds that such a form cannot comprehend the evil and divisiveness which he so effectively portrays in these plays. What happens to the audience's involvement as a result is that we are split; we are asked for an acceptance which the play cannot ease us into providing.

In the tragedies, Shakespeare finds different ways of connecting the psychological action on stage and that within the audience, ways which depend on a revived sense of the value of being involved in illusion or show. By a species of paradox similar to, but not the same as, that operating in the high comedies, an increased emphasis on the unreality of the play's action results in a deeper penetration of reality as we know it. Our awareness of the fictive is heightened, and its power thereby increased. This issue leads directly to the main theme of the romances, *The Winter's Tale* and *The Tempest*, both of which explore the power of art in its relation to nature, especially theatrical art and its effect on the psychological nature of man. For these latter plays, Shakespeare devises a form which has much in common with that of the earlier comedies, and reinstates, especially in *The Tempest,* many of the old techniques. As a form, however, the romance is both more inclusive than the earlier comedies, and more specifically reflexive, more consciously artificial.

The Tempest thus solves some of the problems posed by *Hamlet*. For one thing, the value of illusion and, by extension, of theatrical art, is once again manifest. For another, since Shakespeare shifts the focus from an actual political to a purely imaginative place, an enchanted island, Prospero, the playwright's stand-in, can effect transformations unavailable to the struggling young prince. The two men face similar problems and adopt similar means to deal with them, but where Hamlet can find no solution, Prospero is able to transform his world. His success is limited to the three hours on the island, however, just as the playwright's success is limited to the three hours in the theatre; both must abjure their magic when the time is up. But *The Tempest* leads both its characters and its audience back into a public world where the island's illuminations may still, it is hoped, push back a few shadows, and if the play has any enduring value at all, this is surely where it resides.

Frank Kermode relates the whole fictional enterprise to the task of making sense of life. We construct fictions so that we may order our lives, and confer significance on the interval that we occupy.[2] The very fictions that Shakespeare creates, and the consciousness of them as fictive that he encourages in both characters and audience, convince us of the sense of value that he saw in the effort (though, as noted above, he cast a cold eye on that sense of value somewhere in the middle of his writing life). The idea that fiction confers significance is, I think, the best justification for seeking to understand the processes studied in this book. We persist, and rightly, in trying to clarify meanings, in rounding out the fictions to which we give our ironic assent.

INDIRECTIONS: SHAKESPEARE AND THE ART OF ILLUSION

1

The Merchant of Venice

In approaching *The Merchant of Venice*, we are faced almost immediately with the problem of Shylock. How are we to respond to him? Are we to listen to our moral sense or our theatrical expectations? Do we react to the treatment of Shylock with outrage and indignation, seeing his final punishment as an appalling example of Christian smugness and hypocrisy, or are we filled with a profound sense of satisfaction at seeing the 'biter bitten,' the comic butt ridiculed? It is difficult to come down on one side or the other of this question without either oversimplifying or dislocating the play.

It may be best to begin by suggesting the various levels of reality that the play presents. For one thing, the play is, in Middleton Murry's phrase, 'a matter-of-fact fairy tale.'[1] It is based on source material built around two different folklore motifs, combined here for perhaps the first time: the flesh-bond story and the three caskets motif.[2] The first of these is invested with a more gripping and 'modern' kind of reality than the second. The story of the flesh-bond is set into, and presented as a part of, the cold harsh world of Venice, with its emphasis on legal and commercial values. The caskets motif is not shorn of romance to nearly the same degree; Belmont is a fairyland world with an aura of unreality. In it, an enchanted princess, both rich and beautiful, is held captive by an arbitrary bond and is not set free until the romantic hero arrives on the scene. It is a place where the fulfillment of desire – at least the right kind of desire – is not only possible but ennobling. Unworthy knights, of course, are unable to capture the castle or set the damsel free. The frame for both Venice and Belmont is the play as a whole. Our consciousness of the variously real unrealities within the frame depends on the way our attention is deliberately called to the fact of play itself.

Within the world of Venice, there are important moments when the realism cracks and we see the more schematic substructure underneath. (The romantic aura of Belmont is treated similarly.) The clearest examples are those moments when Shylock slips back into a stock figure – especially the gulled miser – slough-ing off the accrued humanity which he has gained in other scenes. When Jessica has run off with Lorenzo, Shylock's reaction is one of impotent rage; but we are not invited to feel this with him. Instead, we *hear* about his misfortune from Solanio, who presents it as ridiculous: '"My daughter! O my ducats! O my daughter! / Fled with a Christian! O my Christian ducats ..."' (II.viii.15-16). Hav-ing this *told* to us distances us from Shylock's emotion to such an extent that it can only strike us as ludicrous, not pathetic. When we next see Shylock, we are ready to ridicule, especially since Solanio and Salerio are again on the stage. But Shakespeare does not allow such an easy response. Instead, Shylock appears at his least 'stock,' his most fully human. He is cunning, disguising his pleasure at Antonio's losses: 'There I have another bad match! A bankrout, a prodigal ...' (III.i.46-7); he is threatening: 'Let him look to his bond' repeated three times in a few lines (49-53); he seeks sympathy: 'Hath not a Jew hands, organs, dimen-sions, senses, affections, passions ...' (61-3); and, most compellingly, he is an unrelenting and self-justifying critic of Christian society: 'If a Jew wrong a Chris-tian, what is his humility? Revenge! If a Christian wrong a Jew, what should his sufferance be by Christian example? Why, revenge!' (71-4). But as soon as these aspects have been fully elicited, there is a sudden shift to the farcical again with the entry of Tubal. He taunts Shylock with the loss of his daughter and ducats and at the same time buoys him up with the news of Antonio's failures. In this scene, Shylock really is a puppet, though there is a short stab of genuine human feeling even here, when he is suddenly reminded of Leah and the ring.[3] This re-minder has the effect of pulling us back from simple ridicule and thus prevents Shylock's automatism from dominating our imaginative conception of him.

In a similar vein, there are moments in the trial scene when Shylock is a ludi-crous caricature, whetting his knife and slavering like a vampire, and others when he is perceptive, shrewd, and frighteningly justified. His speech criticizing the Christian practice of keeping slaves, and the analogy he draws between the Christians' moral position and his own, are examples of the latter tendency. But a moment later he is sharpening his knife and unconsciously mocking himself.

Shakespeare is obviously in control of this kind of shuttling. (That this oscil-lation accounts for much of the critical disagreement described below goes with-out saying.) The question is why he put it there. Sometimes Shylock's humanness is his most vicious and terrifying quality. His hatred and cruelty are embodied, realized; and sympathy in the ordinary sense is quite impossible (as his first appearance exemplifies). At such times, however, a certain theatrical sympathy does accrue to him. He is alive, more so than any other character except, perhaps, Portia. Shakespeare seems interested in defining certain modes of reality and unreality and the possibilities these provide. Suddenly to reduce a human being to a stock figure is to draw attention to the theatrical mode itself as a form of presenting reality as unreality or unreality as reality. We are thus made aware of the artificial way in which comedy forms reality and we recognize that such a reduction is a way of re-establishing comic control and of diminishing the threat. Shakespeare, I think, was aware of the potential power of Shylock (just as Milton was aware of the potential power of his Satan) and he took pains to control and channel that power so that response to it would not be so overwhelming as to drown the rest of the play.

Most criticism has tried to come to terms with the problem of Shylock, but a good deal of it, unfortunately, tends to find oversimplified solutions which fit neither the action nor the humanity of the characters. Many critics have developed allegorical interpretations of the play, seeing it as a conflict between Good and Evil, the Old Law and the New, or, more commonly, Justice and Mercy.[4] Interpretations like these pay no attention to the emotional, human context in which such conflicts - if they exist at all - are played out. Also, they depend too heavily on a speech that Portia (in disguise) delivers, rather than on what she, or anybody else, actually does. To see her from the first moment of the trial scene, leading an unsuspecting Shylock to his sudden downfall and then striking him with the full rigour of the law, may satisfy us, but hardly makes Portia a personification of godlike mercy.

A smaller number of critics tend to see the play from Shylock's point of view, as a tragedy gone sour and artificially sweetened in the end. This was the view common in the later nineteenth century. It was popularized by various productions of the play (such as Henry Irving's in the seventies) where the star actor took the role of Shylock and played it for every drop of pathos that could be wrung from the hearts and eyes of nineteenth-century audiences. The notorious interpolated scene where Shylock returns to a darkened, empty house after Jessica's flight is a clear reflection of this critical tendency. Some modern criticism, in emphasizing the traditional aspects of Shylock as a stage figure, has effectively denigrated such a view. Shylock is regarded as a miser, an old spoilsport who hates festivity,[5] a 'blocking character'[6] who is structurally as well as psychologically opposed to comic action. His treatment at the hands of Lorenzo and Jessica is nothing more than a recasting of the old Plautine-*commedia* plot where the clever young lovers dupe the old father (or husband). The problem with overemphasizing this approach, however, is that it is based rather on a plot summary than on an analysis of the whole play. One of the first critics to adopt such a view was E.E. Stoll, who argues that Shylock is a puppet and a comic butt, worthy of nothing but ridicule; for, he says, 'sympathy at the theatre traditionally is for the debtor and against the money-lender, just as it is for the amorous son or eloping daughter and against the hard-hearted, stingy father';[7] but he forgets that Shakespeare is never simply traditional in that sense.

Stoll spells out an important corollary of his opinion in the following comment: 'How can we for a moment sympathize with Shylock unless at the same time we indignantly turn, not only against Gratiano, but against Portia, the Duke, and all Venice as well?'[8] A.D. Moody, in reaction to the views of what he calls the 'romantic or idealizing' critics (Coghill, Kermode, etc.), has done precisely that. Arguing that the play is thoroughly ironic, Moody insists on the 'humanity' of Shylock and claims that this humanity is perverted through his treatment by the Christians.[9] His conclusion is essentially that the play is a criticism of the false Christianity of the Venetians, who claim to live by true Christian principles but do not. Ralph Berry has offered an analysis which, though much more moderate than Moody's (he exempts Portia from ironic attack for example), stresses some of the same problems. For him, 'the chief characteristic' of the play is 'the rigorous objectivity of its analysis,' especially in its 'exposure of underlying motivations' and in its depiction of the exploitative side of human relationships.[10]

The main problem with Stoll's analysis is that he does not recognize the possibility of entertaining two different, or even contradictory, responses to one work. He fails to see how Shakespeare has deliberately deepened and complicated the traditional figure. Moody's analysis, on the other hand, is too strenuously thematic and neglects the theatrical elements that Stoll, and later critics in more detail, emphasize. As a critique of the 'romantic' or allegorizing critics, it is successful. However, Moody's argument does not meet Stoll's major points; it is too academic, too much a product of the study rather than the theatre. He ignores the fundamental issue of how the audience will respond to the play's situations, and hence provides an interpretation that is unactable.* Berry faces a

---

* For example, to play Morocco as worthier than Bassanio would violate the audience's expectation that the right man will necessarily choose the right casket. The irony that would result from this situation runs counter to the dramatic purposes of the play, even if it can be argued that it enhances the thematic point. And in Shakespeare, questions of dramatic impact and significance are never clearly and deliberately at odds with thematic issues.

In 1976, the Westcoast Actors of Vancouver staged a performance of the play which made quite a hit and was subsequently televised. The interpretation was close to that of Moody and Berry, in that the play was treated as a savage attack on Christian society, all of the Christians being hypocrites and/or opportunists. Portia was an aging husband-hunter, though not without charm and wit, Antonio a bitter old homosexual, Gratiano a hissing racist, and Bassanio the king of opportunists, who, in order to insure his victory with Portia and her gold, came in disguise as Morocco and Aragon before presenting him-

similar difficulty. He describes the trial scene as 'a savage ikon of human relationships,' but admits that his interpretation emerges more clearly in the reading than '(often) on the stage.'[11]

I would like to offer a different approach to the problem by examining Portia's role and function in relation to both Shylock and the other characters, especially Bassanio. Such an approach should make clear how our attitudes towards Shylock are controlled and, ultimately, contained by other interests. My aim is to suggest a way in which the play manipulates our responses so that the contradictions just reviewed may be given full play and yet supported within a larger comic framework. If we examine the play in terms of its use of illusion and levels of comic detachment, we may see at work a different kind of irony from that described by Stoll, Moody, or Berry – a theatrical and a much more sympathetic irony – by which our responses are controlled and through which the different claims of different justices are measured. Portia is the central figure in an analysis of this kind since it is she who manipulates the concluding action of the play and she who, in so doing, directs not only our reaction but that of the other characters.

In a sense, Shylock and Portia are opposite sides of the same coin; though the play is nominally about Antonio, the central antagonism is between these two. Both are manipulators, both are somewhat given to duplicity, both are disguisers. They are, as well, complementary in that when the one is active, the other is passive. They gradually shift during the play. At the outset, Shylock is at his most active and dominant, devising his treacherous bond, working things most effectively to his own advantage. At the same time, Portia is at her most passive. She is at the mercy of her father's will and must suffer the consequences. As the play goes on, Shylock becomes more and more acted upon, less in control of his situation: first there is Launcelot's defection, next Jessica's elopement and theft; then the good luck of Antonio's losses puts Shylock in a position of power; and finally there is the trial scene where he appears to have control but in fact does not. Once again he is acted upon, this time by Portia and the law of Venice. Throughout the play he comes more and more under the domination of external events while Portia comes more and more to control the events of the play. This movement begins with her active love for Bassanio and is greatly aided by the release from her bond which allows her to enter the public world. Before that release, her action is defined by her role as sought-after maiden; our sense of her

self as himself and choosing the leaden casket. Shylock did not escape the acidity of the director's vision either, nor did Lorenzo and Jessica, who emerged as vacuous and tainted, their love twisted into an elegy of bitterness. The production was highly effective, but the interpretation made nonsense of the play as Shakespeare wrote it.

liberation is confirmed by her subsequent action. She assumes a disguise, defeats Shylock, devises the ring plot, is somehow instrumental (magically we are to assume) in the retrieval of Antonio's argosies and, in short, brings events to a happy conclusion back in her now not-so-remote retreat at Belmont.[12]

It is Portia's disguise that enables her to get into the public world, to pass from 'romantic' Belmont to harsh, 'realistic' Venice. She passes, as it were, from one level of stage reality to another and, through the adroit use of her disguise, encompasses both. As noted above, Belmont's reality has been that of a fairy-tale. But although Portia has been cast in the part of the fairy-tale princess, that is not the role she actually plays. She is *perceived* as romantic princess but is not in fact so remote and unworldly. Rather, it is Bassanio who is romanticizing her, as well as himself, when he speaks of her:

> Nor is the wide world ignorant of her worth;
> For the four winds blow in from every coast
> Renowned suitors, and her sunny locks
> Hang on her temples like a golden fleece,
> Which makes her seat of Belmont Colchos' strond,
> And many Jasons come in quest of her. (I.i.167-72)

Bassanio's casting of himself as a Jason in search of the legendary golden fleece (which beyond its romantic associations suggests the 'fortune' Bassanio needs) reflects his own misperception of what Portia really is. In making a myth of her, he goes beyond classical parallels to make her somehow central to the natural world: she sits where the four winds meet and is associated with the sun. The money that she has is included in his romantic vision: he speaks of her as being 'nothing *undervalu'd* / To Cato's daughter, Brutus' Portia' (165-6, my italics); he never clarifies what meaning he is ascribing to the many different phrases he uses which connect moral and financial 'worth.' (Words like 'value' and 'worth' consistently have a double meaning in the play and emphasize the commercial aspect of the play's world.)[13] His very use of a word like 'quest' (so central to romance) and his belief that his quest will be 'fortunate' (176) re-emphasize the point that his romanticism is causing him to blur important distinctions.

Portia does not conform to this kind of description. The woman we meet in the scene following Bassanio's romantic portrait is clever, witty, and worldly. At the same time, she is 'aweary of this great world' (II.i.1-2). Her sadness, such as it is, is the result of her father's bond, which is thwarting her ordinary human desires. It is, then, more of a mood than a condition and contrasts with that of Antonio, whose motiveless melancholy has puzzled critics and led to a good deal of psychological speculation.[14] The greater part of this scene is taken up with

Portia's sharp-eyed satirical commentary on her various suitors, who exist primarily as national types. She shows herself shrewd but humane (her criticism is without rancour), witty, at ease with sex ('I am much afeard my lady his mother played false with a smith'), and mature (she can remain detached enough to comment as she does, and she avoids self-pity).

There is thus a counterpoint in the treatment of Belmont similar to that in the depiction of Shylock. Into what is essentially a fairy-tale situation which is, as well, perceived as such by other characters, a note of 'realism,' or fully drawn human character, is injected. This is analogous not only to the occasional reduction of Shylock to stock figure (from psychological solidity to two-dimensional type), but also to the larger movement of the Venice story which, while predominantly realistic, nonetheless revolves around a story (the flesh-bond) as primitive and undisplaced as that of the three caskets.

It is Portia's main function to mediate between these two worlds and, in the process, educate Bassanio and defeat Shylock. Bassanio, though he lives in Venice, is much more romantic than she and hence much less able to deal with the real situations he must face. This is reflected in his inability to master the financial necessities of Venice. He thus gets himself deeply in debt to Antonio. Furthermore, he is ignorant of how to defeat Shylock; only Portia can do that. He must master his illusions if he is to live in real society. Portia is able to help him, partly at least, by bringing the different worlds of the play together into one emergent reality that the play 'bodies forth.' The values of each must be transcended by a more inclusive vision that is at once both imaginative and socially productive.

Certainly the emphasis in this play is on living in society, in a civilized, 'modern,' economic society where wonder or beauty appear to have no place. This is the effect of the emphasis on law and justice, the social norms by which Venice functions, and of the concern with trade and individual, differentiated economic enterprise. But the source of energy for a full life within such a society is discovered to be in those very things which the spirit of Venice seems to negate: love, beauty, music, magic, and imagination. The attempt to unify the two worlds is the basis for the mingling of the commercial and love vocabularies in the scene immediately after Bassanio has chosen the right casket. Venice and Belmont suddenly merge in this language and we see how the energy of the latter quickens the deadness of Venice's cold commercialism. It is, of course, Portia speaking:

> I would be trebled twenty times myself,
> A thousand times more fair, ten thousand times more rich,
> That, only to stand high in your account,

> I might in virtues, beauties, livings, friends,
> Exceed account. But the full sum of me
> Is sum of something – which, to term in gross,
> Is an unlesson'd girl, unschool'd, unpractic'd. (III.ii.153-9)

She is aware not only of the ways in which economic considerations can impinge on love, but also of the fuller vision that can emerge out of their combination. Such language differs from Bassanio's romantic view of her wealth, not only financial but social and spiritual, in that it seems to allow for the possibility of love's survival in an economic society. Bassanio is moving out of society, mythologizing, confusing meanings, not clarifying them. Portia is using economic terms as metaphors to describe her own love and Bassanio's estimation of it. Furthermore, there is a (somewhat ingenuous) recognition that she is *not* a romantic princess but an 'unlesson'd ... unpractic'd' girl.

The same scene has opened with Portia trying to convince Bassanio not to hazard, in case he lose and be forced to retire. She detains him with playful talk just to delay his moment of choice. In the midst of this, she states that 'a maiden hath no tongue but thought' (III.ii.8), something which she instantly belies by confessing, in a relatively straightforward way, her love for Bassanio. If we were to be severe moral judges (like Moody), we might accuse Portia of falsehood and dissimulation. We might even suggest (as Moody does) that she seems so given to such duplicity that she is not above foiling her father's will by hinting to Bassanio which is the true casket. But this would be to judge her out of context; she must be seen first as the heroine of a comedy. (What would we think of Rosalind if we were to judge her on naturalistic, ethical grounds alone?) The main point of Portia's role-playing here (now the demure maid, now the clever young lover) is to deal with the seriousness of the situation, to transmute it into comic terms and to get things under comic control. This seems the impetus behind two short sequences, the joking about the rack which follows her opening speech and the invocation of classical parallel in the story of Alcides a little farther on.

Bassanio protests against Portia's pleas that he wait longer before choosing by saying, 'Let me choose: / For as I am, I live upon the rack' (24-5). Portia immediately challenges this kind of vocabulary and the seriousness it implies:

> PORTIA Upon the rack, Bassanio? Then confess
> What treason there is mingled with your love.
> BASSANIO None but that ugly treason of mistrust,
> Which makes me fear th'enjoying of my love.
> There may as well be amity and life
> 'Tween snow and fire, as treason and my love.

PORTIA Ay, but I fear you speak upon the rack,
Where men enforced do speak anything.
BASSANIO Promise me life, and I'll confess the truth.
PORTIA Well then, confess and live. (III.ii.26-34)

This passage has a double function. First, it introduces a comic tone at a moment of potential high tension; as such it is part of the process by which Portia moulds the situation, transmuting it into comedy. Second, it shows us Portia probing Bassanio's romantic suppositions about love and the conventional rhetoric in which he expresses them. Portia takes his metaphor literally and hands it back to him to scrutinize. He doesn't respond to her tone, however; he remains implacably serious, seemingly not understanding her efforts to deflate his rhetoric nor recognizing the over-earnest romanticism at the heart of his love. So he advances to his choice.

Just before he is to choose, Portia creates a scene in which he becomes Alcides and she Hesione standing for sacrifice:

Now he goes,
With no less presence, but with much more love,
Than young Alcides when he did redeem
The virgin tribute paid by howling Troy
To the sea monster. I stand for sacrifice;
The rest aloof are the Dardanian wives,
With bleared visages come forth to view
The issue of th' exploit. Go, Hercules!
Live thou, I live. With much much more dismay
I view the fight than thou that mak'st the fray. (III.ii.53-62)

This passage moves from comparison to identification, from simile to metaphor. Its effect is, on the one hand, to heighten the splendour of the scene and, on the other, to disengage us from the seriousness of it, to remind us that it will, indeed, turn out as we hope. This is implicit not only in the fact that Hercules was successful in the original story but also in the lessening of tension by the creation, literally, of a 'scene' in which Portia, Bassanio, and the others are enacting certain parts in a pre-established plot. Because it points to a further illusion, this 'scene' draws us back to an awareness of the basic illusion and of the mythological story's inevitable outcome.

The effect of this is, as I said, lost on Bassanio, though not on us. He moves to the caskets without comment. It is strange that, though Shakespeare altered his source to make the inscription on the lead casket read, 'Who chooseth me must give and hazard all he hath,'[15] such a consideration is hardly obvious in Bassanio's choice. He seems more interested in philosophizing, rather absurdly, on the manifold relation between appearance and reality. His philosophy, by an amusing irony, leads him to the correct choice (appearances aren't always false, after all), but since he ignores the mottoes altogether, are we to assume a moral superiority or a moral obtuseness? Is Bassanio really hazarding? 'All he hath' belongs to Antonio. His moral righteousness is certainly ambiguous, and Shakespeare indicates this by postponing the consummation of his love (as with Berowne at the end of *Love's Labours Lost*) while he and Portia are put through a series of tests in the real world. This postponement, which is a departure from the source, is not adequately explained by Portia's remark that Bassanio's soul is 'unquiet.' Bassanio must not only clarify his perceptions and meanings (for example, by coming to a fuller understanding of the relationship between apparent and real worth), he must also recognize the necessity of genuine hazarding on his own part before he can be judged worthy of comic integration, before he can be said to have attained some sort of identity within the comic framework.

A moment of intensity for Bassanio follows immediately after his choice. With the news of Antonio's misfortune, he is moved to confess things about himself that he was unable to reveal before. He thus tells Portia of his indebtedness, his near betrayal of his 'true friend,' in a speech whose harsh but lyrical simplicity contrasts markedly with the more elaborate rhetoric of his earlier speeches, giving us a sense of intense emotion for perhaps the first time:

> When I told you
> My state was nothing, I should then have told you
> That I was worse than nothing; for indeed
> I have engag'd myself to a dear friend,
> Engag'd my friend to his mere enemy
> To feed my means. (III.ii.258-63)

The reiteration of plain words and phrases, the straightforward syntax, and the use of the strong metaphor implied by 'feed,' especially because of the echoes of Shylock's insistent use of the metaphor in more wolfish contexts, all heighten our sense of Bassanio's new commitment. This feeling prepares him for the growth that he must undergo in Venice before he can return to Belmont and the fulfillment of his love for Portia.

It is at this point that Portia dons her disguise, and with it her public responsibilities, and enters the world of Venice. From then on, she is presenting a play, both for our benefit and that of the other characters. The reality of the play-world is thus broadened by the introduction of a further element of illusion. We have the confluence of Belmont and Venice and, beyond that, the creation of a 'scene' within the total illusion of the play itself. Portia's disguise enables her to play other roles besides the enchanted princess or the intelligent young woman in love. It offers her an opportunity to perform a valuable social function within the public world depicted in the play, something which no one in Venice seems able to do, and, further, to control the events of the play itself. Thus, as she adopts the role of lawyer, she also adopts that of stage-manager, directing the action as a kind of play within a play but with the difference that for the other people involved, it is terrifyingly real and has real consequences within the context of the play. It is neither parodic like the Pyramus and Thisbe playlet, nor a reflection of the main action like the play in *Hamlet*; it is *part* of the main action while at the same time it is consciously enacted by Portia and Nerissa as a play within a play. This redefines Portia's relationship to the audience, putting her in collusion with us since we alone are, with her, aware of the playful aspect of this scene. This makes us see how serious issues like those raised by the trial can be harmlessly surrounded by the beneficence of illusion, a process effected not only by this scene but by the play as a whole.

Before her entrance, the trial scene is predominantly gloomy and threatening. Shylock is a destructive force ironically sanctioned by the laws of Venice. There is, however, the same kind of alternating portrayal of him noticed elsewhere in the play. At one time he seems fully, if terrifyingly, human. A moment later he is nothing more than a caricature. This process carries over into his mental activities during the trial. Hence he argues his case with a cogency that may seem rigid but which is quite convincing; he inveighs, with vigour and moral weight, against the Christian practice of slavery and the ownership of people that practice implies. On the other hand, he performs like a conventional stage villain, ostentatiously whetting his knife; intellectually as well, he is mechanistic, seeing human motive in terms of involuntary reflex:[16]

> You'll ask me why I rather choose to have
> A weight of carrion flesh than to receive
> Three thousand ducats ...
> Some men there are love not a gaping pig,
> Some that are mad if they behold a cat,
> And others, when the bagpipe sings i' th' nose,
> Cannot contain their urine ...
> As there is no firm reason to be rend'red
> Why he cannot abide a gaping pig,
> Why he a harmless necessary cat,
> Why he a woolen bagpipe ...

> So can I give no reason, nor I will not,
> More than a lodg'd hate and a certain loathing
> I bear Antonio. (IV.i.40-61)

This kind of argument is the intellectual and verbal counterpart of his knife-sharpening or his shuttling back and forth between his daughter and his ducats. At the same time, it is very effective and sets an ominous tone as prelude to the actual business of the trial.

We know, of course, that Portia and Nerissa have invented some saving plan; we have seen their preparation in III.v. From the moment Portia enters, she takes charge and we feel that we are in safe hands. Her method is to present these events in as consciously theatrical a way as possible; this allows the audience to recognize the artifice of comedy and react accordingly. She moves slowly, carefully building up suspense, pleading for mercy which she knows will not be granted and offering money which she knows will not be accepted. Then, between her last appeal to Shylock and her ultimate solution, lies an interval (some eighty lines of conversation) which she prolongs to stall the outcome. She plays, as well, the comic game of dallying with the puppet, raising Shylock's hopes with seeming concessions to the justice of his cause, only to dash him down again after she has revealed the full extent of her judgement. Towards the end of this interval comes Bassanio's protestation, spoken in reply to Antonio's farewell speech, that he would sacrifice life and wife to deliver his friend. Portia interjects:

> Your wife would give you little thanks for that
> If she were by to hear you make the offer.
> GRATIANO I have a wife who I protest I love.
> I would she were in heaven, so she could
> Entreat some power to change this currish Jew.
> NERISSA 'Tis well you offer it behind her back.
> The wish would make else an unquiet house. (IV.i.288-94)

Here we have a major shift in tone, once again engineered by Portia, which undercuts the seriousness of the scene and brings it home to us as play-acting. The naïve irony that we, along with the two women, perceive reminds us of what is actually going on, that a show is being presented, a trick being played. The force of the previous debate, the threatening tone arising from Shylock's imposing presence, has caught us up in the suspense and so we are recalled to a more detached, comic viewpoint. Portia continues the theatrical playing once she has turned the tables on Shylock. She toys with him, insisting that he take his bond or nothing. Once again she moves very slowly, eventually revealing the penalty for attempted murder and subjecting Shylock to the mercy of the Duke and all the court. In her hands, Shylock becomes more and more a puppet as she gains and asserts control.

It is worth noting the change in Bassanio that can be measured in the trial scene. Berry's view of him as one of life's 'winners,' as a shrewd aristocrat who exploits his charm to get ahead seems basically just up to this point.[17] But now he seems to respond to the test which separation from Portia had imposed. As I have said, Bassanio learns important truths only under intense pressure and such seems to be the case here. The situation is a desperate one and he is intimately involved. As the scene develops, he comes to recognize the necessary range and depth of his commitment. A realization, which his earlier romanticism had inhibited, of the difficulty of life in the real world seems to come home to him during the scene. He is still extravagant and excessive, but he learns something about the meaning of hazarding: 'The Jew shall have my flesh, blood, bones, and all / Ere thou shalt lose for me one drop of blood' (iv.i.112-13); and something about the responsibility of binding himself: 'If that will not suffice, / I will be bound to pay it ten times o'er / On forfeit of my hands, my head, my heart' (210-12). Thus the scene depicts Bassanio moving towards a more serious and generous conception of human relationships.

Portia pursues the comic game with her introduction of the ring plot. It is essentially a comic improvisation woven tightly into the play's fabric, both thematically and structurally, and emphasizes the power and significance of Portia's comic sense, a feature of her character and her role which seems to me the most important thing about her. Her sense of comedy is the basis not only of the ring-game but also of her transmutation of tension before the caskets and her defeat of Shylock at the trial. Portia has been said to represent mercy. I would argue that, if she represents anything, it is comedy itself (though, of course, such allegorization ultimately defeats itself). The point is not that she has a more developed sense of compassion or Christian mercy than Shylock; it is that she has a more finely attuned sense of comedy, a sense that is sometimes quite *un*merciful. The unmercy of the ring plot is merely teasing; it revels in the squirming that Bassanio and Gratiano are forced into. That of the main plot, however, is considerably more disturbing and is the source of the marked critical disagreement outlined earlier. Comedy often contains action which may seem unmerciful or unjust and, in this play, Portia is the agent of such action. It is the function of the ring plot to drive home this comic point in a harmless way and to complete the comic transmutation begun in the earlier scenes.

The ring plot is set in motion by a clever improvisatory twist in which Portia-Balthasar asks first for Bassanio's gloves as her reward, evidently with the intention of uncovering the ring which she can then demand. It is essentially a theatrical complication which Portia introduces for the sheer joy of playing. She is at this point manoeuvring towards a happy ending to the drama that she is now controlling. By adding this bit of complication, which is not essential to the rest of the action, she consolidates her control and incidentally helps to make us aware of the illusion inherent in the play as a whole. For we are immediately and continuously aware of the illusion of this particular business. It is an enactment in miniature of the movement of the whole play; it is the comic process distilled to its basic elements and can therefore show us in a condensed way how comic drama functions. This is revealed in these scenes by the way serious issues, as I shall discuss presently, are treated in a comic fashion and the whole action is kept on a harmless level. The ring plot thus exaggerates and presents in a schematic, skeletal way elements inherent in all romantic comedy.

Like the original disguise, this game has other purposes besides the depiction of multi-levelled illusion. It completes the disillusioning of Bassanio; it brings up the theme of the relation between love and friendship that runs through the rest of the play; and it provides an opportunity for bawdry which affects the tone of the final scene and contributes to our assessment of the reality of the whole play. All of these purposes are related to each other and to the element of theatricality inherent in the ring plot.

The demands of friendship and love create unforeseen difficulties for Bassanio who, through his involvement in this illusory game, learns something actual about life. The ring is an external sign, a pledge of his fidelity. As such it is related to the crucial theme of bonds and promises which is woven into both plots. Until conflict arises, Bassanio is unaware of the complexities of the various claims of love and friendship. But it does arise; the ring of love is relinquished at the friend's request: 'Let his [Balthasar's] deservings, and my love withal, / Be valued 'gainst your wife's commandement' (IV.i.450-1). This is the only place in the play, except for the brief exchange between husbands and wives during the trial (quoted above), where the values of love are in conflict with those of friendship. At the beginning, Antonio is entirely willing to put himself in danger to aid Bassanio's romantic quest, despite his sadness (which may, as some critics maintain, be due to the prospect of losing his friend).* And when need calls, Bassanio returns from Belmont, at Portia's insistence, to help Antonio. Only here does Antonio ask for something *against* Portia's apparent wishes. Such a confronta-

---

* If I have neglected Antonio, it is because I view him, with many critics, as essentially passive, and thereby peripheral to the main action though central to its tone. His presence provides an atmosphere of sadness and unfulfillment that adds depth to the conflicts which culminate in the trial scene and that tempers the final festivity.

tion forces Bassanio into a choice and the necessary reappraisal of his stance that a choice implies. The advantages of such a situation are evident; I have already given examples showing how Bassanio responds to and learns from situations of crisis and this, though on a less serious level, is another instance. He decides to part with the ring at the request of his friend and, in so doing, indicates a willingness to de-emphasize the externals of love. He bows to the more telling demands of gratitude, courtesy, and friendship, which are brought to his attention by Portia's creation of an artificial situation.

In v.i, the little play that Portia has constructed and the larger one converge in the resolution of their respective plots. Characters and plots are now moving towards a final, conclusive, comic celebration. In the early part of the scene, Lorenzo and Jessica sit in the moonlight and speak of love and harmony. They invoke classical parallels to their love in a high romantic vein:

> In such a night
> Stood Dido with a willow in her hand
> Upon the wild sea-banks, and waft her love
> To come again to Carthage. (v.i.9-12)

The fact that all these parallels are tragic is an odd feature of this lyric moment, but it too may be explained by the pervasive sense of tragic possibility being transmuted into comic triumph enacted in the main plot, and again, though less seriously, with the rings. It is fitting, then, that as their conversation continues, their romanticism is modulated into a gentle self-mockery which indicates a clear awareness of themselves and a confidence in their mutual love of the kind which Bassanio must come to possess:*

> JESSICA   In such a night
> Did young Lorenzo swear he lov'd her well,
> Stealing her soul with many vows of faith,
> And ne'er a true one.
> LORENZO   In such a night
> Did pretty Jessica (like a little shrow)
> Slander her love, and he forgave it her. (v.i.17-22)

This irony, this sense of humour about themselves, is very appealing and adds a dimension to this couple that Bassanio lacks. The latter is very serious about

---

* The situation here is parallel to that in *As You Like It*, where Oliver's relationship with Celia stands as a model for Orlando's to Rosalind.

himself and his love. This seriousness is effectively met by Portia; her mockery and manipulation force Bassanio to see the irony of his position and eventually to laugh at himself. She mocks the romantic view much more emphatically than Lorenzo and Jessica. Their association of love, music, moonlight, and harmony (especially in Lorenzo's famous speech, 'How sweet the moonlight sleeps upon this bank') is challenged by Portia's considerably less romantic description of the moonlit night: 'This night methinks is but the daylight sick; / It looks a little paler' (v.i.124-5). Another effective attack against Bassanio's seriousness is Portia's bawdry: as a response to his romantic exaggeration, she greets her husband with a sexual joke: 'Let me give light, but let not me be light; / For a light wife doth make a heavy husband' (129-30). This remark sets the stage for a whole series of mocking, and slightly salacious, comments on the part of the two women. For example, the way in which they finally reveal that they do have the rings is delightfully bawdy: their mock jealousy turns into triumph when Portia produces the ring and announces: 'I had it of him. Pardon me, Bassanio; / For, by this ring, the doctor lay with me' (258-9).

Portia and Nerissa derive a good deal of pleasure from dragging out the dénouement to cruel lengths, making the men squirm with embarrassment and jealousy before finally resolving the whole business. Portia handles the whole scene with great polish, taking everything at the right pace and in the right order. Her final acts as stage manager are even more in the direction of the happy ending and an inclusive celebration. She brings Lorenzo and Jessica the deed of inheritance and, more interestingly, she produces a letter to Antonio of which she knows the contents and of which she says: 'You shall not know by what strange accident / I chanced on this letter' (278-9). It tells him the good news of argosies come home, an event with which, we are to understand, Portia has had something to do. Here we have the fairy-tale aspect of the story reasserting itself and Portia is its magic agent. Portia's magic role is deliberately unrealistic, and allows us a further glimpse of the artificiality of the story. This 'strange accident' stands as a small model for the way comic processes order reality, allowing us our wishes, but keeping us aware of the distance between such wishes and actuality; while in the very awareness of that distance lies the power of comedy, not only to delight, but to teach as well.

In rounding out the play in this way, Portia is emphasizing some of the important facts of social life, especially sex, but also obligation, humour, and the intricate relations between reality and appearance. It is satisfying that Bassanio finally enters into the joking: 'Sweet Doctor, you shall be my bedfellow. / When I am absent, then lie with my wife' (284-5). And it is worth observing that the play, far from ending on a romantic note, closes with a bawdy pun: 'Well, while I live I'll fear no other thing / So sore as keeping safe Nerissa's ring.'

Throughout the play, especially in the latter part of it, we can observe a distinction between private and public spheres and their corresponding virtues. Venice and Belmont, in their broadest outlines, represent these two spheres. An important part of what Portia and Bassanio learn, through her disguise, is the way private virtue can be transformed into public action. The sense of reality requisite for this transformation is a basic aspect of the identity which they finally achieve, an identity both personal and social. This is emphasized in the way they come together at the end, stripped of the romanticism and role-playing which have been a part of the process by which these two finally come to terms with themselves. It is the way in which the play can both reduce the illusion in the end *and* confirm it that makes the process specifically dramatic or theatrical (ie, which distinguishes the process here from that in, say, a novel). We might say also that the movement of all the characters from Venice to Belmont suggests the movement back, or better, the possibility of easy passage in both directions. Belmont then is finally presented as both an illusion and a reality; it is a place of nurture and rest, not a mysterious romantic island, where the characters, especially Bassanio and Portia, can live in social and personal harmony and from which they can emerge to meet the larger demands of society.

2

As You Like It

As You Like It seems both more balanced and more fragile than *The Merchant of Venice*. Though it manifests many of the same concerns, it brings us closer to the centre of Shakespeare's comic vision. For one thing, the theme of love is expanded; for another, the movement from public world to private and back to public in the later play is like a schematized version of analogous movements in the earlier. Arden, like Belmont, is both an illusion and a reality, and Shakespeare exploits both of these potentialities more fully than in *The Merchant of Venice*. He does so by making disguise and illusion central not only to the comic action, but to the development among the characters of a richer attitude towards love and a more perceptive view of their own experience. At the same time, he moves back from the confrontation of public issues typical of *The Merchant of Venice* to consider the traditional pastoral themes of retreat, time, and love (among others). Varying points of view towards these problems are juxtaposed within a deliberately artificial, created framework, with the result that both characters and audience are involved in a game of irony which illuminates even as it fools.

The game begins and ends with Rosalind. Her disguise, first of all, has no function on the level of plot beyond getting her safely away from the court and into the pastoral forest of Arden. Once she has arrived there, her original purpose in donning the disguise loses its importance. So she turns to other uses irrelevant to, or even at odds with, the strictly narrative function depicted in the early parts of the play. Her use of the device to go *into* the enchanted world, where love is the primary concern, contrasts with that of Portia, who moves in the opposite direction, from Belmont to Venice. Again unlike Portia, who goes to solve the comic problem, Rosalind uses her disguise to create it. Indeed, it is worth noting that this is Shakespeare's only comedy in which the heroine's disguise constitutes the primary stumbling block to the working out of the comic resolution.[1]

But on another level, maintaining the disguise makes it possible to bring about a significant kind of resolution. The role of the disguise becomes almost purely educative. Portia's disguise leads her to perform important public action, indicating her gifts for affecting the public world. Rosalind's sphere is the more private one of personal relations and the kinds of illusions such relations are subject to. She is more interested in manipulating attitudes than events. Here, even more than in *The Merchant of Venice*, enlightenment involves the undercutting of romantic notions by the presentation of contrary forms.

This is particularly true of the different views of love presented in the play and the way they are made to comment on each other. Love (different ways of experiencing it, of viewing it, of presenting it, or talking about it) is certainly the main subject of *As You Like It*. Characters are hurried off to the forest as quickly as possible so that the real business of the play can get under way. This haste explains the unreality of the early scenes, especially the unblushing portrayal of stock folklore types like the evil older brother and the usurping ruler.[2] Shakespeare is merely establishing a *donné* – an exterior threat that is really not threatening at all (quite unlike Shylock or even Don John) – to allow himself the opportunity to set up a standard polarity between court and country and to circumscribe a comic space within which the important action can take place. Evidence may be derived from a comparison of this part of the play to its source, Lodge's *Rosalynde*. Shakespeare, contrary to his usual practice, treats events less 'realistically' and establishes more schematic relationships than his source. (Such schematic treatment is characteristic of *All's Well* and *Measure for Measure* too, and for similar reasons.) Lodge's treatment of his material could itself/hardly be described as realistic, but he does assign some psychological motivation to both Saladyne (Oliver) and Torismond (Duke Frederick). Shakespeare compresses the incidents and makes them less motivated and more arbitrary. There is, of course, very little plot and virtually no development of the fairy-tale beginning;[3] rather, the whole sense of fairy-tale is soon dropped to make room for the more literary pastoral form and then taken up when needed to provide the convenient conversions of Oliver and Duke Frederick. Still, the first act is important both for its creation of a deliberate sense of artifice and for the public place that, in spite of its unreality, it establishes.

Once in Arden, the characters do not have to confront any threat to the comic world from the 'real' world outside. Such stumbling blocks – 'irrational' laws as in *A Midsummer Night's Dream* or *Measure for Measure*,[4] Shylock's bond, Don John's plot etc. – are part of the standard Shakespearean plot structure. Here, such a 'real' obstacle is replaced by an essentially artificial one created by the heroine for the purpose of complicating the narrative and manipulating the various characters. Such deliberate complication is consciously theatrical – Rosalind is playing a part which involves her and those she encounters in a process analogous to that which we as an audience undergo and which is crucial to their, and our, enlightenment.

Rosalind uses the role-playing to manipulate events in such a way as to make them concur with the attitudes that she is inculcating. A good example of this is what she does with Phebe. She breaks down her self-conscious stance as haughty love mistress and shapes events to a conclusion in which Phebe happily accepts her constant swain. The Phebe-Silvius plot is essentially a farce which is both a literary parody and an example of a restricted, self-involved attitude towards love which must be tempered. It is a parody of the conventional literary pastoral, the sad love of a swooning swain for a cold-hearted mistress. In this sense, it is artificial even within the play-world; it is another kind of theatrical performance. Also, it is the focus for an artificial language which re-emphasizes the distance between such action and sentiment and genuine human feeling. Both these aspects are mirrored in Corin's announcement to Rosalind and Celia: 'If you will see a pageant truly play'd / Between the pale complexion of true love / And the red glow of scorn and proud disdain, / Go hence a little ...' (III.iv.55-8). We are advised not only of the 'show' which we will see performed but also of the abstract, dehumanized, almost allegorical quality of the performance. Silvius is playing the role of True Love and wears the traditional pale mask; Phebe is Scorn and sports a red mask. The trouble with this kind of posing (in contrast to Rosalind's) is that it is unconscious. It is divorced from true feeling since it is controlled by the mask it wears and, beyond that, it is unaware of itself as role-playing. Rosalind recognizes the shortcomings of their situation and decides to take a part in the proceedings: 'Bring us to this sight, and you shall say / I'll prove a busy actor in their play' (III.iv.61-2).

Silvius's rhetoric is a good indication of his lack of self-awareness, his inability to see his own absurdity, and his failure to recognize the possibility of other experiences of love besides his own:

> If thou rememb'rest not the slightest folly
> That ever love did make thee run into,
> Thou hast not lov'd.
> Or if thou hast not sat as I do now,
> Wearing thy hearer in thy mistress' praise,
> Thou hast not lov'd ... (II.iv.33-8)

Even the rhythm of such a passage – repetitive, unvarying – reinforces our sense of Silvius's unwavering self-assurance. His personality is circumscribed by his elaborate love talk, which defines him and his feelings but which is undercut by the variety of love experience presented in the rest of the play. In the 'pageant' that follows Corin's invitation quoted above, Phebe, in her first appearance, challenges Silvius's rhetoric directly; and in so doing, gives us a hint about her own character and view of love:

> Thou tell'st me there is murder in mine eye:
> 'Tis pretty, sure and very probable
> That eyes, that are the frail'st and softest things,
> Who shut their coward gates on atomies,
> Should be call'd tyrants, butchers, murtherers ...
> Lie not, to say my eyes are murtherers.
> Now show the wound mine eye hath made in thee.
> Scratch thee but with a pin, and there remains
> Some scar of it ... (III.v.10-22)

Phebe is here challenging one of the commonest of courtly love metaphors (the capacity of the mistress's eye to wound the lover) on the grounds of its literal untruth. Like Touchstone, whose literalist tendencies are examined more fully later on, she is unable to accept metaphor as a way of talking about love (though her reaction is very different from his). Her position is thus the exact opposite of Silvius's, but it has a similar effect of blocking feeling, of denying or turning away from real experience. She is in the anomalous position of denying the relevance of the language of courtly love while at the same time unwittingly playing the role of courtly love mistress. For this situation to be righted, Silvius's extravagance must be toned down and Phebe must come to see the folly of her posing. It is Rosalind who is the catalyst in both processes.

Rosalind, who has been a witness to the scene discussed, suddenly steps in as stage manager, taking precisely the tone needed to thrust Phebe out of her self-absorption – 'chiding.' Shakespeare's irony is heavy here; just before Rosalind's interruption, Silvius says: 'If ever ... you meet in some fresh cheek the power of fancy, / Then shall you know the wounds invisible / That love's keen arrows make' (III.v.28-31). His wish comes true sooner than he could hope. Phebe's frozen attitude crumbles quickly under Rosalind's chiding and the beginning of her 'regeneration' (to deliberately overstate the case) is established. The point is to broaden her own experience, since this is the only way she can understand the experience of others. She can only understand Silvius's love for her through her love for Ganymede. The necessary first step is for her to stop adopting the literary pose and admit genuine, if illusory, feeling to herself; as a corollary, she comes to admit the miraculous power of eyes:

If the scorn of your bright eyne
Have power to raise such love in mine,
Alack, in me what strange effect
Would they work in mild aspect. (IV.iii.50-3)

This reversal of roles is effected by Rosalind, who consciously uses illusion to bring Phebe to an awareness of the illusion that she has been living. At the end, therefore, Phebe can accept Silvius on the grounds of *his* experience and his faith, since she now understands what this means: 'I will not eat my word, now thou art mine; / Thy faith my fancy to thee doth combine' (v.iv.155-6). Silvius, upon winning Phebe, has no more need for his role and thus can pass out of that stage of the relationship with a sense of liberation. What has begun as a farce ends as a comedy, in the sense that the characters involved have reached some degree of self-awareness, some sense of their own identity, and have turned away from the fixed attitude and the literary pose.

The foregoing analysis gives us an idea of how illusion can be used to break down stereotypes: the act of playing a role is itself a part of the process of developing self-awareness. A reversal of role was necessary in Phebe's case since only then could she recognize her previous behaviour as a role. Now, the relationship of this action to the whole play is analogous to the relationship of the play to us, the audience, and our sphere of action. Both are 'pageants,' both self-consciously artificial, both consequently lead to awareness, though the Silvius-Phebe pageant is one level further removed from our reality. We can see, then, that this type of process needs theatrical form; it requires various levels of illusion, all of which illuminate each other and cast light on what we call reality. We are asked to take a detached view of the whole play just as Rosalind does of the Silvius-Phebe plot; such a view engenders irony and it is this ironic sense, critical yet gentle and amused, which the play invokes and Rosalind embodies.

At the same time, we realize that the function of the play as a whole in relation to us is similar to that of Rosalind's masquerade in relation to Silvius (and, as we shall see later, to Orlando). The play challenges our assumptions, presents us with varying and opposing attitudes, and tries to steer us away from stereotyped responses. The treatment of pastoralism, for example, is both accepting and critical, whereas in the play's source, Lodge's *Rosalynde*, there is no ironic awareness of the artificiality or even the silliness of pastoral conventions.[5] In *As You Like It* such awareness is built into the structure of the play. Hence the response of an Elizabethan playgoer, bred on plays like *Mucedorus* and romances like those of Lodge or Greene, would be displaced, his expectations would be deflected, and room would be made for new, more complex responses. The technique which serves Shakespeare best in effecting this change is variety, especially variety of attitude. The structural correlative of variety is juxtaposition, which he here uses so successfully. The immediate result of such comic juxtaposition is irony and the final product of the irony is balance, which is why the role of Rosalind and her balanced view are so central to the development of the whole play. Before turning to the working of the process of illusion-making in the main plot, then, it will be useful to look briefly at this variety and juxtaposition, and the irony produced through the encounters of the various characters and their various attitudes towards life in the pastoral world.[6]

Let us consider for a moment the role of the pages and the banished lords. They are part of the trappings of the traditional pastoral and embody the 'holi-day humour' which is an important aspect of the play's mood.[7] The songs they sing crystallize this mood, and express an attitude towards time and love that is essentially lyric and present-minded. The lyric is, in fact, the form most per-fectly attuned to their attitude and it is no accident that it is so prominent here. Of course, it is also no accident that Jaques, who stands firmly against this atti-tude, parodies 'Under the greenwood tree,' making it an invocation for fools, or that Touchstone mocks the amorous lyric of the pages, 'It was a lover and his lass.' In fact, even within his portrayal of the most traditional pastoral ele-ments, Shakespeare suggests another viewpoint towards them. In one of the most beautiful songs, he reminds us of winter and bitter weather, and he keeps before us the 'uncouth' and 'desert' qualities of the pastoral scene which both Orlando and Adam, and Rosalind's party, encounter upon entering Arden.

The role of Duke Senior presents us with a different view of pastoral. He is preoccupied with the past rather than the present. His memory of past events provides the energy for his present action and the rationale for his very social attitudes towards love and the future. Even his opening speech, in which he em-phasizes the value of his present life in Arden in contrast to the life of 'painted pomp' (to which he is nonetheless very willing to return at the end), reaches back to the old world for its metaphors. The cold winds are spoken of as 'coun-sellors / That feelingly persuade me what I am' (ii.i.10-11). It is noteworthy that he is the lord of the pastoral world, since the pastoral is really the mode of mem-ory, of looking back with the eyes of the imagination at childhood or at a lost golden age. The Duke's memory is not strictly nostalgic, however. It is a source for his life in the present:

> True is it that we have seen better days,
> And have with holy bell been knoll'd to church,
> And sat at good men's feasts, and wip'd our eyes
> Of drops that sacred pity hath engend'red;

And *therefore* sit you down in gentleness,
And take upon command what help we have ... (II.vii.120-5, my italics)

He repeats, we might almost say intones, Orlando's preceding speech in the manner of oral epic, emphasizing his knowledge of the past and the direct connection between what he has done, his memory of it, and what he is doing here 'in
gentleness.' Such a speech, like his first speech, reveals a more realistic and more
social view of pastoral than that of the pages and lords. The connection between
the real world and the pastoral is neither so distant nor so unfruitful as they
imply. The Forest of Arden is, for the Duke, less of an escape and more of a re-
fuge. Another instance of the still lively connection between his past life and his
life now is his acquaintance with old Sir Rowland (like that of the King with
Bertram's father in *All's Well*) which informs his acceptance of Orlando. We are
thus given a sense of continuity and harmony between the generations. Perhaps
continuity is the key word in an interpretation of the Duke's role, since he me-
diates not only between past and present but also between court and country,
artifice and nature. His position as overseer of the final festivities is an aspect of
this mediating function; he places the present festivity in perspective by declar-
ing it a prelude to a return to the public world:

First, in this forest let us do those ends
That here were well begun and well begot;
And after, every of this happy number
That have endur'd shrewd days and nights with us
Shall share the good of our returned fortune,
According to the measure of their states.
Meantime ... Play, music, and you brides and bridegrooms all,
With measure heap'd in joy, to th' measures fall. (V.iv.176-85)

Touchstone and Jaques are, of course, the most important qualifiers and un-
derminers of the attitudes of the other characters.[8] Touchstone's view of the pastoral world, time, and love is essentially materialistic.[9] It is in a sense the lowest
common denominator of all the views that the play presents. His thoroughgoing
materialism is an important part of his wit: he replies to Rosalind's exclamation
'O Jupiter, how weary are my spirits!' by saying 'I care not for my spirits if my
legs were not weary' (II.iv.1-3). In a similar vein, he tells her a moment later, 'I
shall ne'er be ware of mine own wit till I break my shins against it' (II.iv.59-60).
Touchstone is a Midas in reverse; everything he touches turns to dross. His style
is one of continual and relentless reductionism; he brings all the rarefied experiences of the other characters down to the most basic level. The most far-reaching

of his reductions is naturally of love itself, which most of the others are celebrating as the most sublime of experiences. His love for 'Jane Smile' and for Audrey makes this point clear. Love for him exists primarily on a simple physical level: 'As the ox hath his bow, sir, the horse his curb, and the falcon her bells, so man hath his desires; and as pigeons bill, so wedlock would be nibbling' (III.iii.80-3). All the usual trappings of love are only 'mortal in folly.' His view of the pastoral life and time is consistent with this. He manifests his disdain for the former in his dialogue with Corin (III.ii) and time for him (as Jaques reports it) is nothing but hourly progression and physical process:

> 'Tis but an hour ago since it was nine,
> And after one hour more 'twill be eleven;
> And so, from hour to hour, we ripe and ripe,
> And then, from hour to hour, we rot and rot;
> And thereby hangs a tale. (II.vii.24-8)

Such a view is a far cry from the *carpe diem* songs of the lords and pages. It reduces their rather unrealistic joy to the pallid, literal facts emphasized here by the very physical metaphor of ripening and rotting. At the same time, it is not a melancholy view; rather, it is alert, cynical, and amused, and as such is a strong spice in the play's recipe.

If Touchstone's role is to keep us aware of the basic physical reality behind all the efflorescence, Jaques' is to cast a shadow on that very efflorescence. His view of life and love is self-indulgently tragical. His influence is carefully modulated, however. His first entrance, for example, is prepared for by the first Arden scene in which he is discussed at length but does not appear. He is identified as 'the melancholy Jaques' and his tendency to 'moralize the spectacle' is deliberately alluded to, so that when we do meet him we are ready for his affectations. Yet it is he more than anyone or anything else that focusses our attention on the artificiality of pastoral and on the evils in life which everyone else would rather ignore.[10] He is essentially a defeated idealist who is outraged by the hypocrisy in the world but is unable to extirpate it even in himself. As satirical railer, he is effective but limited, especially in his famous 'ages of man' speech. Social hypocrisy and the brutality of time's passage produce for Jaques a sort of weary bitterness towards each of the succeeding ages. The ghastly state of 'mere oblivion' crowns this sharply anti-romantic, but nonetheless inflated and delusive, image of human life. It is clear that Jaques' nihilism is foreign to both comic and tragic affirmation. As if to repudiate Jaques' final statement, Orlando enters with Adam the minute he is finished. Adam, though old, has not shown himself 'sans everything' and his disappearance right after this scene seems to indicate that

Shakespeare introduced him here at least partly as a foil to Jaques.[11] It is one more example of the way juxtaposition works as a corrective in the play.

A view of life such as Jaques' naturally includes a cynical attitude towards love and society so that he regards the one as foolish and sentimental ('And then the lover, / Sighing like a furnace, with a woful ballad / Made to his mistress' eyebrow.' ii.vii.147-9) and the other as vain and undesirable. These feelings prevent his being included in the final resolution just as they make him a misfit in the forest world. But his attitude, like that of Touchstone, keeps us aware of the alternative possibilities and hence allows us to remain detached from the final resolution to the extent that we can see its limitations and maintain a sense of irony.[12] This distancing effect is heightened in Jaques' 'ages of man' monologue through the use of the theatrical metaphor which, like the disguises and the 'pageants,' makes us more aware of the illusory as a mode by which we can gain a perspective on experience and thus deepen our perception of reality (even if Jaques himself is incapable of doing so). Just as we, like Orlando, have been separated from our illusions and romantic expectations through Rosalind's irony, so we are kept from taking the conclusion sentimentally[13] because of the complex web of ironies resulting from Jaques' role.

All these different views are juxtaposed with one another in a careful pattern of alternation, and the result, as I pointed out earlier, is balance. The play manifests a critical spirit at the same time that it establishes a moderate view of love, time, the pastoral, and all the other issues it raises. Rosalind is the focus of both the critical spirit and the balanced view; she gives them substance and makes them effective. It is, after all, her show. She is the stage manager and the comic conclusion is in her hands. That she is aware of her moderate position and consciously trying to maintain it is evident in her remark to Jaques: 'Those that are in extremity of either [mirth or melancholy] are abominable fellows ...' (iv.i.5-6). As her interference in the affairs of Silvius and Phebe indicates, her most effective way of moderating and balancing is her ability to play roles. This is where the structure of juxtaposition just outlined and the structure of illusion-making discussed in relation to Silvius and Phebe connect. Rosalind's play-acting with Orlando is the most important instance of her using the techniques of illusion to realize her moderate role. With him, not only is she using her disguise to manipulate attitudes and provide critical detachment, but she is also using it to test herself and her own illusions.

It is here that the educative aspect of her role comes most fully into play. The immediate and mutual love of Orlando and Rosalind has been prevented from growth through the perversity of external circumstances and the viciousness of Duke Frederick and Oliver. We may suppose that these external inhibitions have their internal correlatives. At any rate, both lovers are forced to wander far from their places in society and in so doing lose their social or public identities. Both are children of noble blood whose birthrights have been thrust aside. They are homeless, dis-placed in terms of their public lives, and this too has its inner or private correlative. The action of the play will be to establish private identity leading to a return to proper public place. As is often the case in sophisticated pastoral (*The Winter's Tale* and Book VI of *The Faerie Queene* are other examples), the pastoral world exists as a source of energy and private fulfillment, but only a temporary one; the movement out is as important as the movement in.

The process really gets underway in III.ii, a scene which offers us a glimpse of nearly all the attitudes towards love and experience encountered in the play. It begins with Orlando dashing through the wood, carving courtly verses on the trees, playing to the fullest his role as adoring lover. The parallel with Silvius is immediately established. He sighs:

> O Rosalind! these trees shall be my books,
> And in their barks my thoughts I'll character,
> That every eye which in this forest looks
> Shall see thy virtue witness'd everywhere. (III.ii.5-8)

The trees-as-books metaphor, which Orlando is here making into a literal relation, recalls Duke Senior's introduction to Arden, which had established a connection between the natural life of the forest and verbal 'counselling'; their life, he says, 'Finds tongues in trees, books in the running brooks, / Sermons in stones ...' (II.i.16-17). Amiens's reply to the Duke extends the image: 'Happy is your Grace / That can translate the stubbornness of fortune / Into so quiet and so sweet a style' (19-20), suggesting that control over nature and fortune is similar to control over language. Orlando's inability to control his language, his windy rhetoric and poetizing, is an indication of his vulnerability. His lines do not truly describe Rosalind or witness her virtue; they are too conventional and external. Furthermore, Orlando's view is considerably more arrogant. He sees himself as the teacher, making the trees into *his* books to teach the glories of love and the virtues of Rosalind. The Duke, on the other hand, *finds* a lesson in the trees and winds, emphasizing the educative nature of the retreat.

Orlando's appearance at the beginning of III.ii is brief. He is soon replaced by Touchstone and Corin, who enter discussing the relative merits of court and country. This polarity has already been emphasized in the preceding action where the corruption of the court – usurpation, arbitrary use of authority, ingratitude, dandyism, etc. – has been set off against the mingled beauty and harshness of the country. Similarly here, Corin's unaffected rusticity makes Orlando's courtly plaints look silly. Through such means, we are brought to accept the moral superiority of the country, the traditional outcome of such contrasts. However, Touchstone's amusing observations on the advantages and disadvantages of country life introduce a more critical frame of mind which coincides with our growing perception of the artificiality of this pastoral world, itself a created 'poetic' world. Shakespeare is treating the court-country dichotomy in the same way that he is treating the other traditional materials in the play – with double-edged irony. He induces us to take a critical view, not only of court or country but of the literary nature of the whole conflict. At the same time, the value of this country life is quite definitely asserted within the structure of the play, while the rich potential of court life too is implied in Touchstone's witty repartee ('Wast ever in court, shepherd?' 'No, truly.' 'Then thou art damn'd') and even more in the eventual return to court of all the noble characters. The implication is that a great part of the value of a particular way of life is derived from a critical view of that very way of life. Touchstone's humour is instrumental in the development of such a view since it makes us aware of the built-in limitations inherent in any set pattern of thought or action.

Rosalind's entrance a moment later is introduced by Touchstone's final accusation against the 'vices' of the country:

That is another simple sin in you: to bring the ewes and the rams together and to offer to get your living by the copulation of cattle; to be bawd to a bell-wether, and to betray a she-lamb of a twelvemonth to a crooked-pated old cuckoldy ram ... (III.ii.82-7)

Such an attack reflects more on the vices of the court than on the work of the country; I point to it, however, for the tone that it establishes, coming as it does immediately after Orlando's romantic sonneteering and immediately before Rosalind's bewildered reading of his verses and Touchstone's acute parodies of them. Rosalind reads: 'From the east to western Inde, / No jewel is like Rosalinde. / Her worth, being mounted on the wind, / Through all the world bears Rosalinde ...' (93-6). Touchstone revises the little poem, creating a bawdy version of the original with the same dog-trot rhythm and repetitive rhymes, but with the addition of pointed references to animal sexuality:

> If a hart do lack a hind,
> Let him seek out Rosalinde.
> If the cat will after kind,
> So be sure will Rosalinde.
> Winter garments must be lin'd,

So must slender Rosalinde.
They that reap must sheaf and bind,
Then to cart with Rosalinde ...
He that sweetest rose will find
Must find love's prick and Rosalinde. (III.ii.107-18)

Rosalind is reduced from dominating courtly love mistress to the butt of a series of sexual jokes, most of them degrading. If Orlando is making her into Phebe, Touchstone turns her into Audrey. The final couplet is characteristic of the whole method: a traditional romantic image (the 'sweetest rose') is invoked and then made wittily, anatomically, and bawdily explicit by the introduction of 'love's prick.' Once again a critical attitude undermines a romantic stance. It is especially this emphasis on the physicality of sex, amusing as it so often is, which deflates the romantic idealism of Orlando or Silvius (or even Rosalind at times) and sets things on an earthier foundation. Touchstone lives up to his name by once again re-establishing a sense of basic reality.

Rosalind learns enough from Touchstone's reaction and parody to be able to react in the same kind of way to the wildly hyperbolic verse which Celia then enters reading: 'O most gentle pulpiter! what tedious homily of love have you wearied your parishioners withal, and never cried, "Have patience, good people"' (III.ii.163-6). The metaphors of the religion of love are here deliberately reduced to their homeliest expression. Rosalind is half-consciously readying herself for a consideration of various attitudes towards love; she is learning to examine her own feelings and see them in perspective. The process continues during the sub-sequent conversation with Celia, who begins by telling her that it is a man who is writing the verses but then refuses to say who it is. Her stalling, of course, only whets Rosalind's curiosity. In the process, Celia uses sexual innuendo to remind Rosalind of the realities of the situation: replying to Rosalind's wine bottle metaphor ('... pour this conceal'd man out of thy mouth as wine comes out of a narrow-mouth'd bottle ... that I may drink thy tidings'), she says: 'So you may put a man in your belly' (210-15). This kind of chatter is typical of Shakespeare's comic heroines (compare Portia and Nerissa's similar banter) and indicates their maturity and moderation, their ability to balance opposing points of view and styles of behaviour. But Rosalind, it should be emphasized, is only half-way there; her balance needs testing, strengthening, evening out. Celia soon tells her it is Orlando and this brings Rosalind's real feelings and excitement into the open – witness the speech where she breathlessly poses a dozen questions and then demands, 'Answer me in one word.' She reveals her most 'feminine' aspects here, just before she begins playing the male role in earnest; she asks Celia: 'Do you not know I am a woman? When I think, I must speak' (263-4). Celia, however, continues to play the balancing, corrective role, tempering our reaction to Rosalind's excitement and making her aware of its extravagance. To Rosalind's joyous interruptions to her story, she keeps making pointed responses, causing us more to smile at, than to feel with, Rosalind: 'It is as easy to count atomies as to resolve the propositions of a lover ... Cry "holla" to thy tongue, I prithee. It curvets unseasonably' (245-6, 257-8).

Their conversation is cut off by the entrance of Orlando and Jaques in mid-quarrel. Jaques' attitude is thus added to provide another dimension; and his is a more severely critical one than the festive bawdiness of Touchstone or the gentle irony of the heroines. We have been alerted to the pitfalls of Orlando's romanticism but we are not totally unsympathetic to it; Jaques too we have seen before and are hardly surprised by his point of view. We are thus in a position to be able to examine critically their various attitudes and evaluate what they have to say to each other. Jaques has nothing but scorn for Orlando and his verses: 'I pray you mar no more trees with writing love songs in their barks' (276-7), to which Orlando can only reply rather petulantly, 'I pray you mar no more of my verses with reading them ill-favouredly' (278-9). But the balance soon shifts and Orlando gets the better of Jaques on the next parry: 'I do not like her [Rosalind's] name.' 'There was no thought of pleasing you when she was christen'd' (282-4). In the end, Jaques can only complain to Orlando that 'The worst fault you have is to be in love' (300). The introduction of such a viewpoint at this stage provides us with a further reminder to be watchful even as it establishes another level of psychological reality: lest we be carried away by Rosalind's excitement, we have Jaques' cynicism to bring us back; lest we wholeheartedly accept Orlando's exuberance, we have Jaques' melancholy as an alternative focus.

The last part of the scene shows Rosalind taking charge of the situation; she has made up her mind what to do with her 'doublet and hose' and has hit upon a way to use them to her own and Orlando's advantage. It is a crucial decision for her, as it is for Shakespeare. Taking the lead from Lodge's romance, which is his main source, he decides to use the fact of Rosalind's disguise to allow her to play herself. The distinction between illusion and reality becomes somewhat more complicated at this point, since there is a double role-playing being presented: a woman disguised as a young man will play the part of the woman herself (not to mention the fact that the role is being played by a boy). In Lodge, the double role-playing (which is relatively brief, taking up a much smaller proportion of the whole) is done not to 'cure' Rosader (Orlando) nor to test Rosalynde's feelings. Rather, Lodge's Rosalynde pursues it both for her own satisfaction and with the hope of driving away her lover's 'amorous melancholy.' She invents it as a means of keeping him with her since she 'was loath to let him passe out of her presence.'[14] The fact that Shakespeare changed the whole thrust of this scene indicates a good deal about his intentions. He is eager to emphasize the value of this double role-playing in developing insight and self-awareness in the young lovers.

It is evident that this doubling provides the opportunity for many small ironies, statements in which we see the ambiguity though Orlando does not: 'ORLANDO Fair youth, I would I could make thee believe I love. ROSALIND Me believe it? You may as soon make her that you love believe it' (III.ii.404-7). But such talk, though amusing, is of no great importance. The more significant kind of irony which this device makes possible is that produced by the various levels of awareness and consequent detachment which it provides. Just as Ganymede retains a certain detachment about his role as Rosalind, a detachment which is built into the very nature of playing a part, so Rosalind maintains a detachment about her dual role. This allows her to see herself in perspective and to say things to Orlando that she could never say directly. This process begins even before the adoption of the second role, as when she accuses Orlando of not looking the true lover and deduces the reason 'as loving yourself, than seeming the lover of any other' (III.ii.402-3); or when she blithely claims that 'Love is merely a madness, and, I tell you, deserves as well a dark house and a whip as madmen do' (III.ii.420-2). Such statements bring Orlando up against a firm obstacle and force him to look into himself in a way that ordinary wooing never would.

Orlando does not want to be cured, but he agrees to act out Ganymede's little play. In so doing, he accepts the role-playing, the theatrical aspect, and almost unwittingly opens his attitudes to the kind of detached perception that the theatrical mode can provide. In theatre, there are ways of distancing the audience from the action in order to provide further perceptions and ironies of which the characters may not be aware.[15] (Even in 'realistic' drama this phenomenon is observable; Chekhov is a master of it.) Similarly, here, through this playing, Orlando is going to be both an actor in, and an observer of, something that to him is real. He agrees to act it out with someone else and thus removes it from the realm of (for him) the real to the illusory. This eventually will give him more of an insight into his behaviour than simple action would. The same principle applies to Rosalind, who is playing the role of herself and so, as mentioned above, is distanced enough from her own real emotions and action to look carefully at them and test them. This is why the disguise and subsequent role-playing are necessary for the development of awareness; for without the theatrical element, the requisite detachment or emotional distance cannot be achieved. Thus illusion is important to provide a deeper understanding of the reality of experience. This same principle is at work in the relationship established between the play and the audience. We too must enter into the structure of illusion and juxtaposition that the play creates, surrendering our hard-nosed attachment to actual experience, in order to allow that experience to be illuminated. Such is the rationale behind the play-acting within the play, behind the whole play as illusion, and indeed behind most (perhaps all) drama.*

Most of iv.i is devoted to the process just outlined. The scene begins, however, with a short dialogue between Jaques and Rosalind, a structural parallel to the dialogue between Jaques and Orlando that introduced the first Rosalind-Orlando scene. Once again, Jaques' view reminds us of an alternative possibility, but here he gets much the worse of the argument, and Rosalind's moderation is seen as the norm. Jaques' sadness is no match for Rosalind's gaiety; his rarefied pleasure – the garnering of melancholy from all his 'experience' – is gently mocked by Rosalind who thus *places* him for us as well when she remarks: 'I had rather have a fool to make me merry than experience to make me sad' (26-8).

She begins the assault by attacking the genuineness of Orlando's love, continuing the approach which led her to accuse him of self-love in iii.ii. This time it is his late arrival which indicates his half-heartedness. She thus gets him off balance from the start. Next, she launches into a full-scale attack on his illusions. His destiny is to be a cuckold or a henpecked husband. Most of all, however, she attacks the rhetoric which is a reflection of his romanticism, his refusal to allow realities to cloud his ideal vision. Two particular extravagances are singled out for special treatment. The first is Orlando's claim that he would die if his Rosalind refused him. Her reply is quick-witted, cynical, and, above all, realistic, even in its physical detail: 'The poor world is almost six thousand years old, and in all this time there was not any man died in his own person, videlicet, in a love cause ... Men have died from time to time, and worms have eaten them, but not for love' (iv.i.95-8, 106-8). Orlando struggles to avoid the relevance of such talk, which is for him very disillusioning, but he can only repeat 'I would not have my right Rosalind of this mind, for I protest her frown might kill me' (109-10). The point is, of course, that his Rosalind *is* of this mind (though it is not her *whole* mind either), something which he must accept before he can call her his. This same little speech emphasizes the similarity of Orlando and Silvius, whose metaphors on the deadly power of the mistress's eyes we have just heard in the scene immediately preceding this. Once again, the juxtaposition is not accidental; Orlando too is shown to be adopting a conventional stance and he must be brought face to face with the human realities of experience. Rosalind, like Phebe, rejects

* The therapeutic technique of 'psychodrama,' in which patients confront each other, adopting their own or someone else's role in a relationship and acting out a typical 'scene' (for example, a wife plays the role of her husband, or of herself relating to her husband, who is played by a third person) is based on exactly this principle.

the extravagant metaphor: 'By this hand, it will not kill a fly!' Unlike Phebe, however, she is very much aware of her own feelings at this point. What the recurrence of this motif in both plots suggests is that a certain literalism, a 'realistic' outlook which sees the metaphor for what it is, is an important step on the way to enlightenment. But to be frozen in this literalism, as Touchstone is or as Phebe is until she is moved by Rosalind, is no better than being an extravagant romantic.

The second major illusion which Rosalind cuts from under Orlando in this scene is his insistence that he will love her 'forever and a day.' In response, she launches into a tirade against lovers in general and Rosalind in particular:

Say 'a day' without the 'ever.' No, no, Orlando! Men are April when they woo, December when they wed. Maids are May when they are maids, but the sky changes when they are wives. I will be more jealous of thee than a Barbary cock-pigeon over his hen, more clamorous than a parrot against rain ...
(IV.i.146-52)

When the catalogue is over, Orlando can only ask in astonishment, 'But will my Rosalind do so?' To which the clever and ironical Ganymede-Rosalind naturally replies: 'By my life, she will do as I do.' Orlando is thus led to reconsider his feelings and their expression, to admit to himself some of the less desirable consequences of his love. Such self-questioning is even more important for Rosalind since she is using all these conjurations as a kind of exorcism. Not only is she testing her own feelings, but she is also purging herself spiritually by expressing all of these more or less unpleasant possibilities. Even to speak about them she must recognize them as possible and prevention can only follow upon such recognition. And it is her disguise which allows for this process by providing the emotional distance from the love she genuinely feels (and admits to Celia after Orlando leaves), a distance which is necessary for her to say the things she says and face the perceptions she develops.

The point where the role-playing ceases is an important one. It marks the time when hero and heroine have reached a different perspective and are ready for the comic resolution and the promise of life in the public world thereafter. By v.ii, Orlando has learned a good deal about love from Ganymede and has been told of his brother's forthcoming marriage to Celia. He has, as well, saved his brother from the lioness, an act of forgiveness indicative of a greater ability to love. When Ganymede-Rosalind suggests to him that he-she should serve him in place of his 'real' Rosalind on the next day (the wedding day), he replies, 'I can live no longer by thinking' (v.ii.55). Role-playing and the whole theatrical game are no longer of much use to him; he now needs and is ready for the real thing. Rosalind also understands and immediately begins preparations to bring him to his 'real' Rosalind and thus to steer the whole business to a neat comic conclusion.

As with Silvius and Phebe, only on a firmer and more significant level, we have finally a sense of re-established identity, with both hero and heroine ready to assume their legitimate places in the social world. In the case of both shepherds and courtiers, arriving at this distinctively comic form of identity has involved a theatrical process which tempered or transformed real feelings by playing them, by drawing a circle of illusion around them (a circle which is not entirely broken even at the end). The movement towards clarification experienced not only by Rosalind and Orlando, but by us as well, thus depends on an exposure to opposing viewpoints within a consciously artificial framework.[16] The irony which results, and the complicated perception of illusion and reality which it entails, means for them and for us a sharper, more complex, and ultimately comic vision of life.

The end of the play affirms and confirms this idea. The final solution to all the riddles is *presented* to us as yet another 'pageant.' This may seem odd if we think of the play's action as working through 'shows' or 'appearances' to arrive at some basic reality. The problem disappears, however, when we think of the specific role of the pageants and shows. For the illusion involved, as I have tried to show throughout, is designed as a means of insight as well as delusion, and of insight on a deeper level. Rosalind's final pageant with Hymen (together with the reintroduction of pure fairy-tale elements like Frederick's conversion) is meant to remind us of the artificiality of the play as a whole, and of playing. It keeps us aware of the fact that, though the disguises have been dropped and the confusions straightened out, the role-playing remains under the control of the stage manager. At the same time, *within* the pageant, important bonds are formed and the marriages take place – the most important realities are imbedded in illusion. (This idea gains strength when we note that Hymen's song, unlike the earlier pastoral songs, stresses the *social* nature of love and thus points back to the society which the characters will soon rejoin.)[17] Once again we are aware of the centrality of the theatrical dance and of its effect in manipulating and distancing our responses.

At the very end, we are released from the theatrical illusion in the same way as the role-players in the play – ambiguously, since the disguise is dropped but the 'pageant' is still going on. In the epilogue, Rosalind, stripped of her role and appearing as the real boy actor who plays the part, speaks directly to us in his own person while at the same time retaining an echo of the persona of Rosalind:

It is not the fashion to see the lady the epilogue; but it is no more unhandsome than to see the lord the prologue ... My way is to conjure you, and I'll begin with the women. I charge you, O women ... to like as much of this play as please you ... If I were a woman, I would kiss as many of you as had beards that pleas'd me ...

We may note that at the beginning the speaker is female ('Rosalind'), and at the end, male (boy actor), though still with undertones of his original femininity. The result is that the illusion of the play is slowly and consciously dissolved and we are returned to everyday experience with a richer sense of the theatrical and a more expansive view of reality.

3

Hamlet

Hamlet, though it employs many of the same devices, marks a significant shift from *As You Like It*. In *Hamlet*, the techniques I have been discussing – disguise, roles, manipulation – become for the first time in Shakespeare's career dangerous and threatening. They serve primarily as political tools.[1] Comic manipulation becomes political intrigue, and the sympathy of the audience, our sense of the value of 'playing,' is reduced and finally alienated. As has often been noticed, the play is full of spying and counter-spying, device and 'indirection.' Such activity is a strong tonal element in the play and bespeaks the corruption of its political world. One commentator has even suggested that *Hamlet* can be seen as a key document in the changing history of views of the court, representing a turning point in the transformation from the older, medieval notion of the court as the moral centre of the nation (typified by the Arthurian stories) to the later seventeenth- and eighteenth-century commonplace that the court is a centre of sycophantic flattery and ambitious scheming (exemplified by Swift's Lilliputian court or by the story of the emperor's new clothes).[2]

As J.D. Wilson pointed out long ago, though few critics, including Wilson himself, have pursued the matter, the political background of the play is extremely important.[3] The play, in fact, defines a struggle between political forces, with Hamlet, who considers himself the rightful heir and whom an Elizabethan audience would naturally regard as dispossessed, lined up against the overtly political craftsmen, Claudius, Polonius, and their lackeys. The confrontation of these forces is, of course, personal as well as political, and the chief antagonists are Hamlet and Claudius. Although their conflict underlies the play, they do not face each other very often. Only once, after the death of Polonius, is there a direct confrontation between them. The one time they are alone together on the stage, in the prayer scene, there is no confrontation whatever, but rather a peculiar realignment and oblique connection between them, with Hamlet seeming more the Machiavel and Claudius the suffering self-accuser.[4] In the second scene, the struggle between the two men is tempered by the presence of the Queen as well as by Claudius's phony good will, and, in the last, Laertes, not Claudius, is the actual antagonist, though our attention is focussed on the latter. The duel with Laertes, coming at the climax of the play, serves as a theatrical symbol which refers to and caps the various conflicts,[5] and expresses their consistently strategic and indirect nature.

If we look first at the styles used by the antagonists, we can begin to understand the issues raised by the conflict. As George Orwell has reminded us, style and rhetoric have a real political dimension and this was as true in the sixteenth as it is in the twentieth century. Shakespeare's culture believed implicitly in the value and power of language; and English humanism found support for this belief in an idea derived from classical rhetoricians, the notion of *eloquentia*, or the power of words well spoken to move men in the direction of the good. For Cicero, whose *De Oratore* is the major source of the tradition, the social fabric itself was woven on the loom of words; civilization depended on eloquence:

To come, however, to the highest achievements of eloquence, what other power could have been strong enough either to gather scattered humanity into one place, or to lead it out of its brutish existence in the wilderness up to our present condition of civilization as men and citizens, or after the establishment of social communities, to give shape to laws, tribunals and civil rights?[6]

Eloquence was both a good in itself and an indispensable adjunct of the good ruler. In *Musophilus*, a poem written only a year or two before *Hamlet*, and one that restates all the principal optimistic doctrines of Renaissance humanism, Samuel Daniel writes of eloquence:

> Powre above powres, O heavenly Eloquence,
> That with the stronge reine of commanding words,
> Dost manage, guide, and master th'eminence
> Of men's affections, more than all their swords:
> Shall we not offer to thy excellence
> The richest treasure that our wit affords?
> Thou that can do much more with one poor pen
> Than all the powres of princes can effect:
> And draw, divert, dispose, and fashion men
> Better than force or rigour can direct ...[7]

This passage is a simple hymn to eloquence, ascribing to that virtue extraordinary powers of persuasion. Eloquence is a pre-eminent public virtue; it is honest, and effective by the very clarity of its honesty. In *Hamlet*, however, ambivalent, negative feelings towards this tradition predominate, public utterance comes under severe scrutiny, and the whole notion of eloquence as a public *good* exists only far in the background.

Let us listen to Claudius's eloquence:

> Though yet of Hamlet our dear brother's death
> The memory be green, and that it us befitted
> To bear our hearts in grief, and our whole kingdom
> To be contracted in one brow of woe,
> Yet so far hath discretion fought with nature
> That we with wisest sorrow think on him
> Together with remembrance of ourselves.
> Therefore our sometime sister, now our queen,
> Th'imperial jointress of our warlike state,
> Have we, as 'twere with a defeated joy,
> With an auspicious and a dropping eye,
> With mirth in funeral, and with dirge in marriage,
> In equal scale weighing delight and dole,
> Taken to wife ... (I.ii.1-14)

Claudius's rhythms – of both metre and meaning – strike us as too perfect, his balancing too precise, his tone too unctuous. The parallelisms and oxymorons are too neat for us to believe in the sentiments expressed; the speech has a rehearsed quality about it.[8] The view of the state as a body politic, an essential feature of Renaissance political theory, is here twisted into a tortuous conceit: 'Our whole kingdom [is] contracted in one brow of woe.' We get the impression, one that is corroborated later in the play, that Claudius and the court in general regard the organic metaphor as something to use to their own advantage, not as a moral given of political life.

A similar tendency is apparent in Claudius's speech to Hamlet on mourning a little later:

> ... you must know, your father lost a father,
> That father lost, lost his, and the survivor bound
> In filial obligation for some term
> To do obsequious sorrow. But to persever
> In obstinate condolement is a course

Of impious stubbornness ...
               Fie! 'tis a fault to heaven,
A fault against the dead, a fault to nature,
To reason most absurd, whose common theme
Is death of fathers, and who still hath cried,
From the first corse, till he that died today,
'This must be so.' (I.ii.88-106)

Again here, we have an unctuous, almost sententious public style, one that we perceive as untrue to private feeling. This is suggested by the elaborate, patterned repetition in the first two lines, by the sonorous combination of latinate nouns and adjectives in the next four, and by the skilled but slightly excessive alliteration (obligation, obsequious, obstinate). The manner is smooth and persuasive, but under it there is a hardness, an implacability. In the latter part of the speech, Claudius outdoes himself. He invokes the great humanist abstractions, nature and reason, links them in traditional fashion with Christian doctrine, and lines them up against Hamlet, only to undercut himself with an unconscious irony, the mention of the 'first corse,' that of Abel, the first victim of fratricide.[9] *Eloquentia* has become a mask and a political tool; in the new political world, there is no longer any trust in public speech or faith in public metaphor. As Bacon, whose *Essays* are a kind of handbook of the new polity, writes, 'Discretion of speech is more than eloquence.'[10]

    The ideological flattery of Rosencrantz and Guildenstern and the maxims of Polonius provide us with a similar sense of falsehood and hypocrisy. In III.iii, Rosencrantz and Guildenstern flatter the king with an exaggerated rhetoric which depends on the traditional theory but veers significantly away from it. They respond to Claudius's fear of Hamlet and his decision to send him to England in the following terms:

Most holy and religious fear it is
To keep those many many bodies safe
That live and feed upon your majesty ...

            The cesse of majesty
Dies not alone, but like a gulf doth draw
What's near it with it. It is a massy wheel
Fix'd on the summit of the highest mount,
To whose huge spokes ten thousand lesser things
Are mortis'd and adjoin'd; which when it falls,
Each small annexment, petty consequence,

> Attends the boist'rous ruin. Never alone
> Did the king sigh, but with a general groan. (III.iii.8-10, 15-23)

In their desire to please the king, the anxious courtiers distort the traditional view by making the king more important than he is, so that the old metaphors can be used to justify new treacheries.[11] In the first speech quoted, Guildenstern makes the king into a kind of Christ figure, a god who 'feeds' the many; in the second, Rosencrantz, in a subtle divergence from the 'Upon the king' soliloquy in *Henry V*, makes the life of the nation rest specifically and entirely on the life on the monarch.[12]

Polonius's style is not ideological, merely sententious. He is pedantically concerned with verbal expression: he dislikes Hamlet's use of 'beautified' ('a vile phrase') but to him 'mobled queen is good.' He delights in formulae and conceits, in manner over matter. He is incapable of not trying to be eloquent, even when the situation calls for brevity. (A notable exception to this, as Charney points out, is the direct and colloquial style he sometimes adopts with his family.)[13] When faced with this tendency, Gertrude, like Bacon in the *Advancement*, can only call for 'More matter, with less art.' As Gertrude's rejoinder indicates, Polonius's 'eloquence' is debased and self-conscious; it is another instance of the disintegration of public speech in this political world. Osric, of course, provides us with the most extreme example of self-conscious 'eloquence'; with him, eloquence serves exclusively for courtly self-display. The rehearsed quality of all such speech is ironically manifested by the fact that Osric soon runs out of pretty words, much to Hamlet and Horatio's amusement.

Hamlet's response to all this is to create his own cryptic, punning, private style to be used for political, or any other public, confrontations: 'Now, Hamlet, where's Polonius?' 'At supper.' 'At supper? Where?' 'Not where he eats, but where he is eaten' (IV.iii.17-21). That this style is a new addition to Hamlet's verbal repertoire is indicated earlier by Polonius's surprised approval: 'How pregnant sometimes his replies are! a happiness that sometimes madness hits on ...' (II.ii.212-13). Hamlet's most eloquent language is reserved for those times when he is talking to himself. And even the eloquence of the soliloquies is entirely private, serving primarily to express the vehemence of his emotions and their own powerful, non-rational logic.[14] He seems to regard a shared public language as no longer viable in the political arena. Yet he is not entirely willing to relinquish his humanism. His famous speech to Rosencrantz and Guildenstern is directly in the humanist tradition – until the twist at the end of each section:

... this most excellent canopy, the air, look you, this brave o'erhanging firmament, this majestical roof fretted with golden fire – why, it appeareth nothing to me but a foul and pestilent congregation of vapours. What a piece of work is a man! how noble in reason! how infinite in faculties! in form and moving how express and admirable! in action how like an angel! in apprehension how like a god! the beauty of the world, the paragon of animals! And yet to me what is this quintessence of dust? (II.ii.310-21)

From the point of view of both style and content, the juxtaposition here shows as clearly as anything Hamlet's double attitude towards the traditions behind him.[15] He can spontaneously elaborate a rich picture of the universe and man's place in it, and with a wave, dismiss it. Here, both in the presentation of the traditional doctrine and in his rejection of it, he is still using a rich, culturally shared language.

At the end of the play, at least once, he seems to be looking for a different kind of speech, one that is pared down, prosaic, yet with a distinctive, individual rhythm and order:

There's a special providence in the fall of a sparrow. If it be now, 'tis not to come; if it be not to come, it will be now; if it be not now, yet it will come; the readiness is all. (V.ii.230-3)

It is difficult to assess this speech. It seems to arise out of a felt need for a sustaining religious order, a support which has been conspicuously absent during most the play. At the same time, the style is personal, simple, direct.[16] As such, it seems to represent some achieved awareness and order (if we take style to be an aspect of a larger harmony). But there are other styles and other needs crowded into the last part of the play which seem to contradict this (the tough-minded dismissal of Rosencrantz and Guildenstern, for example; and the polished, courtly apology to Laertes, to which I shall return later). So I would say that this speech arises out of an important *part* of Hamlet – the need for a place to rest, for an order that is fulfilling and self-validating. The complexity and difficulty of meeting that need should become clearer as we go along.

Even from such a brief analysis, it is evident that the style of the participants in the game of traps and strategies which is *Hamlet* expresses a good deal about the personal and political conflicts in which they are embroiled. In turning now specifically to the action of the play, I want to explore how the comic devices I am concerned with in this book are fitted into a tragic pattern. Hamlet emerges as a figure bent on discovering and asserting an order which goes beyond words. But in spite of, or partly because of, his efforts, an uncertainty is created which embraces not only the life of the protagonist but the responses of the audience as well.

Endless debate over whether Hamlet is actually mad or simply playing indicates that Shakespeare wants us to feel somewhat uncertain about the degree or limits of Hamlet's mental confusion. At no time, however, is he completely out of contact, as Ophelia becomes in her mad scene. Moreover, he declares that he will 'put an antic disposition *on*.' I think therefore that his madness can be regarded as a role, a disguise like those in the comedies we have been looking at. Which is not to deny the very real symptoms of disorder that he periodically manifests, especially in the scene reported by Ophelia. The fact that the madness is a response to the ghost's revelation shows clearly that the disguise is also a deeply personal truth. For the purposes of this book, however, I am interested in Hamlet's madness less as a psychological phenomenon and more as a manipulative device, as something, in the particular context in which it is set, with political as well as personal significance.

He first adopts the disguise in an effort to establish control over a volatile political situation. In the same speech in which he resolves to put on the antic disposition, he recognizes that the *time* is out of joint and that he was born to set it right. The disjointed nature of the time arises from a disrupted political and social order and so Hamlet, the disinherited prince, uses madness in an attempt to reconstitute that order; or better, he uses madness in an attempt to clarify the situation, to root out the 'vicious mole of nature' which the Ghost has revealed at the centre of the state. Claudius's kingship is based on a lie, an illusion, and Hamlet turns the penetrating light of a further illusion against it. This latter illusion is theatrical, like the illusions of the comedies. Hamlet 'acts' mad, and thus he 'acts' against the vicious mole of Denmark.

As the disguises in the early comedies liberate the heroines, so too, Hamlet's madness frees him from ordinary social constraints, thereby allowing him a detached, ironic view of the play's events and an opportunity for manipulation. On the simplest level, this role-playing is exemplified by the game with Polonius. In the 'fishmonger' dialogue, for example, his acting allows him to challenge Polonius's complacent self-importance. Combining the style of Rosalind's criticism of Orlando's easy love and Feste's probing of Malvolio's 'madness,' but with more incisive irony than either, Hamlet strips Polonius of his pretensions and lays bare his role as a psychological pander. As with Rosalind, Hamlet's disguise is what gives him the licence to speak freely, but his intentions in doing so are different from hers. She tests Orlando's rigid love in order to soften it and make it more durable; he attacks Polonius as a representative of an authority he despises, an authority which is both illegitimate and corrupt.[17] He has no illusions about actually changing Polonius's attitudes.

On a deeper level, Hamlet dons the disguise in order to set things right, politically and ethically. This effort, too, stands in an important relation to the earlier comedies, especially *As You Like It*, where the comic impulse leads towards the establishment of a new social order embodying the insights which the main characters achieve during the course of their role-playing. In the comedies, the specific politics of the new society are not an issue, although similar political evils – usurpation, banishment, ambition – are as important to *As You Like It* as to *Hamlet*; nor is the struggle to achieve a new society presented as a political one, as it is in *Hamlet*. Nevertheless, the impulse in the latter play is similar to that in the comedies, and we can thus see a political dimension to the comic process. The comedies, that is, do make statements about society and social forms of identity as well as about individuals and personal identity. This becomes more explicit in *The Tempest* which, preserving the comic form, resolves some of the problems of *Hamlet*.

Hamlet, then, is a comic figure (from the point of view of his structural role) trying to cope with potentially tragic problems by using the techniques of comedy. But in this play, there is a moral ambiguity at the very centre of illusion and of role, an ambiguity not present in the high comedies but pervading the 'problem' plays. The first decisive mark of this ambiguity is that the disguise is no longer a shifted identity, but an inverted one, a madness. Another important mark of the ambiguity is the insistent, almost obsessive concern of the language with inner and outer and the discrepancy between them:

> Seems, madam? Nay it is; I know not 'seems' ...
> But I have that within which passeth show;
> These but the trappings and the suits of woe. (I.ii.76, 85-6)

To 'act' is itself a suspect activity, liable to corruption, akin to the 'plast'ring art' which beautifies the harlot's cheek. And yet in order to *act*, Hamlet must 'act.'[18]

Illusion and manipulation, considered as aspects of human relations, thus come under severe scrutiny in the play. Such activity in a political context becomes, as I have said, spying and intrigue. The play emphasizes this in its structural use of juxtaposition (a favourite technique of Shakespeare's around this time; it is the basic principle of composition in *Troilus and Cressida*, for example), which, at the same time, calls into question the more innocent forms of playing. In II.i, Polonius sends Reynaldo to Paris to spy on Laertes and to 'put on him what forgeries you please' (12-20). His purpose, as he explains, is that 'Your bait of falsehood [will take] this carp of truth,' a phrase which, interpreted innocently, might serve as a motto for the playing of the earlier comedies but which here has an ugly aspect, given the corrupt policy of the play. In the next scene, we have a whole series of intrigues: first, Claudius welcomes Rosencrantz and Guildenstern and describes to them their new task – to spy on Hamlet; then Polonius and Claudius plot to 'loose' Ophelia to Hamlet to see if his melancholy is a product of frustrated love; next, we have Rosencrantz and Guildenstern's efforts to probe Hamlet, to test him for ambition; then the players enter, into a situation so full of counterfeiting that theirs can hardly have a positive ring. Finally, Hamlet develops a plot to trap Claudius – with a *play*! All this in one, admittedly long, scene.

The next scene, III.i, shows us Claudius questioning Rosencrantz and Guildenstern for the results of their first efforts, then relapsing into guilty knowledge of his own counterfeiting in the speech about the harlot's cheek mentioned above. Hamlet enters with the 'To be or not to be' soliloquy, a rumination which questions the value of the whole illusory enterprise, setting the temporal scheming into focus by providing a context of eternity. Ophelia enters and, with Claudius and Polonius watching from behind the arras, plays a scene with the hostile Hamlet, who himself knows the plot and acts accordingly.[19] After this, with the causes of Hamlet's madness still not apparent to the schemers, Polonius suggests a further device: 'Let his queen mother all alone entreat him / To show his grief ... I'll be plac'd, so please you, in the ear of all their conference' (III.i.190-3). Here the spying is feeding on itself. It is being suggested less as a way of finding things out (at this point, Polonius has no reason to suspect that Gertrude will hide things from them) than as a continuation of a mode of action that is fundamental to the relations of the Danish court. The next scene is the play-scene which, coming on the heels of such tortuous intrigue and scene playing, has been set into a highly ambiguous moral context.

It is important to recognize that, because of this distrust of disguise and 'play,' the relationship established between audience and action is different from that typical of the earlier comedies or the tragedies. Since, within the play, acting is associated with intrigue and entrapment, the feeling the audience is likely to get is one of alienation, even sometimes of threat. It seems to me, and the feeling is shared by many other spectators, that our experience of *Hamlet* and the hero's predicament is less immediate and more distanced than our experience of plays such as *Othello, King Lear, Macbeth, Antony and Cleopatra*, even *Romeo and Juliet*; and our involvement in the festivity of the comedies, while very different, is sometimes equally engaging. *Hamlet*'s appeal is more intellectual than emotional; a good production will fascinate more than it moves. Even though we get to know Hamlet more fully than any other Shakespearean character, we are hardly ever brought to feel with him the way we do with characters like Othello, in whom there is so much less of ourselves. Hamlet, as I have said, attempts to use illusion as an instrument of illumination and control, and to some extent he succeeds. But the ultimate failure of his efforts suggests a certain incompleteness (deriving perhaps from Shakespeare's apparent distrust of his own forms) in the audience-play relation; the very sources of our pleasure (we enjoy being an audience) are called into question by the fact that a certain scheming or guilty consciousness is so often associated in the play with listening and watching. This suggests that the play does not carry within it its own theatrical justification, as plays such as *As You Like It, King Lear*, or *The Tempest* do[20] (which of course does not mean that the role-playing is without a great deal of psychological and cultural significance). If we follow Hamlet's manipulative efforts, we can get a clearer picture of both their significance and their failure.

At the beginning of the play scene, Hamlet gives his famous advice to the players, in which he says that 'the purpose of playing' is to show 'the very age and body of the time his form and pressure.' Earlier, in talking to Polonius, he says of the players that they are 'the abstract and brief chronicles of the time' (II.ii.548-9). At the outset, he had realized that 'The *time* is out of joint.' The play-within, by the very fact that it is a play, as well as by the fact that it mirrors 'real' events (showing them to be out of joint) does show the time its 'pressure' (just as the play, *Hamlet*, shows the pressure of its time, as this whole chapter argues) since 'the time' finds its most characteristic stamp in 'playing,' in corrupt or ambiguous intrigue. Hamlet's madness, his disguised presence within his real world, stands in the same ambiguous relationship to the events of the play as the play-within; it is an expression of the world of the play and an attempt to control it, to make it into art. Now, Hamlet is stage manager, chorus, and part author of the play-within, as well as a member of the audience, and we may, I think, take that multiple role as an emblem of the position vis-à-vis the rest of the court that he wants to achieve. He wants to make a play of them, in a sense, not unlike the way Portia and Rosalind make a play out of 'real' situations. The problem is that Claudius is not so easy to manipulate as the Player King (or as Orlando). Still, the mousetrap is partially successful and we may take Hamlet's elation after it works as the elation of the artist whose *plot* (again the ambiguity) is working out.

His excitement manifests itself as a consolidation of his control. In the scene which follows the abrupt interruption of the play and Hamlet's exclamations to Horatio, Hamlet brings Rosencrantz and Guildenstern face to face with their own crafty purposes through the game with the pipe:

HAMLET Will you play upon this pipe?
GUILDENSTERN My lord, I cannot.
HAMLET I pray you.
GUILDENSTERN Believe me, I cannot ...
HAMLET It is as easy as lying ...

GUILDENSTERN ... I have not the skill.
HAMLET Why, look you now, how unworthy a thing you make of me! You would play upon me; you would seem to know my stops; you would pluck out the heart of my mystery ... (III.ii.365-82)

This, again, is a kind of 'scene' created by Hamlet for his own moral and psychological purposes. It is like the playing that Rosalind does with Phebe and Silvius, although here, of course, the situation is more serious and the issues political rather than amorous. There is a strong, significant contrast between this scene and the similar ones (IV.ii and IV.iii) that follow the closet scene. In IV.ii Hamlet appears again with Rosencrantz and Guildenstern, but this time without the confident control he manifested in III.ii. He is now on the run, and on the defensive: 'Besides, to be demanded of a sponge, what replication should be made by the son of a king?' (12-14). He is still a verbal master, able to make fools of Rosencrantz and Guildenstern, especially in the development of the sponge analogy (16-22). But there is a tonal difference; now we get the sense that the verbal mastery and wit stand as a substitute for the more firmly based control of the earlier scene. This sense is corroborated in the next scene when Hamlet faces Claudius. The latter's decisiveness, as he solidifies his decision to send Hamlet away, is contrasted with Hamlet's mercurial oscillation. He is brought before Claudius and dodges his questions with fiendish cleverness: 'Where's Polonius?' 'At supper.' 'At supper? Where?' 'Not where he eats, but where he is eaten. A certain convocation of politic worms are e'en at him ...' (17-21). Hamlet goads Claudius, insults him, but does not stand up to him. The extreme verbal wit, whose very extremity is emphasized by the morbid preoccupation with the processes of physical decay, serves as a camouflage covering the disintegration of that inner vitality which prompted his attempts at 'comic' control through Acts II and III. He therefore accepts without question Claudius's decision to send him to England and seems to let himself fall passively into a trap (though he does have vague, but unconvincing plans to doublecross Rosencrantz and Guildenstern, or so he suggests to his mother).

If we ask what has intervened between the first of these scenes and the latter two to cause the apparent loss of control, the event which assumes the most importance is the impulsive, panicky slaying of Polonius. This is, I think, the turning point of the action viewed in the context of Hamlet's attempt at theatrical manipulation. It is the first instance of an *uncontrolled* action on Hamlet's part and marks the point where Hamlet's 'comic' efforts are finally and irrevocably deflected. What this means is that a potentially comic structure is transformed into tragedy through a loss of 'theatrical' control. This becomes clearer if we contrast the play with Marston's *The Malcontent*, written around the same time, in which a prince, robbed of his throne, stays at the court disguised as a madman. He gradually manipulates the action to a successful comic conclusion and, in the process, clears up the corruption, both sexual and political, which theatened to overwhelm the court. Shakespeare has turned this kind of conventional situation into a penetrating analysis of the difficulties and delusions of such comic control.

Related to the murder of Polonius are the surrounding scenes in which Hamlet is unable to take the opportunity to kill Claudius and instead manufactures a pretext for not acting (as readers as diverse as Coleridge and Ernest Jones have argued),[21] and then attacks his mother in a scene in which his unconscious incest wish manifests itself in an aggressive, phallic brutality ('I will speak daggers to her, but use none,' iii.ii.414) and in an inordinate fascination with and revulsion from her sexuality ('Nay, but to live in the rank sweat of an enseamed bed, / Stew'd in corruption, honeying and making love over the nasty sty' iii.iv. 92-5). The conjunction of these three events, the unwillingness to kill Claudius, the killing of Polonius in the mother's closet, and the attack on his mother for her sexuality, lend weight to the psychoanalytic interpretation and reveal a point of convergence between that interpretation and the theory I am trying to develop. As we have seen, the techniques of comic manipulation have an important relation to identity, and this is as true for Hamlet as for Rosalind and Orlando. It is significant, therefore, that the comic effort flounders on the very reefs that psychoanalytic thought stresses as the obstacles to Hamlet's achievement of full identity. The struggle towards a personal identity has as well an important public, political dimension, a dimension which reveals a decisive contradiction in traditional society, related to the contradiction, psychological and moral, within the central figure. And it is to this broader issue that we now turn.

Hamlet's 'madness' is expressed not only by his behaviour and his language but by his dress as well. Ophelia describes him as 'Lord Hamlet, with his doublet all unbrac'd, / No hat upon his head, his stockings foul'd, / Ungarter'd, and down-gyved to his ankle, / Pale as his shirt ...' (ii.i.78-81). As Dover Wilson shows, he wears the uniform of madness throughout most of Acts ii and iii.[22] This dress bears a similar relation to his madness as his mourning dress did to his very unfeigned melancholy. It is an external appearance with an ambiguous but nonetheless fundamental relationship to the inner reality. There is, however, a contrast as well, since in the case of his madness the external appearance is *more* than the inner reality while his mourning clothes represent less than what's inside. But, in a sense, both modes of dress are an act. As Hamlet says of his grief, a man 'might play' at mourning (even if he have 'that within which passeth show'), just as a man might play at madness and still be a little bit mad.

Dress in Elizabethan society had what we might call an emblematic function, that is, it was related to the social hierarchy, each 'place' having its appropriate mode of dress which was then an emblem, a public manifestation, of that place.[23]

To violate this code was in some cases (as with the wearing of swords) against the law. The eventual result in court circles was self-conscious elaboration of costume (Osric's clothes would presumably be as flowery as his speech) which bespoke for an individual courtier a higher 'place' – in the Baconian rather than the traditional sense* – than someone else. At court, the notion of dress as an emblem slides easily into the use of dress as a status symbol.

Hamlet's costume, however, is a symbol of a very different order. His clothes are the badge of a different kind of status, that of the madman or fool. His role as fool is what gives him the licence to speak and act as he does without, at first, arousing too much suspicion or hatred. The fool's freedom was, of course, conventional in the theatre as was the notion that the fool's wisdom, though hidden, was indeed real. This convention was undoubtedly related to the ritual role of the madman in society as Michel Foucault describes it.[24] According to Foucault the madman was located at the centre of a tension between exclusion and passage, passage to a profoundly perceptive confrontation with a kind of cosmic Unreason. And, interestingly, Foucault describes a comic process of enlightenment through madness which is strikingly close to the point I have made about illusion dispelling illusion. Madness is

the most rigorously necessary form of the *quid pro quo* in the dramatic economy, for it needs no external element to reach a true resolution. It has merely to carry its illusion to the point of truth ... In madness equilibrium is established, but it masks the equilibrium under a cloud of illusion ... Madness is the great *trompe-l'oeil* in the tragicomic structures of preclassical literature.[25]

Madness, then, besides being a manipulative device, is also a step out of the traditional order (an 'exclusion'), and a step which offers a new perspective on the very ground of one's being and heritage (hence a 'passage'). Hamlet's madness thus becomes a test of the authenticity of his culture. As such, it represents a threat to the traditional system which, as I mentioned, is the official ideology of the Danish court. Claudius recognizes this and therefore thinks Hamlet dangerous and has him watched. Hamlet is floating free, he has no fixed 'place' as he ought to have, and this is what worries people. Rosencrantz and Guildenstern's suspicion of Hamlet's ambition (primed by Claudius) is an attempt to fit Hamlet into their ideological mold, to 'rationalize' him, as it were. But his sense of dis-

* By 'traditional' I mean the sense as in Ulysses' speech on degree when he speaks of all things standing 'in authentic place.' For Bacon, 'high place' did not refer to a stationary rung on a hierarchical ladder but a position to be reached by ambitious but circumspect social climbing. See his essay 'Of High Place.'

placement is deeper and more ambiguous. His clothing is an important theatrical symbol for his ambiguous position because it is an ironic manifestation of 'place' and self. The moral bankruptcy of conventional self-display (that typical of the late Elizabethan and Jacobean court) is clear from Osric or Rosencrantz and Guildenstern; Hamlet is seeking a more authentic kind of behaviour as of speech (though outside of his 'authentic place' in the traditional sense) in a different kind of acting, an acting which expresses the self instead of masking it.

The political and what might be called the philosophical significance of the role-playing in the play seems to me to rest in this relation between Hamlet's acting and the traditional order. Politically, the role-playing represents an abdication of his princely role (we might say that he is not the prince because he is not dressed like one – 'the apparel oft proclaims the man') in an effort to test the traditional polity by which he should be king. Philosophically, the disguise (like those in *As You Like It* and *The Merchant of Venice*) allows Hamlet to test abstractions, but this time the abstractions are not those of unexamined love but concern the whole issue of man's place in a political and moral universe. What his test reveals both to himself and to us in an unbridgeable contradiction built into the old system, a contradiction which he expresses in his 'What a piece of work is a man' speech and which provides the basis for all the imagery of corruption in the play, imagery that arises out of the organic metaphor, the conception of the state as a *body* politic. Hamlet recognizes that such a conception depends on the humanist assessment of man, not on man as quintessence of dust. The play, I think, lays bare the dilemma of the Christian humanist synthesis even as it expresses the nobility of that synthesis.[26] What it records is a transition from a collective to an individualist consciousness in the political as in the philosophical order. We need not wonder, then, at Hamlet's hesitation and tentativeness; his delay can be seen as the result of his need to test the traditional system and his gradual loss of faith in its validity. His problem is that he has no order, no heritage, to sustain him, and so he must try to create his own, a compulsion which soon overcomes the injunction to kill Claudius.

At the same time, there is a very powerful nostalgia in the play for the loss involved in the collapse of the old faith. The record of this nostalgia is the pastoral, conceived of as an *impulse* rather than a convention. The world, for Hamlet, is a 'sterile promontory' where no growth is possible; it is an 'unweeded garden / That grows to seed; things rank and gross in nature / Possess it merely' (I.ii.135-7). A general sense of loss pervades the play. We are introduced to it in the first scene with the news of the recent death of the king and it grows when we are introduced to Hamlet mourning for his dead father. The loss of innocence in woman (both Ophelia and Gertrude – 'Frailty thy name is woman'), of friendship among men (Hamlet and Rosencrantz and Guildenstern), of wholesomeness in the state, all add to the heavy atmosphere of loss.

In *Richard II*, a similar perception of the state finds expression in a static, emblematic scene in which a gardener tends his garden as the country ought to be tended but is not (III.iv). In both plays, the use of the pastoral implies the notion of a good, well-ordered society, the vision of an ideal which is not being realized. In *Richard II*, the ideal seems both clear and attainable; in *Hamlet*, it is envisioned mostly as the opposite of what exists at present; in *Richard II*, again, the perception of disorder is externally presented while in *Hamlet* it is internalized. It becomes a dominant element in Hamlet's most intimate experience. The result is agony and disgust. Disgust, particularly, is the dominant emotion of the play; it is expressed in the language of rankness, sickness, and corruption which runs throughout. Sexual disgust especially, a kind of revulsion from and fascination with physical processes. Hamlet's attacks on both Ophelia and his mother reveal the extreme ambivalence he feels about women: his demand that they be excessively virginal and non-physical linked with his fear that they are rampantly and aggressively sexual.

Disgust is a kind of inverted pastoral feeling. This seems to be at the basis of Hamlet's accusation of his mother, that she has taken 'off the *rose* / From the fair forehead of an innocent love,' his love for Ophelia.[27] She is responsible for his disgust and has thus destroyed their pastoral love. It is important that both Hamlet and Ophelia are elsewhere referred to as roses. After the nunnery scene, Ophelia laments that Hamlet is no longer what he was, 'the expectancy and *rose* of this fair state'; Laertes calls to Ophelia as she enters, mad, to strew *flowers*, 'O rose of May.' All of these are evocations of a lost past, a broken vision, a truncated potentiality: Hamlet and Ophelia's springtime love, Hamlet's young, blooming princeliness, Ophelia's flowerlike innocence. In the first scene, which contains the germ of so many important elements in the play, there is a beautiful evocation of Christmastide, set in language very different from the rest of the play:

> Some say that ever 'gainst that season comes
> Wherein our Saviour's birth is celebrated,
> The bird of dawning singeth all night long;
> And then, they say, no spirit dare stir abroad,
> The nights are wholesome, then no planets strike,
> No fairy takes, nor witch hath power to charm,
> So hallow'd and so gracious is the time. (I.i.158-64)

The point is that this is not *now* – now the nights are not 'wholesome' (the word provides a brief, nostalgic counterpoint to the powerful, pervasive language of corruption), ghosts *are* walking, something is rotten in the 'fair state.'

In *Richard II*, as I have said, the pastoral is a static allegory representing a perception of disorder. But even there, the allegory has a significant ambiguity. On the one hand, the garden scene acts as a focus for the pervasive plant and growth imagery in the play.[28] As such, it is associated with Richard himself, who invokes the traditional, hieratic imagery and the divine right of kings as a justification of both his actions and his identity. On the other hand, the kind of action that the garden scene advocates is tough, effective political action like that of Bolingbroke:

> GARDENER Go thou and, like an executioner,
> Cut off the heads of too fast growing sprays
> That look too lofty in our commonwealth.
> All must be even in our government ...
> MAN Why should we, in the compass of a pale,
> Keep law and form and due proportion ...
> When our sea-walled garden, the whole land,
> Is full of weeds, her fairest flowers chok'd up,
> Her fruit trees all unprun'd, her hedges ruin'd ...
> GARDENER   Hold thy peace.
> He that hath suffer'd this disordered spring
> Hath now himself met with the fall of leaf.
> The weeds which his broad-spreading leaves did shelter,
> That seem'd in eating him to hold him up,
> Are pluck'd up root and all by Bolingbroke ...
>   Bolingbroke
> Hath seiz'd the wasteful king. (III.iv.33-5)

The scene, then, is actually praising the actions of Bolingbroke, the usurper. Built right into the scene, therefore, there is a paradox: the language and style of the traditional order are used as a justification for activity destructive of that order. The paradox, I think, is an indication of a shifting attitude within Shakespeare's society, a transition of political or cultural consciousness signalling the decline of the old order and its political imperatives. In *Richard II*, this transition is reflected in the play as a whole (its political relevance was not lost on the followers of Essex, who commissioned a performance of the play on the eve of their rebellion); in *Hamlet*, the transition is internalized as part of the hero's consciousness and embodied in the play's language.

In the comedies, the political reverberations of the pastoral are far in the background. The 'green world' is a region of play and illusion, an illusion which usually results in some kind of clarification. But the political overtones are not entirely absent. We should not forget that part of the pastoral experience in *As*

You Like It, for example, depends on the contrast between court and country and that the result of that experience is the restitution of the Duke to his rightful throne. In general in the comedies, disguise and manipulation work *within* the pastoral, towards the restitution of a new order, both psychological and social. In *Hamlet*, on the other hand, these devices are working *against* the pastoral, that is, they are presented as part of a world for which the pastoral is a lost potentiality. This marks *Hamlet* as a key play in the transition from *As You Like It* to *Measure for Measure*, in the shift, that is, from a relatively uncomplicated and optimistic view of comic potentiality and comic devices to a sometimes bitter awareness of their limitations and failures. It also marks the play as the halfway point in the psychic distance between *As You Like It* and *The Tempest*.

In the latter play, again about a ruler who has lost his kingdom, the only pastoral is that created by the artist, Prospero, the image of the playwright within the play. Prospero's island is both a 'real' (in the same sense that Arden is 'real'), magic, pastoral place and, more importantly, an *imaginative* place, created and sustained by the theatrical imagination. It is, in a sense, both playground and theatre, a place where all events are produced through Prospero's power and achieve a kind of dual reality, as shows created by the artist-magician and as events perceived as real by the people involved. *The Tempest* explores the relationship between these two aspects of reality and depicts the transforming power of the theatrical enterprise both within plays and within theatres. The pastoral world thus becomes identified with the world of the theatre and the responses of the various characters to Prospero's creations are intimately linked to the audience's responses to Shakespeare's. Through this linking of the imagined and the actual, the whole problem of personal and political restitution is resolved in the formation of a complex attitude, a vision of human possibility created by art but depending on reason and virtue to make it work. At the end of the play, the courtiers return to 'civilization,' to a society which still has real human problems; but the viewpoint which the play has created and fostered is alive in them and occupies a vital place in the new polity.[29] What Prospero does is what I think Hamlet is trying to do with his role-playing and his sense of personal and political loss. But instead of a magic island, the ultimate pastoral vision in *Hamlet* is a graveyard.

The archetypal pastoral story is, of course, the myth of the Garden of Eden and the most powerful pastoral impulse is that leading back to Eden. In *Hamlet*, the grave becomes a kind of ironic parody of Eden. Just before we meet the gravediggers, we watch Laertes and Claudius plot to kill Hamlet. Their contriving is like a recapitulation of the major themes of the play: for one thing, they devise a *show*, the duel, which is also a trap; for another, Claudius's language is peppered with references to sickness and corruption ('For goodness, growing to a plurisy, / Dies in his own too much.' IV.vii.118-19); in addition, Laertes describes the poison which will so easily gall the life out of Hamlet, reminding us as he does so of the poison that killed Hamlet senior, and Claudius acts as if to emphasize this memory by adding to the plot the melodrama of the poisoned cup. As they complete their plans, Gertrude flies in with the news of Ophelia's death. Her very beautiful description of the circumstances is no sooner over than the gravediggers enter, engaged in a burlesque discussion of suicide and the legalistic niceties of Christian burial. Death, in its tragic and comic aspects, rules. Gertrude's description of Ophelia is a picture of innocence gone blank, of the drowning of spring:

> ... fantastic garlands did she make
> Of crowflowers, nettles, daisies, and long purples,
> That liberal shepherds give a grosser name,
> But our cold maids do dead men's fingers call them.
> There on the pendent boughs her coronet weeds
> Clamb'ring to hang, an envious sliver broke,
> When down her weedy trophies and herself
> Fell in the weeping brook. Her clothes spread wide
> And, mermaid-like, awhile they bore her up ...
>   But long it could not be
> Till that her garments, heavy with their drink,
> Pull'd the poor wretch from her melodious lay
> To muddy death. (IV.vii.170-8, 182-4)

It is unquestionably a lovely pastoral picture, but it is also a mindless, vacant one. Its placing suggests the ultimate collapse of the pastoral impulse in a world of political intrigue and murder. To live in the pastoral world in this play, one has to go mad; and it all ends in 'muddy death.' (Sexuality, too, an integral part of the traditional pastoral, is linked with madness and death: in Ophelia's songs in her first mad scene, and here in the reference to 'dead men's fingers.') Ophelia's attempt to reach Eden ends in the graveyard. The point is reinforced a moment later when the equivocal gravedigger equates gardeners and gravemakers, who both, he says, 'hold up Adam's profession.' The final death of the pastoral impulse and its burial in the graveyard indicates, I need hardly point out, the impossibility of re-establishing the order and perfection of the lost past.*

---

* The graveyard also registers the death of another important motif, that of Hamlet's role as fool. His dialogue with the clown shows him still to be a master of words – his joking here is almost obsessive – but Yorick's skull reminds us that the fool is dead. It is a kind of symbol for Hamlet's failure to carry through that role.

For Hamlet, the lost past is tied up with his own sense of political and personal identity. His task of reasserting order is not simply a political one (the fact that he is a prince trying to gain back a usurped throne plays an important, though secondary role) but also a broadly human one, just as the pastoral is a universal human impulse. Hamlet's problem is one of identity in the fullest sense, of achieving identity in a world where order no longer exists, where there are no longer any defined rites of passage. This is a key theme of the 'To be or not to be' soliloquy. Suicide is one answer to the problem of identity: 'by opposing, end it.' The alternative is *how* to be, how to act in a corrupt world, a world plagued by the oppressor's wrong, the insolence of office, and the other generalized evils which Hamlet catalogues (and which, though he doesn't relate them directly to his own predicament, clearly arise out of it). The feelings and attitudes expressed here are a far cry from the relatively simple anger and despair of the first soliloquy – a despair kept at a distance by the canon of the Almighty – and represent a complete reversal of Hamlet's determination in the previous scene to catch the conscience of the king. Now there is no scruple about the canons of the church, nor is there the Oedipal despair. And his sense of mission is in abeyance. What prompts this outburst then? I suggest that the speech arises out of an uncertainty (a sense of the absurd, we might call it today) so penetrating that Claudius's death could not assuage it. Such a vision represents the point of convergence between Hamlet's role-playing and his inner self, for his very free-floating quality in his mad role, his state of suspension, has an inner correlative in his insecure identity. This manifests itself in the style of the 'To be ...' speech as well – its loose, ruminative connections, its almost stream-of-consciousness quality. As the play progresses and Hamlet loses his manipulative control, the pastoral begins to merge with the funereal; and it becomes increasingly clear that the whole problem of identity is never solved. Hamlet doesn't find a way to live, only a way to die.

Before concluding, I want to examine the nature of the political world of the play in a little more detail. In the scene where Hamlet encounters Fortinbras and his army on their way to Poland (IV.iv), we move away from a concentration on the corruption of the Danish court to a survey of the world of international politics. To Hamlet's inquiries about the purposes of the expedition, the Norwegian captain replies:

> We go to gain a little patch of ground
> That hath in it no profit but the name.
> To pay five ducats, five, I would not farm it;
> Nor will it yield to Norway or the Pole
> A ranker rate, should it be sold in fee. (IV.iv.18-22)

Hamlet cannot believe the Pole will defend it, but when he is assured that it is 'already garrisoned,' he observes:

> Two thousand souls and twenty thousand ducats
> Will not debate the question of this straw.
> This is th'imposthume of much wealth and peace,
> That inward breaks, and shows no cause without
> Why the man dies. (IV.iv.25-9)

He perceives the whole exploit as an 'imposthume' in the body politic, a hidden ulcer that is as deadly to the state as the more overt corruption of Denmark. All the language of the play is in these lines – images of sickness and death, the discrepancy between appearance and reality, the implicit realization that peace (or any human ideal) is an illusion. Immediately after this exchange, Hamlet speaks his last soliloquy, in which he again upbraids himself for not performing his 'dull revenge.' As he had earlier used the player, he now uses Fortinbras as a foil to illumine his own predicament:

> Witness this army of such mass and charge,
> Led by a delicate and tender prince,
> Whose spirit, with divine ambition puff'd,
> Makes mouths at the invisible event,
> Exposing what is mortal and unsure
> To all that fortune, death, and danger dare,
> Even for an eggshell. Rightly to be great
> Is not to stir without great argument,
> But greatly to find quarrel in a straw
> When honour's at the stake. How stand I then,
> That have a father kill'd, a mother stain'd ...
>   ... while to my shame I see
> The imminent death of twenty thousand men
> That for a fantasy and trick of fame
> Go to their graves like beds ...
>   ... O, from this time forth,
> My thoughts be bloody, or be nothing worth! (IV.iv.47-66)

There is an extraordinary ambiguity in this speech, an ambiguity which is designed to foster in us a double attitude towards Hamlet's assertions, an attitude which we have already formed in response to his previous vows of revenge. He pulls back from his earlier perception of the 'imposthume' and praises Fortinbras for his ability to find quarrel in a straw and to derive honour from such a quarrel.

But the use of 'straw' and 'eggshell,' and the phrase 'with divine ambition puffed,' where the hyperbole of 'divine' is immediately undercut by 'puffed,' creates a sense that runs counter to the primary meaning.

This scene, together with what follows it, the madness of Ophelia and the hasty revolution stirred up by Laertes, gives a clearer picture than even all the court intrigues do of the madness of the political world of this play. Jan Kott writes that 'Politics is itself madness, when it destroys all feeling and affection.'[30] We might add that politics is also mad when it places honour before responsibility, death before life. Shakespeare, in this scene, questions the whole notion of Renaissance honour and, in so doing, undercuts Hamlet's resolution to revenge ('My thoughts be bloody or be nothing worth').[31] We adopt Hamlet's ambivalent response to Fortinbras and, at the same time, we are led to see Hamlet's revenge in a similarly ambiguous light.

Why does Hamlet pull back from his perception of the 'imposthume' in Fortinbras's action to an assertion of the necessity to uphold honour? I think because he senses that without this notion of honour the whole political system, the world of both Hamlet senior and Fortinbras, will collapse. But there is an undercurrent both here and in the graveyard scene a little later that honour is simply not worth it. Hamlet asserts the importance of honour even as he realizes its limitations; he contains within himself both sides of the conflict represented in *Henry IV* by Hotspur and Falstaff. Hamlet, like Falstaff, sees very clearly the mortality of honour ('What is honour? A word. Who hath it? He that died a-Wednesday.') In the graveyard, Hamlet speculates on Alexander and Caesar, the very models of honour:

Alexander died, Alexander was buried, Alexander returneth into dust; the dust is earth; of earth we make loam; and why of that loam (whereto he was converted) might they not stop a beer barrel?

> Imperious Caesar, dead and turn'd to clay,
> Might stop a hole to keep the wind away. (v.i.231-7)

Just as he finishes this little disquisition, the funeral procession enters with the body of his one-time love and, in another of those powerful shifts of tone and feeling which characterize the play and its hero, Hamlet is struck with the utter seriousness of death, and proceeds to assert his own honour in the teeth of Laertes.

This sense of shift, or strong contradiction and resulting inconclusiveness, dominates the last scene of the play as well. Rather than serving as a resolution of the conflicting issues of the play, this scene seems to present them more clearly than ever. Most critics do not seem to have noticed or fully appreciated the problems of this scene. The standard view is that Hamlet returns from England a revitalized and better man, ready to meet his obligations and accept death if necessary. For this interpretation, critics tend to lean heavily on two speeches ('There's a divinity that shapes our ends ...' and 'Readiness is all') without casting a cold enough eye on Hamlet's *actions* and on certain other speeches.[32] Granville-Barker, with his usual perceptiveness, sees the final Hamlet as 'royal' and 'noble' in the Fortinbras mould, emphasizing his kingliness ('I am Hamlet the Dane') and his coldbloodedness in dispatching Rosencrantz and Guildenstern. But the inevitable result of the combination of these latter qualities is a loss in feeling, a drastic emotional narrowing, which for Granville-Barker accompanies Hamlet's new determination to perform his task. He has become 'fit for his task' but 'in the conversion much that seemed lovely in his nature has perished.'[33] Such an interpretation, while bringing some shadowy elements into the foreground, tends to overlook the very facts that support the standard view and is unable to explain the haphazard, arbitrary slaughter at the end (though on this last point the standard view does no better). There seems to me to be little evidence to show that now Hamlet is ready and determined to kill Claudius; he has no *plan* and his talk with Horatio about not letting 'this canker of our nature come / In further evil' (v.ii.69-70) sounds similar to other threats and promises throughout the play. Moreover, the 'Readiness' speech is more passive resignation than kingly determination. On the other hand, there *is* evidence to suggest that his capacity to feel has not been lessened (his friendship with Horatio is as deep if not deeper, and his response to Ophelia's death and subsequent declaration of love seem to me genuine and characteristic of the earlier Hamlet). Furthermore, his awareness of himself and his situation seems as acute as ever.

There appears to be, then, a rather powerful contradiction running through this last act. On the one hand, we have Hamlet's 'divinity' and 'Readiness' speeches, his acceptance of death, the bold statement of his love for Ophelia, his new balanced, personal style that I described at the beginning – all this seems to point to a new Hamlet who has built within himself his own order. But on the other hand, there is his adoption of his political (pragmatic and ruthless) role, there is the manner of carrying out the revenge itself, a deed which could hardly arise out of either the resigned Christian impulse, or the kingly one, and finally there is Hamlet's elaborate, courtly apology to Laertes just before the duel, a speech which has bothered many commentators:

> Was't Hamlet wrong'd Laertes? Never Hamlet.
> If Hamlet from himself be ta'en away,

> And when he's not himself does wrong Laertes,
> Then Hamlet does it not, Hamlet denies it.
> Who does it, then? His madness. If't be so,
> Hamlet is of the faction that is wrong'd;
> His madness is poor Hamlet's enemy. (v.ii.244-50)

This from a man who was mad but north-north-west! It is impossible for me to accept Wilson's argument that this speech represents a sincere outpouring of Hamlet's generous nature.[34] With Bradley, I see it as dissimulation.[35] And, I might add, a shrewdly pragmatic sort of dissimulation, given the situation. Certainly the style, so courtly and contrived, contrasts markedly with the simple, personal style of the 'Readiness' speech; and the distinction between Hamlet and his madness smacks of casuistry.

As I argued above, statements like those he makes in iv.iv, have prepared us to respond to Hamlet's assertions in a double way. His assertion of kingship in the last act is just the sort of ambiguous statement that his praise for Fortinbras is. That is, it arises out of only part of his nature. It is the way, at times, he wants to be – the way, in an uncomplicated world, he would be, like his father or Fortinbras. Similarly, the resigned, Christian speeches and state of mind arise out of a different and contradictory impulse, a nostalgia for a Christian system which no longer provides the absolute order it once did. This feeling harks back to the first scene and Marcellus's speech about Christmastide, a speech which emphasizes the distance between the time it describes and the present.

The ambiguity and oscillation of the last act seem to me explicable only in terms of what Hamlet is trying to do. As I see it, he is trying to establish some kind of permanent order; he is trying in various ways to solidify his fluid world. Out of his vain attempt comes a kind of violent frustration which seems to me to underlie the whole of the last scene. His perception of the corruption of the political world and the illusion of honour prohibits him from taking straightforward political action as Laertes and Fortinbras do in Act iv. Thus, ironically, the very depth and subtlety of his perception tends to foster the violent destructiveness which erupts at the end and which seems to stand behind even the apparent harmony of his peaceful and clairvoyant moments.

Hamlet's ultimate problem, then, is that he is unable to fuse the opposing impulses arising from his far-ranging awareness. He is unable to maintain all his insights and balance all the conflicting forces which the disintegration of humanism and the old polity have unleashed. His tragedy is that he cannot establish a mode of life, an individual and social order, based on his insights. In *The Tempest*, such an order is precisely what the play does create. But in *Hamlet*, the attempt leads to annihilation. Hamlet's act of destruction at the end (the word 'act' retains its ambiguity; he is unable to fuse the role and the man) seems to symbolize the irrevocable split. It is not the calculated act of a Machiavellian prince, nor the cleansing, sacrificial act of the saint. It is the violent, almost anarchic expression of a desperation which is at once both 'theatrical' and real. In a moment of histrionic superfluity, Hamlet forces the poisoned wine down the gullet of his uncle a second after wounding him with the envenomed sword. And he speaks to those around him: 'You that look pale and tremble at this chance, / That are but mutes or audience to this *act*, / Had I but time ...' and he could as easily be speaking to us as to the court. Theatricality and actuality (the act within the play and the act within the theatre) do in fact converge here, but not to solidify love as in *As You Like It*, nor to underline the value of art as illumination as in *King Lear* and, more completely, in *The Tempest*. The effect here is more ambiguous, though no less profound. Hamlet's 'act' does not clarify; it merely ends. The audience is more disturbed than illuminated. Hamlet's consciousness remains divided, and the sense of the value of the techniques he has exploited remains uncertain.

Hamlet's final awareness, then, is a contradictory one, just as his earlier humanism was contradictory (man is the paragon of animals *and* the quintessence of dust). But the paradox of this awareness is itself deeply human and far-ranging. This is what accounts for the enormous sympathy which, despite all the ambiguity, accrues to Hamlet throughout this final scene. Hamlet's problem, and our own, is that such a vision is not and cannot be comprehended by society or social forms, that such a consciousness moves beyond and outside the political or social body.* The play emphasizes this in the final irony of Fortinbras's entry with the English ambassadors. These latter remind us both of the death of Rosencrantz and Guildenstern and of the short time Hamlet had – and used only by chance – to accomplish his purpose. Fortinbras, the stalwart, unthinking man of honour, becomes king. The final society that is established thus moves back from the vision of the tragic hero to the pragmatism of the man of affairs. The irony of this shift is underlined in Fortinbras's final testimony to Hamlet: 'Bear Hamlet like a *soldier* to the stage; / For he was likely, had he been put on, / To have prov'd most *royally*.' By this time, we are aware of the inadequacy of words like 'soldier' and 'royal' when applied to Hamlet and his vision. And the tragic irony only reinforces our sense of the distance between such a vision and the structures of a society to which it is alien.

---

* Implicit in this final part of the play and, I think, in Hamlet's final words, is the realization that societies are not normally built on such a vision; rather, they move to restrict awareness in order to ensure smooth functioning. The business of tragedy (or comedy) within society is to underscore just this point and to extend individual and social awareness.

4

A Midsummer Night's Dream, Twelfth Night, and Troilus and Cressida

Through the three plays to be discussed in this chapter,[1] we can trace a development of changing attitudes and structural forms that to some extent recapitulates the development described in the previous three chapters and that points towards the second half of Shakespeare's career. In *The Merchant of Venice* and *As You Like It*, Shakespeare is moulding a comic structure which is buoyant and optimistic, well suited to the issues raised by the plays. Deception and illusion provide satisfactory solutions to problems of love, of justice, of private and public affairs. In *Hamlet*, Shakespeare first expresses a deep ambivalence towards these comic tools and reveals the inadequacy of even benevolent disguise in the face of personal and political corruption. *A Midsummer Night's Dream* and *Twelfth Night*, without depending strictly on manipulative disguise, extend the range of the comic uses of illusion within an optimistic context. *Troilus and Cressida*, like *Hamlet*, registers a distrust of roles and illusions, depicting them as destructive and self-serving.

For different reasons and in different ways, the world of each of these three plays is fluid and uncertain. Moonlight, madness, and impermanence result in radical changes in personality – comic metamorphoses, abrupt redirection of feelings, violent responses to shifting circumstances. The very ground of life in Athens, Illyria, and Troy, the social reality that upholds the lives of the characters, seems elusive and capricious. But in *A Midsummer Night's Dream* and, for the most part, in *Twelfth Night*, this uncertainty is comic, both funny and life-enhancing; while in *Troilus and Cressida*, it is entirely destructive. In the latter play, we feel strongly the irreducible conflict of opposites, a bifurcation in the world and in the mind; a conflict which is harmoniously resolved through magic and imagination in *A Midsummer Night's Dream*, and through the ingenious circular architecture of *Twelfth Night*.

Looking at the role of the senses in each of the plays yields the same general point. In all three, the senses, especially sight, are highly untrustworthy and 'deceptious.' But in *A Midsummer Night's Dream* this untrustworthiness leads harmlessly to the hilarious complication of partners in the forest and to the absurdly rational justifications that accompany such shifts, and, in *Twelfth Night*, it leads to a host of misperceptions and mistaken identities, all of which find a satisfying resolution; whereas, in *Troilus and Cressida*, the deceptiveness of the senses is a brutal fact, an aspect of the generally unhinged, unfixed nature of things.

In *A Midsummer Night's Dream*, as in *Twelfth Night* and *Troilus and Cressida*, there is no disguised manipulator, no conscious creation on the part of the various characters of illusory or 'play' situations through which they work out their destiny. Magic and dream, rather than deliberate artifice and role-playing, are the elements that bring confusion and clarification. This, of course, does not mean that there is no manipulation at all. Both Oberon and Puck love to interfere in the affairs of mortals and both use the disguise that Prospero adopts to great advantage in *The Tempest* – invisibility. There are, as well, the manipulations of that whimsical and fun-loving fate that Puck acknowledges after he realizes that he has anointed the wrong Athenian eyes: 'Then fate o'errules, that, one man holding troth, / A million fail, confounding oath on oath' (III.ii.92-3).

The scene (IV.i) in which all the characters awaken from their delusions, as morning steals upon them and us, can serve as a focus. On stage are the four exhausted lovers, sound asleep, Titania and Bottom who soon fall asleep themselves, entwisted in each others' arms, and Oberon watching over all. He releases Titania, tells Puck to 'take off this head' from Bottom, and orders music to 'strike more dead / Than common sleep of all these five the sense.' Dancing and singing, the royal train glides away with the dawn, just as Theseus and Hippolyta come in, eager for the hunt. This shift from moonlight to daylight, from the illusive, liquid world of the fairies to the practical, realistic world of the court, is as abrupt and as magical an awakening for us as it is for the characters themselves. Theseus and Hippolyta come in talking of hounds, heroes, and hunting, and evoke a mythological, heroic reality:

> We will, fair Queen, up to the mountain's top
> And mark the musical confusion
> Of hounds and echoes in conjunction.
> HIPPOLYTA I was with Hercules and Cadmus once,
> When in a wood of Crete they bay'd the bear
> With hounds of Sparta. Never did I hear

> Such gallant chiding ...
> ... I never heard
> So musical a discord, such sweet thunder. (IV.i.112-21)

The shift in tone which this effects could hardly be more complete. Within the contrast, however, there is a subtle identity; for in the words these heroes speak is expressed an extraordinary blending and merging of opposites, a process which is being enacted in the story of lovers and fairies. The very symbols which Shakespeare most often uses to express harmony (music) and chaos (storm) are here brought together as an expression of overriding harmony wrought out of a conflict of opposites.[2] It is a relaxed moment in the play, a moment when the madness and illusions of dream give way to the heroic exploits of war and physical prowess. But it is an index of Shakespeare's imaginative grasp on his material that, just when the tension is relaxed and the spells dissolved, at a seemingly unimportant moment, we get a metaphorical enactment of the central action of the play. And just as the power of the poet can effect such metaphorical synthesis, so the power of the magician, or by extension the playwright, can effect the sort of reconciliation of opposites that the plot presents. In the plot, love is generated out of hate, true sight out of blindness, natural harmony out of chaos and disorder.

Earlier in the play, the quarrel between Oberon and Titania had produced a 'progeny of evils' (II.i.115), a whole series of disasters and disorders in nature of which they are the 'parents and original' (II.i.117). Titania's long description of these evils also brings opposites together – natural generation and disnatured chaos – but the product is disharmony. After the reconciliation of Titania and Oberon, the dissolution of her 'unnatural' love for an ass, and the resolution of the other amorous conflicts, Theseus and Hippolyta (standing for the noble couple whose marriage the whole play is honouring) are given speeches entirely appropriate to them but which also summarize in metaphor the symbolic action of the play up to that point. In a sense, what they say may be taken as an answer to Lysander's beautiful complaint early in the play:

> The course of true love [is] ...
> Brief as the lightning in the collied night,
> That, in a spleen, unfolds both heaven and earth,
> And ere a man hath power to say 'Behold!'
> The jaws of darkness do devour it up:
> So quick bright things come to confusion.[3] (I.i.145-9)

But the play shows how brightness and confusion can co-exist, how in fact brightness can arise out of confusion, which is what happens with the four lovers, just as music can arise out of the confusion of baying and echoes.

The process is further illuminated a moment later when Theseus and his followers discover the sleeping lovers. Theseus, though skilled in the knowledge of 'musical confusion' in the realm of sense, cannot understand such merging in the emotional sphere:

> How comes this gentle concord in the world,
> That hatred is so far from jealousy
> To sleep by hate and fear no enmity? (IV.i.146-8)

Again, concord arises out of discord, this time as a result of magic, a power which confuses the lovers even as it brings them to their senses. Demetrius says,

> I wot not by what power
> (But by some power it is) my love to Hermia,
> Melted as the snow, seems to me now
> As the remembrance of an idle gaud,
> Which in my childhood I did dote upon;
> And all the faith, the virtue of my heart,
> The object and the pleasure of mine eye,
> Is only Helena. To her, my lord,
> Was I betroth'd ere I saw Hermia;
> But, like a sickness, did I loathe this food;
> But, as in health, come to my natural taste,
> Now I do wish it, love it, long for it ... (IV.i.167-78)

This speech records a return from disorder to order, from sickness to health, and it does so in a language which is simpler and less consciously artificial than either he or Lysander has used before. Both structurally and thematically, it is connected to the reconciliation of Oberon and Titania and to the evaporation of the latter's love for Bottom. Also, through the terms it uses, the speech links growing up with a realignment of the senses.[4]

Much of the comedy in the play derives from the disordering of the senses, especially sight, which the play makes clear is closely associated with love and judgement.[5] In the first scene, there is a conflict between Hermia's eyes and her father's judgement (56-7) and there is Helena's contrasting statement that 'Love looks not with the eyes but with the mind' (234). During the scenes in the forest, sight and judgement get thoroughly mixed up: the effects of the magic potion with which Oberon anoints the eyes are justified by Lysander in terms of 'reason': 'The will of man is by his reason sway'd / And reason says you are the worthier maid' (II.ii.115-16). Lysander's pedantic introduction of faculty psychology is, at this point, more a mark of his self-deception than his education. Bottom shows a clear, if also empty-headed, view of such matters when he tells Titania (whose own eyes have usurped her true vision): 'And yet, to say the truth, reason and love keep little company together now-a-days' (iii.i.144-5). It is, then, appropriate that, when the lovers awaken, the reordering of love is spoken of in terms of ordered sense perception and there is no attempt to justify their new 'sight' by claims of reason. They are willing to accept the workings of the mysterious power whose effects they feel. That this power is the delusive magic of the fairies in no way undermines their experience, since that magic is equivalent to that woven by Shakespeare in A Midsummer Night's Dream as a whole.

In fact, this readjustment of sight (and incidentally of judgement) depends on acceptance of the dream, on the metamorphoses effected by magic. This means that an acceptance of the confusing, illusory world created by the play is essential before the climactic harmony can be achieved. It is as though Theseus's and Hippolyta's metaphors apply even to the play itself; it too is an example of confusion harmonized into art.

The magic the play uses is, of course, not actually that of potions and spells, but that of the theatre itself, where the magic words are those the playwright puts down and the actors speak. That these two kinds of magic are related is made especially clear in the third act when the magic of the fairies creates a highly confused situation which Puck calls a 'pageant' and which both he and Oberon derive a lot of pleasure from watching. They form an audience for the 'dance'[6] performed by the lovers and, by the end of iii.ii Puck proves to be a choreographer as well, leading each lover through a set of steps and then to sleep. As the action proceeds, both fairies, especially Puck, manifest a consciousness of comic artifice ('Shall we their fond pageant see? / Lord, what fools these mortals be'), which allows them to perceive what happens as not simply humorous but also as part of a process moving towards a naturally happy ending: 'Yet but three? Come one more. Two of both kinds make up four'; and again, 'Jack shall have Jill; / Naught shall go ill; / The man shall have his mare again, and all shall be well' (iii.ii.437-8, 461-3).

Besides such language and attitudes, the action of the play also calls attention to its own artificiality. This is particularly true of the abrupt changes of heart on the part of Lysander, Demetrius, and Titania, together with the extravagant language that accompanies them. The play insists on its own silliness and hence, by a species of paradox, forces us to take it seriously, just as the Pyramus and Thisbe play insists on its own seriousness and ends up being ridiculous. The magic potion is at the centre of the paradox, since it is absurd but at the same time does the job. It is thus a symbol for the effect of the broader action of the play on us; the action certainly does seem absurd, but it too does the job of re-aligning our imaginative sight and hence of opening us to the harmony of musical confusion that the play finally presents.

That the harmony is both a pleasure and a pain, that it involves a deeper perception of life, is clear from the attitude the lovers manifest as soon as Theseus leaves them (IV.i), when they can drop the decorum demanded by his presence and talk freely of their amazement:

> DEMETRIUS These things seem small and undistinguishable,
> Like far-off mountains turned into clouds.
> HERMIA Methinks I see these things with parted eye,
> When everything seems double.
> HELENA   So methinks;
> And I have found Demetrius like a jewel,
> Mine own, and not mine own.
> DEMETRIUS   Are you sure
> That we are awake? It seems to me
> That yet we sleep; we dream. (IV.i.190-7)

One of the fruits of illusion, it seems, is an uncertainty of perception, a double-ness, a tender shaking of the conventional branches, which, though the notice-able effects soon wear off, will presumably leave its mark (a mark which Hippolyta recognizes but which Theseus has never felt).

The attitude that the lovers are impelled to take towards their experience – that it was a dream whose psychic boundaries are unclear – is exactly the same as the attitude we are asked to take towards the whole play (and, by implication, our own experience) in Puck's epilogue. This more than anything else establishes the analogy between what happens within the play and the play itself. The lovers' pageant is truly like a masque, watched over by Puck and Oberon, which becomes an image for the whole play. As such it has much in common with the masque presented by Prospero to Ferdinand and Miranda in *The Tempest*. Both 'masques' are important thematically, both are dreamlike and amazing, both give rise to speculation about dreaming and the uncertainty of 'reality.' Prospero's great speech, 'Our revels now are ended,' is a general statement growing out of particular perceptions like those of the lovers in *A Midsummer Night's Dream* (the image of clouds, suggested by Demetrius, becomes the central symbol in Prospero's speculations); furthermore, the relation of Prospero's speech to the masque is analogous to the relation of his epilogue to the whole play, and the relation of spectators to masque is analogous to that of audience to play, in ways very similar to the way such relations are patterned in *A Midsummer Night's*

Dream.[7] In fact, Shakespeare's earliest 'mature' comedy has more in common with his last than it has with any in between.[8] Both are deeply concerned with a clarification of vision through the medium of dramatic experience and both, even more fully than the other comedies, make the audience participate in the experience of illusion that the characters undergo.

For both Titania and the lovers, the actual awakening from the dream means that they cease to be actors in the pageant that Puck so enjoys. They are no longer watched but left to return, Titania with Oberon, the lovers with Theseus, and this marks the point where our sense of clarification merges with theirs. We become more closely identified with the lovers and so it is appropriate that they now may take their turn at being an audience.

The final movement of the play consolidates the themes I have been discussing through the presentation of the tragedy of Pyramus and Thisbe. The association of comic subplot and main plot is established in the first act when we hear that both the lovers and Quince, Bottom, and company will repair to the woods that night, though for very different reasons.[9] Both groups are concerned with the Duke's wedding day, Lysander and Hermia running away from it because of the judgement, the mechanicals preparing for it because of the revel. The association is intensified when Quince describes the forest as a theatre ('This green plot shall be our stage, this hawthorn brake our tiring house.' III.i.3-4) and we see indeed that it is a stage for the foolish pageant of the lovers. Again, Bottom's 'translation' parodies the metamorphoses thrust upon the main characters and his awakening too is a parody of theirs; he sees the past night as the fierce vexation of a dream, but a totally inarticulate and hilariously confused dream, which he speaks of in terms that recall in an absurd way the immediately preceding conversation of the lovers concerning the boundaries of dream:

I have had a most rare vision. I have had a dream, past the wit of a man to say what dream it was. Man is but an ass, if he go about to expound this dream. Methought I was – there is no man can tell what ... The eye of man hath not heard, the ear of man hath not seen, man's hand is not able to taste, his tongue to conceive, nor his heart to report what my dream was ... (IV.i.207-38)

The speech also parodies the language of the senses and their confusion, so important in the main plot. Bottom's lines, 'The eye of man hath not heard ...,' besides being an amusing lampoon of St Paul, record a crazy synesthesia which erupts again in the Pyramus and Thisbe play: 'I see a voice, now will I to the chink, / To spy an I can hear my Thisby's face'; and again, 'Will it please you to see the epilogue, or to hear a Bergomask dance ...?' Such confusion is as close as the mechanicals get to the harmonizing of opposites characteristic of the main plot; the advertisement for their play brings the point home:

> 'A tedious brief scene of young Pyramus
> And his love Thisby; very tragical mirth.'
> Merry and tragical? Tedious and brief?
> That is, hot ice and wondrous strange snow.
> How shall we find the concord of this discord? (v.i.56-60)

The answer to Theseus's final question can only be, 'in the whole play, in *A Midsummer Night's Dream* itself.' The mechanicals add their element of discord, which does in fact turn out to be part of the concord.

Just before the play is announced, Hippolyta responds to Theseus's rationalistic comments on imagination with an implicit theory of her own:

> But all the story of the night, told over,
> And all their minds transfigur'd so together,
> More witnesseth than fancy's images,
> And grows to something of great constancy;
> But, howsoever, strange and admirable. (v.i.23-7)

The strange is also true; miracle and illusion may be strange but they strike the imagination at a deeper level than Theseus is aware of. As in *The Tempest*, the 'strange' has a 'transfiguring' power, a power to remake and transform. Hippolyta's words confirm what we already feel about the experience of the lovers and they also suggest a further relation between main plot and comic subplot. For Bottom too has been 'transfigured,' but on a purely physical, asinine level, and the experience has washed right off him. His new beastliness gains further significance from the fact that his transformation becomes a focus for the language of cruelty and animality prevalent in the lovers' quarrels.[10] Such language (eg, 'I had rather give his carcass to my hounds') expresses an underlying bitterness and aggression in the game in the forest, feelings which are, however, metamorphosed into laughter (itself, as Bergson and Freud saw, not unrelated to cruelty) in the spectacle of Titania's languishing love for an ass. At last, all the beasts merge in the harmless lion of the play-within, who is, 'truly,' only Snug, the Joiner.

The little play, as has often been observed, is a sort of miniature version of the total play. Taken in the context of what I have been saying, it may be seen as an emblem of what all the opposing elements of the play have come together to do. As we watch the court watching the play of Pyramus and Thisbe, and as we laugh with them at its hopeless inadequacies, we are made aware of ourselves as an audience watching an infinitely more sophisticated play but one which must, of necessity, rest on the same base. We are aware, too, of our relation to the pageant of love earlier and to its audience. When we hear Theseus say, 'The best in this kind are but shadows; and the worst are no worse if imagination amend them,' and Hippolyta reply, 'It must be your imagination then and not theirs,' we recognize the importance of imaginative acceptance in order for any transfiguring to take place. That this is a process operative within the play *and* outside it, between it and the spectators, is made particularly clear since the response needed within the play (such as that typified by Hippolyta herself) is here said to be the basic requirement of any audience.

The play slowly modulates to a close, the fairies entering quietly to bring it to conclusion exactly as they had given it its life. The emphasis is on fertility and generation, the threat of the barren nunnery sunk in the past, the moon no longer 'cold' and 'fruitless,' nor any longer lunatic, but a sign of promise, 'like to a silver bow, / New-bent in heaven' (I.i.9-10). Their dance and charm over, they all drift off, leaving Puck alone on the stage. Moving softly toward the audience, he speaks the epilogue:

> If we shadows have offended,
> Think but this, and all is mended,
> That you have but slumb'red here,
> While these visions did appear.
> And this weak and idle theme,
> No more yielding but a dream,
> Gentles, do not reprehend:
> If you pardon, we will mend ... (V.i.430-7)[11]

As with the epilogues of *As You Like It* and *The Tempest*, and to a lesser extent *Troilus and Cressida*, this speech begins consciously to dissolve the dramatic illusion and at the same time to continue elements of that illusion by bringing into focus important themes and motifs. We are called upon to make up for the 'shadowy' quality of theatrical representation through the use of imagination and to show our appreciation by 'giving our hands.' And we are asked directly, while before it was only implicit, to respond to the play as the lovers have responded to their night in the moonlit wood, to see it as a dream and nonetheless to accept it as valuable. For us to accept the mystery of the theatrical world, where concord can be made out of discord, is the only way that our fancies, like those of the lovers, can be magically transfigured.

Twelfth Night, though it is always classed with the 'happy' or 'festive' comedies, is really a somewhat different sort of play from *As You Like It*, say, or *A Midsummer Night's Dream*. It has affinities with the plays that follow it, too, like *Hamlet* and *Troilus and Cressida*, especially in the uncertainty and instability of the world it depicts. In the earlier comedies, as we have seen, disguises are used to manipulate situations and to involve the characters in some sort of learning process.* In *Twelfth Night*, as in *The Comedy of Errors*, there is no real manipulation through disguise; the working out of the plot is left to time and chance. 'O time,' says Viola, in a remark that Rosalind would never dream of making, 'thou must untangle this, not I; / It is too hard a knot for me t'untie' (II.ii.40-1). The disguise here is not an instrument of illumination at all; its initial function is more or less self-protective (Viola's motives are deliberately left unclear) and its dramatic function is essentially to confuse the action, to bring it to such a pitch that only time can untangle it. The fact that the action of *Twelfth Night* is not encircled by any palpable society – that events do not lead away from and back to some fairly solid social structure – this, too, distinguishes it from *The Merchant of Venice, As You Like It*, and even such an ethereal piece as *A Midsummer Night's Dream*, where the solid presence of Theseus and his court gives weight to the beginning and end of the play.

A unique feature of *Twelfth Night* is its extreme reflexivity. All the plays I am looking at turn in on themselves to a fairly large extent, but *Twelfth Night* most of all and in a rather different way. The play as a whole seems to describe a circle and most of the central characters suffer from delusions which involve a motion out of the self and a reciprocal motion back in – a love that seems to be directed outward but actually forms a circle and returns to the self, the external object being more of an excuse, a catalyst for self-love. Orsino's love for Olivia, Olivia's for her dead brother, for Cesario and finally for Sebastian, Malvolio's for his mistress and even, though to a lesser extent, Viola's for Orsino, all have the same emotional form. The main plot has a similar structure: we begin with a circular situation in which Orsino loves Olivia who loves Viola who loves Orsino; the circle can only be broken by the intrusion of Sebastian, who squares it so to speak, and we end with a gracious changing of partners, not unlike a circular dance. The subplot also describes a kind of circle, as Feste reminds us when he speaks of the 'whirligig of time' bringing in its revenges.

Orsino, in the words of Dover Wilson, is the 'epicurean lover, ever seeking, not the satisfaction of his desires, but their perpetuation.'[12] His language is a reflection of his own illusions about love and, in its extravagant Petrarchanism, acts as a block to real feeling, like the masks of Orlando and Silvius. It is the compass that closes the circle. His opening speech is a masterpiece of self-involvement masquerading as love; the vagaries of love's 'appetites' (a word which con-

---

* This seems true even of a very early play like *The Two Gentlemen of Verona*, though there the whole process is in a rudimentary form. The obvious exception to this is *The Comedy of Errors*, where the disguise motif, derived ultimately from Plautus, is used purely as a way of building a confusing plot.

nects themes treated comically here with *Troilus and Cressida*, where they re-
ceive more serious and bitter treatment) are overcome by only one of Orsino's
other appetites – that for *words*, especially words of love. Love is almost entirely
a verbal matter: 'I have unclasp'd / To thee the book even of my secret soul,'
says he to Cesario and instructs him therefore to go to Olivia and 'unfold the
passion of my love; / Surprise her with discourse of my dear faith' (I.iv.24-5).
Love can only be made real through words. Viola carries both his message and
his metaphor to Olivia, in the saucy jokes about her conned speech especially.
(Both Malvolio and Sir Andrew, whose respective loves for Olivia provide mirrors
for Orsino's, also get caught in verbal webs: Malvolio is fooled by a riddle, Sir
Andrew by his own pretentious foolishness and verbal extravagance.) Orsino's
reliance on the book of love rather than experience seems to lie behind even his
extreme cruelty at the end; just before he threatens to 'sacrifice' Cesario, he
alludes to a Greek romance, *Ethiopica*, as a precedent for what he would like to
do: 'Why should I not, had I the heart to do it, / Like to th' Egyptian thief at
point of death, / Kill what I love ...' (v.i.120-2). Unlike the Egyptian thief, and
unlike Othello, he has not 'the heart to do it,' which makes him a comic figure
and transforms his cruelty to laughter.

The play is like a hall of subtle mirrors where everything is reflected and partially distorted by something else. Characters, situations, themes, all find themselves reflected. Viola and Olivia, for example, are mirror images for each other;
each has recently 'lost' a father and a brother, each loves unrequitedly, each
hides her emotional identity behind a mask (Olivia's veil, Viola's disguise); even
their names are anagrammatic. The situations in the play are a maze of reflec-
tions: the obvious pattern of disprized love, for one thing; the parody in the Malvolio plot of the self-love and amorous pretensions current in the main plot;[13]
the faithful love and service rendered by Antonio (complete with ambiguous sexuality) that parallels Viola's service of Orsino (though in the latter case the sexual ambiguity can be resolved through simple change of clothing whereas
Antonio must be left out of the final festivity); the cowardice and pretense of
Aguecheek mirrored in that of Viola; the adoption, again by Viola, of a role
associated with the Fool's and so on. All Shakespeare's comedies are built on a
series of parallels, but here he outdistances himself.

The constant theme in all this is delusion and misapprehension, especially
self-delusion, and the play emphasizes this theme not only in situation but in its
relationship to the audience. For the elaborateness of the mirroring and the detachment from social realities make the play more self-contained, less related to
the world of the audience than *A Midsummer Night's Dream, Love's Labour
Lost*, or the other comedies. As an audience, we are asked to submit to the artificiality, the delusion and 'madness,'[14] to accept it as an image for our 'reality.'

Put in another way, if the theme is appearance and reality, the play itself is a pattern of shimmering appearances which are all the reality the play presents. We must accept the appearances before we can be released from the hall of mirrors. If we look at it this way we can see that the world of the play is a comic version of the world of *Hamlet*, where deception is equally prevalent but much more sinister and where reality is equally impenetrable. The very distance of *Twelfth Night* from the 'real world,' which is related to its lack of a defined social milieu, drastically reduces the threat of deception and makes the impenetrability of reality a matter of confusion and hilarity.*

To illustrate some of the above points, I want to focus on a short scene, Act IV.i, not a vital one in the play's movement certainly, but one which brings together some important strands that we can follow into other parts of the play. The scene begins with a quick dialogue between Feste and Sebastian, a typical comic interchange based on mistaken identity, but one which brings us close to a central issue in the play. We get only the tail end of the conversation, mainly the Fool's commentary on the confusion:

No I do not know you; nor I am not sent to you by my lady, to bid you come speak with her; nor your name is not Master Cesario; nor this is not my nose neither. Nothing that is so is so. (IV.i.5-9)

The Fool has unwittingly put his finger on the central paradox, 'Nothing that is so is so.' Names and words are shifty and unstable. Cesario, after all, is not even Cesario's name, much less Sebastian's. We might, I suppose, conclude that the Fool is only receiving just treatment for being at other times Olivia's 'corrupter of words,' but a corrupter of words can only operate effectively in an environment where meanings are unmoored.

The dialogue as a whole parallels that between Viola and Feste at the opening of the third act in which they discuss the relation of 'foolery,' wisdom, and the corruption of words. It seems that the former two involve the latter. Language is malleable, inconstant, unstable, and false (again a comic parallel with *Hamlet*):

* *Much Ado about Nothing* provides many parallels with both these plays. The lack of fixity, the prevalence of masks, and the tantalizing difficulty of reading appearances, are all as typical of *Much Ado* as they are of *Twelfth Night*; and the obsession with plotting is as native to its world as it is to that of *Hamlet*. *Much Ado* is full not only of plots, but of messages and reports which must be sifted and interpreted, a task which, ironically, Dogberry performs more aptly than anyone else. How to interpret external signs, whether linguistic or presentational, is in fact a problem which faces the characters of most of the middle plays, from *Much Ado* through *Hamlet* and *Measure for Measure*, culminating in *Othello* where it forms the centre of the tragedy.

'A sentence is but a chev'ril glove to a good wit. How quickly the wrong side may be turn'd outward' (III.i.12-15). Folly and wisdom, Viola concludes, are closer than they seem: 'This fellow is wise enough to play the fool.' She goes on, in the same scene, to play with language and to fool with Toby and Olivia. Her excessively courtly language ('Most excellent, accomplished lady, the heavens rain odours on you'), though taken seriously by Sir Andrew, is of course a burlesque of the extravagant conceits of her master (and other courtly lovers). Her equivocation and wit only serve to bind poor Olivia more firmly; the following exchange immediately precedes Olivia's frank avowal of love:

> OLIVIA I prithee tell me what thou think'st of me.
> VIOLA That you do think you are not what you are.
> OLIVIA If I think so, I think the same of you.
> VIOLA Then think you right. I am not what I am. (III.i.150-3)

The only other Shakespearean equivocator to speak those last words is Iago, but the differences are profound. Iago is boasting of his own clever hypocrisy and masked ambition; Viola is merely stating the equivocal and confusing truth about herself and life in Illyria generally.

Feste's inability to fix anything with words, and his delight in his corrupting skill, is, then, a feature of life in Illyria. Language, too, is a matter of appearances. His joke in the scene following the perplexing conversation with Sebastian focusses the problem and acts as a fitting prelude to his role as Sir Topas:

for, as the old hermit of Prague, that never saw pen and ink, very wittily said to a niece of King Gorboduc, 'That that is is'; so I, being Master Parson, am Master Parson; for what is 'that' but that, and 'is' but is? (IV.ii.14-19)

Contrary to what Feste says, however, nothing that is is, since Feste is not a parson, just as neither Sebastian nor Cesario is Cesario.

The resolution of this failure of stability is, of course, comic. There is no threat involved, no danger of a rift in nature or in the mind, as we get in *Troilus and Cressida*. Troilus's cry that 'This is and is not Cressid,' is one of anguish and doubt, while Orsino's 'One face, one voice, one habit, and two persons – / A natural perspective that is and is not,' expresses amazement but also unity. The confusion of contraries finds its resolution here; the twins are the physical embodiment of the fact that contraries can co-exist. The image here goes beyond the harmony of opposites characteristic of *A Midsummer Night's Dream*; it is not simply a creation of concord out of discord, but an actual co-existence of opposites, an optical illusion made actual.

This aspect of the play shows us another reason why there is a sense of self-containment and circularity about it. It presents a world where opposites curl around to meet each other, a kind of magical world from which the characters are never released. They stay forever on the comic merry-go-round. Even our release is a circular one, for the clown's song describes a pattern of growth and decay which is eternally recurrent (a pattern suggested by the refrain) and ends by inviting us back to the feast the next day. In a manner not unlike Beckett's *Endgame*, the end of the play leads us back to the beginning.

Let us return again to iv.i for a minute. The scene continues with a comic inversion of an earlier scene, 'Cesario' changing suddenly from coward to hero. Sir Andrew quickly gives up in favour of the law ('I'll have an action of battery against him ... though I stroke him first, yet it's no matter ...'), but Sir Toby wants to continue the fight and his blood is saved only by the entrance of Olivia. After she shoos the rowdies away, she turns to Sebastian and speaks quietly and lovingly to him, continuing the mistaken identity joke in a much softer key. Sebastian reacts by questioning himself:

> What relish is in this? How runs the stream?
> Or I am mad, or else this is a dream.
> Let fancy still my sense in Lethe steep;
> If it be thus to dream, still let me sleep! (IV.i.64-7)

Sebastian's willingness to accept the madness and the dream is underscored by the rhymed verse with its regular rhythms; the form of his words itself suggests dreaminess and unreality. There is an obvious connection between this speech and his later one (IV.iii), in which he tries to puzzle out an explanation but ends by simply accepting what is 'deceivable,' the 'wonder' of the situation:

> This is the air; that is the glorious sun;
> This pearl she gave me, I do feel 't and see't;
> And though 'tis wonder that enwraps me thus,
> Yet 'tis not madness ...
> Yet doth this accident and flood of fortune
> So far exceed all instance, all discourse,
> That I am ready to distrust mine eyes
> And wrangle with my reason, that persuades me
> To any other trust but that I am mad,
> Or else the lady's mad. Yet, if 'twere so,
> She could not sway her house ...
> As I perceive she does. There's something in't
> That is deceivable. (IV.iii.1-21)

There is a kind of madness abroad in Illyria, which is a function not only of the present situation but also of the persistent instability of 'is' and 'is not' discussed above. In the present context, Olivia both is and is not mad. The only way to live with the madness is to accept it and enjoy it, which is why Sebastian succeeds and Malvolio doesn't. Sebastian's behaviour contrasts significantly with that of Silvio, his predecessor in Rich's *Apolonius and Silla* (probably Shakespeare's major source for the play). Silvio recognizes that there is something wrong somewhere, but shrugs his shoulders and decides he would be a fool 'if he should forsake that which fortune had so favourably proffered unto him.'[15] He therefore plays along with Julina, takes advantage of her, and promptly skips town, leaving her pregnant. A more cynical, but also more rational, response to the situation. Sebastian immerses himself in the waters of Illyria and teaches us to do the same.

As the outsider thrust suddenly into Illyria, he occupies a place similar to ours. He is a stand-in for the audience. Joseph Summers suggests that, in the final scene, with confusion rampant, he becomes 'what we will' since his entrance will clear everything up.[16] His position as exemplar of the subtitle underlines his special relationship with the audience. For 'what we will' in the realm of comedy demands an imaginative projection, an effort on our part to form a psychological circle within the 'wooden O.' Sebastian's surrender to the salutory madness is an image within the play for the relationship of audience to comedy. As such, it is related to the lovers' acceptance of their dream in *A Midsummer Night's Dream*, to the King's acceptance of miracle in *All's Well that Ends Well*, even to Gloucester's acceptance of what flouts his senses in *King Lear*, and to the acceptance of magic and 'art' in the final plays.[17]

Sebastian's surrender in iv.iii leads quickly to the dénouement, which consists of squeezing the misapprehensions for every possible ounce of tension and then releasing that tension in the abrupt but graceful switching of partners. Whether Olivia and Orsino have actually learned anything is a much disputed point, but I tend to side with those critics (eg, Wilson and Baker) who argue that they shift their 'fancies' too easily, that the Duke's final line (Viola is his 'mistress and his *fancy's* queen') indicates that the whirligig of love is still going round.[18] In another sense, then, the play leads us back to its beginning and a new set of Illyrian delusions.

The stage clears and we are left alone with the clown. It is his task to round out the story, dissolve the illusion, and send us all happily out of the theatre. His song brings us closer to the realities of everyday life, to children, thieves, wives, and drunkards, but contains all this in the beautifully balanced artifice of the refrain. And like a miniature of the play itself, the song circles back and draws us with it, back to the play and its next performance, back to the inescapable illusions of Illyria.

In contrast to the comedies, *Troilus and Cressida* presents us with a situation in which multiple perspective does not lead to a fuller awareness but results instead in a division of the hero's consciousness and a narrowing of focus on the part of the audience. The key scene in this development is v.ii, where we watch Thersites watching Ulysses watching Troilus watching Diomede and Cressida. In a different context, we would expect a scene of this kind to provide us with many different points of view, all of which would blend together, through irony, into a balanced unity. Such is the result of the multiplicity of perspectives in *A Midsummer Night's Dream* or in *As You Like It*, but nothing of that sort happens here. The irony is tougher, more cynical, more divisive.

Sight is deceptive, eyes and ears mislead the characters, and even those of the audience are bewildered. The result is fragmentation. Cressida puts it poignantly after Diomede has left, their harsh, flirtatious game postponed for a while; the language recalls *A Midsummer Night's Dream*, but the context and the tone are utterly different:

> Troilus, farewell! One eye yet looks on thee,
> But with my heart the other eye doth see.
> Ah, poor our sex! This fault in us I find,
> The error of our eye directs our mind.
> What error leads must err. O, then conclude,
> Minds sway'd by eyes are full of turpitude. (v.ii.107-12)

There is a softness in Cressida which is often missed. Actress and director should not accept Ulysses' view of her as Shakespeare's; at this moment, she is genuinely sad about Troilus, but her emotion is quite ineffective. (Emotion throughout the play is typically barren.) There is a split even in her vision itself, her eyes are divided and wandering, her judgement weak.

Troilus develops the same theme when he speaks a moment later. For him, there is a division between the 'credence in my heart' and 'th' attest of eyes and ears, / As if those organs had deceptious functions, / Created only to calumniate.' The lies of the senses are associated with the lies of time which, in the words of Ulysses, is also 'envious and calumniating' (iii.iii.174). Both destroy truth, both create uncertainty and confusion.[19] Thersites can only laugh at Troilus's refusal to accept the evidence of his senses: 'Will 'a swagger himself out on's own eyes?' But far from being a balancing voice, Thersites merely underlines the distance between his view and Troilus's, isolating the latter through irony, but not correcting him. The irony is not comic in the way we have been used to in the other plays; there is no consolation.

The uncertainty of perception manifested in the scene is reinforced by the structure, first in the multiple watching itself, a stage event which keeps the spectator jumping from one focus to another (this flitting attention is also enacted in the behaviour of Diomede, who keeps moving back and forth, threatening to leave and returning); and, second, in the lack of felt connection between the various 'actors' and the various 'audiences.' None of the watchers fully understands the show he is watching. Both Diomede and Troilus misjudge Cressida, though in different ways; Ulysses is confused and a little terrified by Troilus's exaggerated reactions; and Thersites can see nothing but lechery in the whole business. This failure of understanding spreads outward to include us, and, although we can recognize all of these misjudgements, still, in the words of L.C. Knights, the 'dominant imaginative effect is bewilderment.'[20]

This sense is certainly not dissipated by the long, bitter, and abstract speech in which Troilus tries to pull together his responses. 'O madness of discourse,' he moans, 'That cause sets up with and against itself.' That is the scene epitomized. The pageant has led to an unhinging of reason, with a correspondent breakdown of the 'rule in unity':

> If beauty have a soul, this is not she;
> If souls guide vows, if vows be sanctimonies,
> If sanctimony be the gods' delight,
> If there be rule in unity itself –
> This is not she. O madness of discourse,
> That cause sets up with and against itself!
> Bifold authority! where reason can revolt
> Without perdition, and loss assume all reason
> Without revolt: this is, and is not, Cressid!
> Within my soul there doth conduce a fight
> Of this strange nature, that a thing inseparate
> Divides more wider than the sky and earth;
> And yet the spacious breadth of this division
> Admits no orifex for a point as subtle
> As Ariachne's broken woof to enter.
> Instance, O instance! strong as Pluto's gates:
> Cressid is mine, tied with the bonds of heaven.
> Instance, O instance! strong as heaven itself:
> The bonds of heaven are slipp'd, dissolv'd, and loos'd,
> And with another knot, five-finger-tied,
> The fractions of her faith, orts of her love,
> The fragments, scraps, the bits, and greasy relics
> Of her o'ereaten faith, are given to Diomed.
>
> (v.ii.137-60)

Troilus is obsessed with a failure of constancy, not simply in Cressida, but extending into every area of life. First, and most dominant, there is a lack of fixity in the mind, an impossible doubleness which goes against all the tenets of a rational epistemology. There is a fight within his soul, a real fight far different from the conventional 'cruel battle here within' which he bemoans in true Petrarchan fashion at the very beginning of the play. This fight leads to an inner division which he can only image in the cosmic language of sky and earth, huge spaces which yet admit 'no orifex.' He then extends his perception of disharmony to include the cosmos itself; the 'bonds of heaven,' of which Ulysses had spoken so eloquently early in the play, are slipped – and 'hark what discord follows.'

In its formal structure, the speech enacts in miniature the conflicts it describes. It is built on a tension between a highly controlled and regulated syntax and uncontrolled, associative leaps of thought. It begins with a very tight rhetorical pattern which depends on the device of anadiplosis ('If beauty have a soul ... if souls ... etc.). At the 'madness of discourse' passage, the movement suddenly stops and the speech bends back on itself; the mind turns inward, and though the syntax remains regular, the direction of thought is suddenly hard to follow. What Troilus discovers as he bends back his mind is that there is a split in the rhetorical structure itself (the whole play is full of rhetoric); rhetoric, like so much else in the play, defeats itself. It sets up the 'bifold authority,' the cause that supports it and beats it down. The 'madness' consists in the fact that the rational, controlled structure of 'discourse' leads to the utterly untenable position that this is and is not Cressid.

The second part of the speech ('Within my soul ...') builds a metaphorical structure, not a traditionally rhetorical one (the first part of the speech is almost devoid of metaphorical language). There is, again, a tension between the tightly controlled syntax and the sliding metaphorical movement. The 'Instance, O instance' lines maintain a rigid syntactical regularity while encompassing a movement from the depths of the underworld (Pluto's gates) to the height of heaven. This whole solid structure buckles in the next line as the bonds of heaven dissolve and we are rushed into a series of metaphors (though still within an ordered syntax) which brings us from bonds to knots to scraps of food and which turns on the gnomic phrase, 'five-finger-tied.' The speech seems partly designed to set us up with the expectation of ordered discourse and then confuse us with reflexive analysis and metaphorical jumps. In any case, the formal structure of the piece adds to the sense of bifurcation we get from the content and from the scene as a whole. We begin to see that the split goes right to the core of language.

At the end of the speech, Troilus returns to the disintegration of virtue and Cressida's failure to remain constant, which, appropriately, he describes in terms of greasy bits of chewed-over food. I say appropriately because such language, laden with disgust, is the inevitable converse of Troilus's earlier concern with delicate and exquisite taste.[21] Waiting for Cressida prior to their night together, Troilus had said:

> Th' imaginary relish is so sweet
> That it enchants my sense. What will it be
> When that the wat'ry palates taste indeed
> Love's thrice-repured nectar? Death, I fear me;
> Sounding destruction ... (III.ii.20-4)

The extreme refinement in these lines indicates the precariousness of the feeling and represents, in Traversi's words, an attempt to 'extract from ... the sensual a substitute for spiritual experience.'[22] It is as though Troilus would stop time with such feelings, eternize them, but the inevitable consequence is not perpetual swoon, but disgust. And it is precisely nausea and disgust that he exhibits in v.ii; his language and the perceptions it registers are still sensual to an extreme, which results in an inordinate fascination with the disgusting to parallel his earlier fascination with the exquisite.*

Ulysses, throughout the play, is the antithesis of Troilus, the public man set off against the private man, the pragmatist against the idealist. It is impossible not to have Ulysses' great speech on 'degree' in mind as we listen to Troilus puzzle out the problems of division and disharmony. Ulysses' presence helps to keep his earlier words before us and may also remind us of the perversion of degree manifested in the action, not least of all by Ulysses himself. Although Troilus does not mention the problem of inconstancy in politics, restricting himself to microcosm and macrocosm, that problem is never very far away in this play of manoeuvring and shady deals. As has been observed, there is an irony in the presentation of the idea of degree, since Ulysses, instead of acting on his principles, proposes a trick, a sly bit of manipulation, which only ends in more disorder, the pride of Ajax compounded with that of Achilles. The degree speech is really a piece of 'ideology' in the sense that we noticed in *Hamlet*, where the traditional doctrine is used as a screen for self-interested action; it is a weapon to win the argument, gracing Ulysses' scheme with the embroidery of tradition, like a

---

* The language used here to describe the ruins of love is similar to that of Ulysses earlier when he is describing the ruins of that other ambiguous value in the play, honour. Time, the great enemy of constancy in both public and private realms, hath 'a wallet at his back, / Wherein he puts alms for oblivion ... Those scraps are good deeds past / Which are devoured / As fast as they are made ...' (III.iii.145-9). Degradation in both spheres is thus connected.

bloody sword in a beautiful scabbard. The reality of action in the play is described at the end of the speech:

> Then everything includes itself in power,
> Power into will, will into appetite;
> And appetite, an universal wolf,
> So doubly seconded with will and power,
> Must make perforce an universal prey,
> And last eat up himself. (I.iii.119-24)

The rush towards self-devouring – such is the dominant action of the play and it is suggested again and again in the language. Cressida, in Troilus's terms, has 'o'ereaten' her own faith and thus devoured herself and driven a wedge into Troilus's mind. Thersites is delighted that 'lechery eats itself' (v.iv.38) and Agamemnon warns 'He that is proud eats up himself,' leading Ulysses to observe, again in very traditional terms, 'Kingdom'd Achilles in commotion rages / And batters down himself.' (II.iii.164-5, 185-6)

Ulysses' speech describes a value central to Renaissance thinking about cosmology, politics, and ethics, a value which in *Troilus and Cressida* is overrun by the power of appetite. In the Trojan council scene, we again see a situation in which reliance on an old value, in this case honour, triggers an almost automatic response on the part of the listeners, even though what Troilus is calling honourable is at least questionable. As in I.iii, the context of the scene, together with what follows it, undercuts the doctrine being presented. Troilus argues that value resides only in what is valued, that the act of valuing itself is what confers value: 'What's aught but as 'tis valued?' Furthermore, he says, once we have valued something, it is dishonourable to change our minds; it is a point of honour to retain what we have once valued.* His is an essentially relativist position which he tries to shore up with the seemingly absolute demands of honour (itself, though, a relative quality, which thus leads to a contradiction). Hector, much more convincingly, argues that 'value dwells not in particular will,' it is inherent as much in the thing itself 'as in the prizer' (II.ii.53-6). Against the second part of Troilus's argument, Hector makes the following point, clinching the argument: 'Thus to persist / In doing wrong extenuates not wrong, / But makes it much more heavy' (186-8). He can see that Troilus's sense of honour is corrupted by its lack of intrinsic focus, by the fact that in such a view commitment

---

* This tendency to let the 'honouring' of past 'commitments' overbalance and pervert the values of the present is visible in the history of many wars, that in Viet Nam being one of the most overt.

to even the most vicious course of action could lead to honour. Though this is Hector's opinion 'in way of truth,' truth is not so important as 'honour' and so he capitulates, agreeing that to keep Helen is 'a cause that hath no mean dependence / Upon our joint and several dignities.' This sudden reversal shows a weakness in Hector and leads indirectly to his death; but more important it shows a weakness in the structure of ethics in the play. The rational basis of action is undercut; in the moral sphere, as in the political and in the personal, there is no constancy, nothing is fixed or secure. It is impossible to escape a kind of choking relativism.

This is strikingly borne out by the Greeks' view of honour. For them, even more than for the Trojans, although one view merely extends the other and makes it explicit, honour is not a value but something you get.[23] It is equivalent to being praised. That, at least, is the subject of the long dialogue between Ulysses and Achilles, culminating in the former's speech on Time, the great destroyer of honour. Time destroys simply by making people forget, by welcoming the new and leaving the old behind. The metaphor that best characterizes the whole dialogue is that of reflection. Ulysses, following his author ('a strange fellow here'), argues that a man 'Cannot make boast to have that which he hath, / Nor feels not what he owes; but by reflection' (III.iii.98-9). He can recognize no virtues in himself 'Till he behold them formed in th' applause / Where th'are extended' (119-20). Later in the same scene, Thersites gives us an ironic view of reflection when he condemns Ajax as 'a very landfish, languageless, a monster. [a precursor of Caliban?] A plague of opinion! A man may wear it on both sides like a leather jerkin' (264-6). Virtue on both sides is based on the idea of recognition, just as the 'beauty' and the 'worth' of a woman is best proven, not by anything intrinsic, but by her lover's chivalric prowess (I.iii.265-83).

The moral status of action is even more ambiguous here than in *Hamlet*. (Perhaps this is why the great heroes all seem so passive.) Political and personal life are as corrupt as in that play, but in *Troilus and Cressida* there is no central consciousness registering the disintegration, focussing our awareness, and broadening our perception. There is only Thersites, a far cry from Hamlet, whose cynical attacks are divisive and untrustworthy. There is Troilus too but his scope is narrower and his penetration shallower; he is more like Laertes than Hamlet.

He begins as a conventional lover, bemoaning his fate and showing off the wounds suffered in the 'cruel battle here within.' He is full of exaggerated love rhetoric which is highly artificial and self-conscious. But it differs markedly in tone from that of the comedies; at times it is almost febrile: 'I tell thee I am mad / In Cressid's love. Thou answer'st "She is fair" / Pour'st in the open ulcer of my heart / Her eyes, her hair ...' (I.i.51-4). The artificiality and insubstantiality of his world is further suggested by the excessive refinement of sensation already discussed, and it is underlined in his declaration of faith. In this latter speech, he shows his concern with future literary production; he wants to be the ultimate Petrarchan simile:

> after all comparisons of truth,
> As truth's authentic author to be cited,
> 'As true as Troilus' shall crown up the verse
> And sanctify the numbers. (III.ii.187-9)

Again, in IV.iv, he is more upset by the fact that he has no time in which to say goodbye properly than he is, seemingly, by Cressida's actual departure: 'injury of chance puts back leave-taking' and time robs them of farewells:

> As many farewells as be stars in heaven,
> With distinct breath and consign'd kisses to them,
> He fumbles up into a loose adieu,
> And scants us with a single famish'd kiss ... (IV.iv.46-9)

Eventually, in v.ii, he is forced to face reality, to admit some facts. But his reaction then is equally cerebral, manifesting the same attention to what is going on within his own body and mind as in the earlier scenes, and consequently blurring the outlines of the external world. The facts are varnished with an extraordinarily subtle set of distinctions which arise partly from (or are at least consistent with) the structure of the scene. The multiple watching suggests the illusions of the theatre and Troilus's disbelief is like that of an audience at a show; 'This is and is not Cressid' is thus a statement about the reality projected by the theatre. Given a standard comic format, the sort of consciousness exhibited here might lead to clarification.* The hero is brought to a new realization and the context in which the process occurs is highly theatrical. The problem is that there is a confusion of realms (which is predominantly responsible for the bewildering effect mentioned before); the 'real' and the theatrical are looped together in such a way as to blur the subtle distinctions typical of the comedies, with the result that both the value of the theatrical process and the trustworthiness of reality itself are called into question. Troilus does not work through illusion to enlightenment; he simply becomes the victim of another illusion parallel to those he has laboured under previously, though the emotional tone is altered. His case

---

* A major difference between the watching here and that in earlier plays such as *As You Like It* or *A Midsummer Night's Dream* is that the watchers there, as in *The Tempest*, are more or less benevolent controllers. Here the watchers are helpless and even voyeuristic.

is almost a parody of the educative process discussed in connection with the comedies; he does learn something, he does cast off the exaggerated idealism of his Petrarchan role. He even replaces it with an emotion that seems to run deeper, though it is still self-indulgent. But it is ironic that this emotion is not love, but fierce hatred.

The wildest chaos of nature cannot match his ferocity:

> Not the dreadful spout
> Which shipmen do the hurricano call,
> Constring'd in mass by the almighty sun,
> Shall dizzy with more clamour Neptune's ear
> In his descent than shall my prompted sword
> Falling on Diomed. (v.ii.171-6)

This tone, though on a less passionate level, is maintained throughout the last scenes. His feeling drives him to embrace war, from which he had shied away earlier, and he is characterized by feverish activity from now till the end. In fact, all the sleeping giants of the play begin to stir now, shaking off the inactivity and passivity that have weighed upon them. Now that the end of this very unheroic play is in sight, we will have some good old-fashioned heroic action (though not without a few radical twists). We begin with Hector arming for battle, ignoring the warnings of his wife and sister: 'Mine honour keeps the weather of my fate' (v.iii.26). Against his chivalric heroism is set, almost immediately, Troilus's wild abandon. Fresh from the Greek camp, Troilus begins to criticize Hector for his 'vice of mercy ... Which better fits a lion than a man' (37-8). Calling mercy a vice is an extraordinary inversion not only of the values of chivalry, but of Christian virtue itself. Let, he says, the 'venom'd vengeance ride upon our swords, [and] spur them to ruthful work, rein them from ruth.' To which Hector can only reply, 'Fie, savage, fie!'

Throughout the battle, Hector shows his mercy, letting the wheedling Thersites live and allowing Achilles a pause, though this latter favour serves only to enrage Achilles the more and proves mercy to be a very impolitic virtue in this environment. But even Hector is partially infected by the prevailing savagery, especially in his attack on the warrior in sumptuous armour ('Wilt thou not, beast, abide? / Why then, fly on, I'll hunt thee for thy hide').

After Thersites' big scene, where he beats off Hector with his cowardice,* the Greek generals assemble (in v.v) and for the first time in the play we hear the straightforward language of heroic activity:

---

* Thersites' role on the battlefield is a little like Falstaff's (especially in the exchange with the Bastard), but more cynical and less amusing. Besides, his voice is almost superfluous since there is little genuine 'honour' to be tempered and balanced, no Hotspur or Hal. Thersites' hollowness merely makes the hollowness in the others resound the more.

> AGAMEMNON   The fierce Polydamas
> Hath beat down Menon; bastard Margarelon
> Hath Doreus prisoner,
> And stands Colossus-wise, waving his beam ...
> NESTOR Go bear Patroclus' body to Achilles,
> And bid the snail-paced Ajax arm for shame.
> There is a thousand Hectors in the field ...
> ULYSSES O, courage, courage, princes! Great Achilles
> Is arming, weeping, cursing, vowing vengeance!
> Patroclus' wounds have rous'd his drowsy blood ...
>   (v.v.6-9, 17-19, 30-2)

That this language should precede the very unheroic murder of Hector is indeed ironic, and deliberately so. It is as if Shakespeare is invoking the traditionally heroic only to throw it away. The death of Hector means the death of heroic ideals and impulses. Achilles is the new warrior, and he is no hero.

Troilus represents a different response to new realities, a more honest one perhaps, but one that's doomed. His ferocity will be no match for Achilles' cruel pragmatism. We have Ulysses' testimony that his attitude has not changed since he spoke to Hector: Troilus, he says, 'hath done today / *Mad* and *fantastic* execution, / Engaging and redeeming of himself / With ... a careless force and forceless care ...' (v.v.37-40). When he hears of the death of Hector, his rage is increased and it becomes the sole focus for his response to the complicated events which he has lived. The result is a considerable narrowing of range and increase in intensity which erupts as a kind of wild abandon, a primitive, non-moral violence:

> You vile abominable tents,
> Thus proudly pight upon our Phrygian plains,
> Let Titan rise as early as he dare,
> I'll through and through you! And, thou great-siz'd coward,
> No space of earth shall sunder our two hates;
> I'll haunt thee like a wicked conscience still,
> That mouldeth goblins swift as frenzy's thoughts. (v.x.23-9)

In the struggle between Achilles and Troilus we have a situation parallel to that between Claudius and Hamlet. In both cases we have a young idealist casting around for a way to come to grips with a powerful pragmatist, someone who has come to accept and manipulate new realities, ways of acting that grow out of a perception that the old metaphors no longer apply. Historically, it is significant that both Hamlet and Troilus lose; the effective power of the traditional metaphors and values was slipping.[24] In *Hamlet*, the struggle is much more extended and the different possible postures explored with great acumen. Troilus is narrower and more self-absorbed than Hamlet; he fixes on an emotional position that disregards the external world and tries to bull his way through. His sheer power is impressive, but his lack of intellectual grasp on his situation narrows the range of our response. Much of the penetrating ethical and metaphysical awareness focussed on Hamlet himself is here abrogated and its place filled by the violence that is an undercurrent at the end of *Hamlet*, but the dominant note in *Troilus and Cressida*. Troilus is simply unable to see clearly enough; and his rage and frustration are partly a response to his inability to understand as well as an effect of his not understanding. Our awareness, too, is partially narrowed at the end since we are, in a sense, forced to choose between Troilus and Pandarus, between one kind of self-devouring or another.

Troilus's last stage is probably best viewed as a kind of self-consumption (to recall one of the key metaphors). We have already noticed his tendency to self-absorption throughout the play, his concern with his own body, his own mental and physical motions. His extreme behaviour at the end grows out of his absorption with himself in love; it is a kind of self-indulgence, though impressive. I think we can view his violent abandon as an outgrowth of the abandon and self-consumption he sought in love, the 'sounding destruction' to be brought about by one's own extreme delicacy of taste. It is ironic that such an attitude should lead to his violence at the end, but the two, as Shakespeare makes us see, are closely related.

The last word is given to Pandarus, whose final act is to go between audience and play. His task, rather like that of Rosalind or Puck at the end of their plays, though in a different tone, is to dispel the illusion of the play and bring us back into reality. The sudden use of London slang in the reference to the 'galled goose of Winchester' is calculated to have this kind of effect. But the reality he brings us to is that of a brothel in which we are all bawds. Our reaction is likely to be one of resistance and distrust, and the final result a confusion about the value of theatrical processes (in contrast to the endings of *As You Like It* or *A Midsummer Night's Dream*). If we cast our minds back over the play, we realize that the various devices associated with the comic processes I have been describing in this book (the multiple watching, the spying, tricks, and manipulations) have all been ambiguous and have led to decidedly non-comic conclusions. This play, even more than *Hamlet*, expresses a profound ambivalence about the value of illusion and playing, especially as they confront the *realpolitik* world depicted in the Greek and Trojan camps. Thus, *Troilus* leads us forward to *All's Well that Ends Well* and *Measure for Measure*, where this ambivalence is a central consideration.

5

All's Well that Ends Well

Structurally, *All's Well that Ends Well* depends on the comic modes described earlier, even as it registers a similar distrust of illusion as *Hamlet* and *Troilus and Cressida*. In some ways, Helena is reminiscent of the earlier, manipulating heroines discussed in the first two chapters. Like Portia and Rosalind, she has the task of reordering her world both psychologically and socially. Like them, too, she uses disguise and stage managing (most obvious in the final scene) to do it. But the results are not at all the same. She has none of their power over *attitudes*, though she does succeed in moulding events to her satisfaction. Even simply in the realm of event, she lacks their extensive control; there is in the play an excessive reliance on providential guidance, a kind of failure of human exertion. Such a reliance is closely related to the folklore roots of the story and to Shakespeare's deliberate attempt to make his version less realistic, closer to folklore, than his immediate sources. But at the same time it reduces the individual power of the heroine. The most important difference from the earlier plays, however, and that which makes the manipulation much more difficult, is the removal of the evil threat from the sidelines into the very centre of the action. Portia and Rosalind do not have to worry about changing the *attitudes* of Shylock or Jaques (the latter, of course, not evil, just anti-festive), they merely have to outwit them. But in *All's Well that Ends Well* the evil attitudes are more pervasive and, most significantly, have a firm hold on the mind of the hero. Bertram is not just innocently deluded; like Orlando, or Orsino, or the lovers in *A Midsummer Night's Dream*, he is a walking monument to the very vices which the play portrays as the plague of the real world. There is no pastoral here.

Another contrast between Helena and the earlier heroines is that her disguise, in the words of Anne Righter, is 'negative, a symbol of death.'[1] I do not agree that it is only this, but its relationship with death is certainly important. For one thing, a sense of death and dying runs through the play. Within the first few lines, reference is made to two recent deaths and a king who is wasting away with a mortal disease. Helena, in order to cure the king, offers her own life as surety; she must metaphorically take the king's death upon herself in order to purge him of it. Her pilgrim's disguise she turns into a message of her own death, as though her quest for the spiritual life of Bertram must be preceded by a symbolic death of her own, as was her quest for the physical life of the king.

In fact, one of the marks that distinguishes Helena throughout is that she must somehow become involved in the evils (both moral and physical) she is trying to outdo. She is like Hamlet, another disguiser faced with evil not easily affected by typically comic manipulations. Like Hamlet, too, she is an equivocator. Her first words, like his, prepare us for a character versed in the complexities of seems and is: 'I do affect a sorrow indeed, but I have it too' (I.i.62-3). Her mourning for her father, unlike Hamlet's, *is* a show; her interest, as she tells us in her soliloquy (placed, like Hamlet's first one, so as to explain the earlier equivocation), is in gaining a lover, not in mourning a father. Her love, however, will involve her in a morally ambiguous course of action (just as Hamlet's mourning eventually does) of which she as yet has no knowledge; but which we, troubled perhaps by her mask and her lack of sympathy, may reasonably expect.

As I said, death hovers over the beginning of the play. The older characters dominate; yet they are not 'blocking' characters,[2] they are not intent on interfering with the pleasures of the young (it is surprising but typical that the Countess should welcome, rather than attack, Helena's confession of love in Scene iii). Instead, they provide, through remembrance, the ideals by which the young ought to live.[3] The paradox that the dying and the dead should be sources of light and energy for the young is resolved in the notion of inheritance. Helena's spiritual inheritance is strongly contrasted to that of Bertram; it is described as an accomplished fact. Instead of bestowing her *wishes* on Helena, as she does on Bertram, the Countess makes the direct claim that 'her disposition she inherits, which makes fair gifts fairer ... she derives her honesty and achieves her goodness' (I.i.47-52). Helena has already made good the succession of virtue (in both senses: not only moral qualities but her father's medical secrets too) from father to child, something which Bertram is supposed to be working towards. The Countess, in her parting advice to her son, makes this point most strongly:

> Be thou blessed, Bertram, and succeed thy father
> In manners as in shape! Thy blood and virtue
> Contend for empire in thee, and thy goodness
> Share with thy birthright! Love all, trust a few,
> Do wrong to none; be able to thine enemy
> Rather in power than use, and keep thy friend

Under thy own life's key. Be check'd for silence,
But never tax'd for speech ... (I.i.70-7)

Although this has some sentiments in common with Polonius's speech to Laertes, it is kept on a different level by the dignified and sympathetic position in which Shakespeare has placed the Countess and by the fact that her precepts are invested with vitality because they are said to be part of Bertram's inheritance from his noble father. Not only blood, but virtue, too, is inheritable. The King emphasizes the same thing when he greets Bertram, 'Youth, thou bear'st thy father's face ... Thy father's moral parts / May'st thou inherit too!' (I.ii.19-23).

But Bertram (with Parolles) does not respond to these possibilities. The memories of their elders do not really affect them. It is these memories which keep the Countess and the King alive and relevant to the younger people. But their relevance is missed, at least by Bertram. He is, as his mother tells Lafew, 'an unseasoned courtier' and he is not open to the growth wished upon him by his mother and the King. He will not easily be 'advised,' except by Parolles. He is, in fact, interested in only one kind of succession, that of title and the 'honour' that goes with it. Helena, of course, can inherit nothing of this sort, and is thus rejected by Bertram. But the King, in his important speech on honour, makes it clear that there is a more significant kind of succession:

> ... She is young, wise, fair;
> In these to nature she's immediate heir;
> And these breed honour ...
> > Honours thrive
> When rather from our acts we them derive
> Than our foregoers. (II.iii.138-44)

Just as the potential for good action is passed down from one generation to another and Helena is heir to this, so honour succeeds from good action in an equally natural way. The succession of virtue is more 'natural' than that of title. Helena is heir to nature and honour is *bred* in her.[4]

At the beginning, then, Helena is more or less uncontaminated (the fact that she has 'become' her father makes her failure to mourn for him forgivable). She is, and has been, isolated from the world in a kind of pastoral retirement which ends as the play starts. In emerging from her isolation, she has to learn to face evil, to deal with it, even be infected by it, in order to overcome it. She must develop and manifest a more complex moral sense than anyone else, one which involves an awareness of the interpenetration of good and evil. She has somehow to use this knowledge to cure the sickness of the play's world, moving from the relatively easy task of curing the King's physical illness to the more difficult one of healing Bertram's spiritual blindnesses.

Such a process is perhaps first symbolized in her conversation with Parolles on the subject of virginity, which at times seems a little compromising for such a chaste maiden. She carries on the debate because the whole question of the role of virginity in the world is a germane one to her; in order to use her virginity in a morally and socially effective manner, as she does with the King and later with the bed trick, she must expose herself to some of the dangers posed by the threat from without. It is a matter of an 'uncloistered' virtue. But the effectiveness of her virtue depends, in part, on an ambiguous involvement with the forces she is fighting, and so it is understandable that verbal thrusts at her virginity should be met in an apparently unseemly manner.

This view is corroborated by the ambiguous way she is introduced to the King and proceeds to heal him, in a scene which connects her virginity and her sexual power. Her magical ability to heal is closely related to her virginity and to her sexual role generally;[5] her cure for the King, in fact, is presented as a kind of symbolic intercourse. Lafew introduces her as if she were coming to a tryst: 'I am Cressid's uncle, / That dare leave two together. Fare you well' (II.i.100-1). This cosiness may prompt us to find sexual meaning in Lafew's earlier description of her:

> I have seen a medicine
> That's able to breathe life into a stone,
> Quicken a rock and make you dance canary
> With sprightly fire and motion, whose simple touch
> Is powerful to araise King Pippen ... (II.i.75-9)

Clearly, she is invested with vitalizing qualities, and a double entendre in the last line quoted seems inescapable. The paradox is that it is her virginity that gives her this power. She draws attention to this when she 'ventures' her reputation on her ability to cure the King (an element not in the source): 'Tax of impudence, / A strumpet's boldness, a divulged shame, / Traduced by odious ballads; my maiden's name / Sear'd otherwise' (II.i.172-5). A failure would result in a destroyed reputation. This indicates that her power over nature is directly associated with her virginity; failure of this power would rightfully result in a loss of maidenly reputation.

The virginity debate with Parolles occurs between Helena's first and second soliloquies. In the first of these, she reveals her love for Bertram, mourns 'th' ambition in my love,' and resigns herself to doing nothing about it: 'In his bright radiance and collateral light / Must I be comforted, not in his sphere' (I.i.99-100). In the second, however, immediately after Parolles leaves, she expresses her decision to seek out Bertram by healing the King, evincing a determination totally absent from the earlier soliloquy. The discussion with Parolles, inasmuch as it leads her and her virginity out into the world, is evidently effective.

Her decision to seek out Bertram derives from both her own desires and a concern for Bertram's moral safety. Her imagination pictures Bertram at court, Bertram as courtly lover, using the language of love sonnets to insinuate himself into the affections of some 'goddess' or 'sovereign':

> There shall your master have a thousand loves,
> A mother, and a mistress, and a friend,
> A phoenix, captain, and an enemy,
> A guide, a goddess, and a sovereign ...
> His humble ambition, proud humility;
> His jarring, concord, and his discord, dulcet ... (I.i.180-6)

This gives us a perspective on Bertram's wooing of Diana, when he does, in fact, use such language and when the falseness of that language is even more apparent. Helena's fear that 'he is one' that will learn such courtly manners is well justified. And she is right to identify such learning with the adoption of a false and precious kind of language.

By the time the conversation with Parolles is over, discrepancy of rank no longer bothers her either; she believes in 'nature' that can join those separated by 'fortune': 'The mightiest space in fortune nature brings / To join like likes, and kiss like native things' (229-30). That such determination faces difficulties she does not deny, but as in *Twelfth Night* and *A Midsummer Night's Dream*, it is faith in, or acceptance of, the irrational which is stressed as a prerequisite for success. 'Impossible be strange attempts to those / That weigh their pains in sense, and do suppose / What hath been cannot be' (231-3). Her understanding of this particular aspect of the play's world allows her partially to control it and establishes a liaison between her and the audience, since the play is asking for a similar kind of acceptance from us.

That Shakespeare seems to be demanding, from both characters and audience, an acceptance of the miraculous as a prerequisite for healing or change is best indicated by his tendency throughout the play to make events seem more remote, more reminiscent of folklore, than in the sources. (A similar tendency is discernible in *Measure for Measure*.)[6] Out of many possible changes to the source which Shakespeare made, let me choose three that illustrate this tendency.[7] The most obvious are related to the healing of the King. We have already noticed how Shakespeare added certain speeches and events which stress the connection between Helena's virginity and her power to heal. We may note, as well, the difference in reaction to the King's cure. In Boccaccio and Painter, the King's acceptance of his new-found health is grateful, but quite matter of fact, and issues in a practical concern for Giletta's future rather than in a sense of miracle: 'And when the king perceived himself whole, [he] said unto her, "Thou hast well deserved a husbande (Giletta)".'[8] Furthermore, there are no commentators around to extol it, as there are in *All's Well that Ends Well.* Shakespeare emphasizes the miraculous quality of the cure: 'They say miracles are past, and we have our philosophical persons to make modern and familiar, things supernatural and causeless' (II.iii.1-3). So claims Lafew, and he goes on explicitly to reject such philosophizing. This speech comes directly to terms with the 'modern' and realistic world of the play (the underside of the elements under discussion) and rejects it as a potential source of the highest knowledge.

Another way that Shakespeare maintains a remoteness from everyday event is his deletion of the public role of Helena. In Painter, it is said of Giletta that she 'was received of all his subjects for their Lady. And perceyving that through the Count's absence all thinges were spoiled and out of order, shee, like a sage Ladye, with greate diligence and care, disposed his thinges in order againe: whereof the subjects rejoysed very much.'[9] Shakespeare makes no mention of this whatever, despite the obvious importance that Boccacio ascribes to it. He prefers to make Helena closer in kind to the folklore heroine who must fulfill the impossible tasks;[10] as such, she is given no political role. Shakespeare treats some of the events in Florence, to move to the third example, as more deliberately magical than they are in the source. This is especially obvious with regard to the pregnancy itself. Giletta continues to meet with Beltramo until she knows she is pregnant; Helena trusts in the single event (as in most folklore analogues) and is, of course, successful.

Another means that Shakespeare employs in order to foster a sense of miracle is the tone and style of the verse. As has often been noticed, the verse in the play varies a great deal, both in style and quality. This has led many commentators to claim that *All's Well that Ends Well* is a version of an earlier play, perhaps *Love's Labors Won,* which Meres mentions in 1598 in his list of Shakespeare's plays. Recently, however, this view has come under attack and G.K. Hunter makes a good case for the dramatic justification of the differing styles.[11] It is certainly true that at particularly miraculous points in the play the quality of the verse does change, often into rhymed couplets which may give a false impression of immaturity. I think, rather, that a suitably 'primitive' effect is being sought. Perhaps the clearest example of this effect occurs in Helena's first conference with the King, which breaks into couplets just at the point when Helena begins her strong petition that he accept her attempt to cure him (II.i.132ff.). From there, the speeches build to what is really a magic incantation spoken by Helena immediately after the King's resistance has been broken:[12]

> Ere twice the horses of the sun shall bring
> Their fiery torcher his diurnal ring,
> Ere twice in murk and occidental damp
> Moist Hesperus hath quenched her sleepy lamp,
> Or four and twenty times the pilot's glass
> Hath told the thievish minutes how they pass,
> What is infirm from your sound parts shall fly,
> Health shall live free, and sickness freely die. (II.i.164-71)

This passage is remarkable not only for its incantatory rhythm but also for its elaborate indirectness and especially for its mythologizing, its personification of natural forces. Even sickness and health are given independent life. And Helena is the vitalizing agent of this whole awakened universe, just as she is of the King himself.

Elements like the ritualized verse and the deliberate attempt to make the action seem more remote and archaic demand from us an imaginative act, an act of belief, just as they do from characters like Helena and the King. This sort of imaginative reach is an important part of Helena's virtue and is set up against the evil in the play, at first the physical evil of the king's disease and then the subtler psychological evil of Bertram's and Parolles' treachery. The King responds to Helena's incantation, just quoted, by expressing his acceptance of what defies 'sense' and thus fulfills a prior condition of his cure: 'And what impossibility would slay / In common sense, sense saves another way' (II.i.180-1). The result is that we are persuaded to accept the romantic and miraculous as real, or as a truer way of representing the real (the process is like our acceptance of theatrical illusion in *As You Like It* or dream and magic in *A Midsummer Night's Dream*), and are thereby led to a richer way of perceiving both the impossibilities that the play presents and the possibilities it represents.

When Helena has to use her virginity to win Bertram, she experiences much more difficulty than with the King. Moral evil is harder to overcome than physical. It is the presence of pervasive evil in the play that sets it off from the earlier comedies, making Helena's control rather insecure, and changing the character of her task and role. This presence, plus an acute, ironic awareness of it typical of certain characters (some of the older generation, the clown, and Helena), provides a sharply realistic, anti-romantic tone which runs in counterpoint to the elements just discussed. The clown's bawdy confession of his 'love' for Isabel, for example (I.iii.17ff.), is an acid comment on Helena's love. Such realism creates a tension in the play which is conducive to the growth of a more complex awareness, possible for the audience at least, if not for some of the characters (Bertram is a notoriously slow learner).

The most brilliant and significant addition to the source, and one which crystallizes the anti-romantic tone, is the introduction of Parolles and the subplot. This goes beyond ironic commentary by bringing to the surface a complex and disturbing awareness of events and moral meanings. The subplot is really the focus of one of the major issues of the play, the problem of language. It deals with many of the same kinds of themes as the main plot – masking and unmasking, verbal and moral dishonesty, appearance and reality – and relates all of these to the use of words and the connections (or disconnections) between words and things.

Parolles' bluff, like Osric's, is almost entirely verbal. He throws up a smokescreen of words to cover the 'nothingness' of his actions. This nothingness is emphasized from the start. At his first entrance, Helena calls him a 'notorious liar ... a great way fool, solely a coward' (I.i.111-12). But it is the clown who sets it down absolutely: 'To say nothing, to do nothing, to know nothing, and to have nothing, is to be a very great part of your title – which is within a very little of nothing' (II.iv.24-7). Images of clothing, so often a symbol of superfluous appearances in Shakespeare, are constantly used, most often by Lafew, to describe him: 'The soul of this man is his clothes' (II.v.48). Such imagery, compounded with the outlandish clothing that Parolles, again like Osric, wears on the stage and which is several times referred to, defines Parolles as a monster of appearances. And the dominant form of these appearances is indicated by his name, 'Words.'

Parolles is an embodiment of a view of language as one-dimensional and deceitful. It is significant, therefore, that his deception involves the use of a false language which he is unable to penetrate and hence accepts as real. The deception is appropriate retribution for Parolles' role in the play. The use of language which he embodies is a denial of genuine communication; his reversal is a token of this denial in that the fabricated 'language' spoken by the French lords and soldiers is a parody of Parolles' own speech: its absurd bombast, its oratorical bravura, and its essential meaninglessness. This is not to say that Parolles' speech is entirely devoid of meaning; it is actually quite the opposite. Otherwise he would not be able to mislead Bertram. The point is that it is lacking in *moral* meaning. Whether he is exhorting Helena to give up her virginity, encouraging Bertram to steal away against the King's orders and to treat Helena in the cruellest possible manner, or reproaching himself for getting into a dangerous situation, the issue is always the same: 'My tongue is too foolhardy, but my heart hath the fear of Mars before it ... not daring the reports of my tongue' (iv.i.32-5). There is no direct relationship between heart and tongue and hence equivocation is almost unavoidable.

Furthermore, Parolles' counsel is always based on false moral conceptions: 'It is not politic in the commonwealth of nature to preserve virginity. Loss of virginity is rational increase; and there was never virgin got till virginity was first lost ...' (i.i.137-8). This advice to Helena to cast off her virginity is based on a pragmatic and materialistic view of nature which shows no understanding for any idealistic motivation or magical usefulness. Furthermore, his argument is based on a kind of equivocal logic which is the source of his humour but which falsifies even as it 'proves.' He sees virginity as a 'commodity' (166) rather than as a personal quality; his point is that to lose virginity is good because that will increase the *amount* of virginity around. The commercial imagery is therefore apt: 'Within ten year, it will make itself ten, which is goodly increase, and the principal not much the worse' (159-61). Further on, virginity becomes an article which 'the longer kept, the less *worth*'; Parolles' advice then is consistent: 'Off with 't while 'tis *vendible*' (i.i.167-8). One further point about Parolles' language is best exemplified by the first passage quoted. There, words like 'commonwealth,' 'nature,' and 'rational' hark back to a traditional system of thought and values but falsify those traditional meanings even as they invoke them. Parolles' meanings are entirely quantitative (thus his use of a word like 'worth' refers to only one set of values) whereas the traditional meanings are hierarchical and qualitative.

I do not mean to deny the humour of his words or his argument. The fact that he is funny, however, does not preclude the fact that he is dangerous. On the contrary, it reinforces it, since the humour arises out of the very attitudes which make him dangerous, his view of nature, for example, which is essentially Hobbesian. But he is not against invoking other meanings of nature to prove, equivocally to be sure, his point. Thus, the 'natural' bond of mother and child is used in another of the virginity speeches: 'Virginity is against the rule of nature. To speak on the part of virginity is to accuse your mothers, which is most infallible disobedience ... virginity murthers itself, and should be buried in highways out of all sanctified limit, as a desperate offendress against nature' (i.i.148-53). In the latter part of the passage, virginity has been twisted into as unnatural a role as suicide and is said to deserve the same treatment – refusal of Christian burial. Besides blurring two different meanings of 'nature,' Parolles exemplifies another feature of his equivocating method in this passage: he treats a metaphorical meaning (and a questionable one at that) as if it were a real one: virginity by not perpetuating itself 'murthers itself,' a misleading metaphor at best, and hence is as unnatural as *real* suicide and should be punished in the same way. Parolles creates his own metaphorical relation, treats it as a real relation, and then uses it as a basic assumption in 'proving' his point.

This sort of obfuscation strongly suggests that Parolles represents a corruption of language which is consonant with a certain kind of moral corruption. He does represent a set of values, but Shakespeare is evidently intent upon portraying them as false ones. They are as sham as their representative, but they are also a genuine threat to order and peace. Though Parolles' words and actions may exist only on the level of appearance, the appeal of these appearances is very strong in the 'modern' world of this play. That is because Parolles' appeal is almost exclusively to individualistic impulse set off against the traditional order of kingship, love, and honour. I have mentioned that his view of nature is Hobbesian; his view of individual action is consistent with this view. Hence he favours aggressive, energetic, individual appetite and cares little for the traditional social or moral order. His views are those upheld by almost all the major characters of *Troilus and Cressida* (Hector at times excluded) whose restless individualism and 'appetite' finally topple the traditional order altogether. Hamlet is caught between such a view of human action and his reverence for the order of the past. In *All's Well that Ends Well* (as later in *King Lear*), Shakespeare takes a much less ambiguous stand with regard to the moral status of such behaviour.

Parolles' views come out not only in his language but also in the action he advises others to take. (He himself seems too cowardly to act on his own principles – another indication of the split between words and actions. Without his cowardice, he might be another Iago or Edmund.) His advice to Helena to cast off her virginity is one example of this. Such action, though it might be 'natural' in one way, a gratification of individual natural appetite, would be neither morally acceptable in terms of the traditional system nor, related to that, socially beneficial in terms of the world of this play. Helena would be unable to heal the King or fulfill her long-range hopes of marriage and ordered love with Bertram. Her clear understanding of the issues involved enables her to see through Parolles' argument and to uphold her own position. His advice to Bertram, however, falls on more fertile ground. His first suggestion is that Bertram 'steal away' to the wars in defiance of the direct order of the King. This too is put in terms of asserting individual will over moral or social considerations. Bertram seems to accept the advice ('By heaven, I'll steal away' II.i.34), which prepares him for another instance of inappropriate self-assertion, his decision to forsake Helena before 'bedding' her. Rather hesitantly and querulously he advances his decision and finds strong corroboration in Parolles: 'O my Parolles, they have married me! / I'll to the Tuscan wars and never bed her.' 'France,' returns Parolles, 'is a doghole and it no more merits / The tread of a man's foot. To the wars!' (II. iii.289-92). Bertram still holds back: 'There's letters from my mother. What th' import is, / I know not yet.' Parolles' rejoinder, though we know it is a bluff, evokes the image of heroic masculinity:

> To th' wars, my boy, to th' wars!
> He wears his honour in a box unseen
> That hugs his kicky-wicky here at home,
> Spending his manly marrow in her arms,
> Which should sustain the bound and high curvet
> Of Mars's fiery steed. (II.iii.295-300)

The bluff, most evident in the last two lines, which seem almost a parody of Marlovian bombast, is apparent to all but Bertram. The hollowness of the heroism is matched by the perversity of the view of masculinity and the concomitant debasement of the idea of honour, so important in the King's speeches earlier in the same scene. To the King, honour is associated with love and virtue; to Parolles it is an external appurtenance which must be shown off (as it is in *Troilus and Cressida*) and which is incompatible with marriage. Furthermore, masculine sexuality is reduced to cuteness and perversity, as indicated by the tone here and by the sexual meanings of 'box unseen' and 'kicky-wicky.'[13] Such a posture seems an effort to cover up a prevailing fear of the responsibility connected with sexuality which both men feel and which is, at bottom, a fear of the power of women over them. This fear is most obvious in Bertram, whose rejection of Helena arises from just such feelings (he will 'never bed her' and refuses even to kiss her). His subsequent infatuation with Diana arises from the same syndrome; it is an adolescent attempt to strike back at Helena and an example of the anarchic and aggressive sexuality of which Parolles would approve; his 'going between' them is completely characteristic. Thus Bertram and Parolles together, both in these speeches and in their subsequent action, turn honour into hollowness and sexual love into adolescent fantasy.

Parolles represents the kinds of forces alive in the play's world which threaten the comic resolution and which Helena must confront. Bertram, of course, provides the major block to a successful resolution. From one point of view, the play can be described as Bertram's movement from Parolles, with all that implies, to Helena. But the conclusion seems tentative and unconvincing. One of the reasons for this is that we have not seen, nor even been persuaded of the possibility of, any growth on Bertram's part. In folklore, characters do not have to be invested with motivations for their actions in order to be convincing. But in a play which is full of subtle psychological probing, we cannot help but demand some reason for Bertram's final change of heart. That we never fully get it is one of the play's major failures, but we do get a penetrating look into Bertram's soul as well as, I think, the outlines of a resolution.

The events surrounding the wooing of Diana, the unmasking of Parolles, and the bed trick, lead us deep into Bertram's character. The trick on Parolles and the bed trick run parallel; they are presented serially and are meant to comment on each other. Bertram is the focus of both actions; Parolles is unmasked to Bertram and Bertram is, after a long struggle, unmasked to himself. The first is an obvious prerequisite for the second, since Bertram must learn to see through Parolles before he can see through himself. Both incidents are described in military terms. This links them not only with each other but also with Parolles' speech, 'To th' wars,' and with the virginity debate in i.i. In the latter scene, Helena asks: 'Man is enemy to virginity; how can we barricado it against him ... Unfold to us some warlike resistance ... Is there no military policy how virgins may blow up men?' (i.i.118-26). She is, of course, playing with Parolles' *miles gloriosus* obsession, but the parallel with later examples is important. Helena says of Bertram, as she prepares to trick him, 'The Count he wooes your daughter, / Lays down his wanton siege before her beauty, / Resolv'd to carry her' (iii.vii.17-19). But Diana, the fort of virginity, and Helena devise a 'military policy' by which to defeat the importunate warrior-suitor. The attack on virginity is foiled and made 'lawful' (iii.vii.45), while the attack on Parolles' falsity succeeds. In the latter case, the whole ploy is a military 'sally' (iv.i.2), and as such enacts the military imagery of the parallel trick.

It is clear that one of Bertram's major difficulties is his inability to distinguish between appearance and reality. The most obvious instance of this is that he cannot see through Parolles, even after all the lords and common soldiers have, and in spite of the warnings of Lafew. Furthermore, his close association with Parolles suggests that he, like his crony, also has serious misconceptions about morality and its relation to language.

Bertram's failure is put in terms of traditional order and loyalty. He is a traitor, a traitor to himself. The lords, having seen him abandon a wife whom they would have been glad to marry, only to pursue a 'young gentlewoman ... of a most chaste renown' (iv.iii.17-18), are appalled. The first exclaims, 'As we are ourselves, what things are we!' The second responds by developing a theory which is central to the psychology of the play and the kind of immorality it presents:

Merely our own traitors. And as, in the common course of all treasons, we still see them reveal themselves till they attain to their abhorr'd ends, so he that in this action contrives against his own nobility, in his proper stream o'erflows himself. (iv.iii.25-30)

The most satisfactory reading of this difficult passage interprets it as saying: just as traitors, by persistence in their essential 'traitorness,' traduce the state, so Bertram traduces himself and his nobility by means of those very qualities and powers which make him noble.[14] This interpretation is corroborated by a glance at another passage on traitors; in the first scene, the Countess says: 'For where an unclean mind carries virtuous qualities, there commendations go with pity; they are virtues and traitors too' (I.i.47-9). As the Countess assures us, this is *not* the case with Helena, who combines 'virtuous qualities' (in both the moral and technical sense) with a clean mind. Bertram, however, later shows his noble skills to be working against him. He is an example of what both the Countess and the second lord describe.

There is a relationship between this self-traduction and speaking about one's misdeeds. Bertram's tendency to talk and brag about his exploits, especially his sexual conquests, seems parallel to Parolles' boasting. This comes out in the passage just quoted and in what immediately follows. The phrase 'o'erflows itself' has been taken to mean 'betray in speech,'[15] an interpretation which is confirmed in the next line when the first lord asks, 'Is it not meant damnable in us to be trumpeters of our unlawful intents?' (31-2). We see this trumpeting enacted a short while later when Bertram lists his exploits of the day and ends by saying, 'And between these main parcels of dispatch [I have] effected many nicer deeds' (IV.iii.103-5). Such talk is an important aspect of his corruption, a fact which illustrates the close connection between words and morality, between verbal and moral misbehaviour. The lords seem to recognize this connection and the concomitant responsibility which it involves. The second lord, admitting that he is not 'of his council,' is quick to make the association: 'Let it be forbid, sir! so should I be a great deal of his act' (54-5). Just as the lords see through Parolles and Bertram does not, so also they see relationships and complexities of which Bertram is unaware.

The most obvious example of Bertram's unconcern for direct connection between word and meaning is his constant lying. Lying in this play is vicious and foolhardy. And Bertram indulges in it, in the last scene especially, but also earlier in the play to the King, to Helena, to Diana. His primary motivation for much of this lying is self-protection; he is afraid of facing others or himself, especially when feeling guilty about something, and hence tries to lie his way out of difficult situations. Most of his lying is the result of his native cowardice. The lies to Diana, on the other hand, spring from desire.

The scene with Diana immediately precedes the one just discussed, so that we first watch and hear Bertram betraying himself and then hear the lords' commentary on his activity. Bertram begins by waxing lyrical over his discovery that his love's name is Diana, whom he apostrophizes as: 'Titl'd goddess; and worth it, with addition' (IV.ii.2-3). He then proceeds to try to seduce her. There is a contradiction here of which Bertram seems unaware: he begins by identifying Diana with the goddess of virginity and then tries to persuade her to give up that which makes such an identification possible. This is akin to, indeed it is something of an enactment of, Parolles' purely verbal assault on Helena's virginity in the first scene. Bertram then adopts the posture of the courtly lover or moaning sonneteer appealing to the cold-hearted mistress. He is thus taking a stance which Helena had predicted would be a danger for him. That such a role seems inappropriate in the world presented in *All's Well that Ends Well* hardly needs to be stressed. This is no longer the Forest of Arden and Diana, despite her name, is a far cry from Phebe. Towards the end of his first speech, however, Bertram shifts his tone by bringing up an argument out of keeping with the courtly style but quite in tune with the mood of the play: 'And now you should be as your mother was / When your sweet self was got.' This brings us back to Parolles and his argument to Helena: 'To speak on the part of virginity is to accuse your mothers, which is most infallible disobedience' (I.i.147-50). The same kind of phony logic is at work in both places; Diana sees through it at once: 'She then was honest' and Bertram is reduced to falsehood, 'So should you be.'

In his subsequent speeches, Bertram piles on the hyperbolic love rhetoric, giving us the impression that he thinks a multiplication of false words will make up for lack of truth. Like Parolles, he mistakes quantity for quality, words for genuine meaning. Diana justly reproves him: ''Tis not the many oaths that makes the truth, / But the plain single vow that is vow'd true' (IV.ii.21-2). She also strikes to the heart of his false vows by exposing their inner contradiction, 'This has no holding, / To swear by Him whom I protest to love / That I will work against Him' (27-9). If Bertram takes 'the High'st to witness' for his oath and yet intends irreligious acts, the vow cancels itself. Diana then can conclude from her argument that there is a disparity between Bertram's words and his meaning: 'Therefore your oaths / Are words and poor conditions but unsealed ...' (29-30). To which Bertram can only respond defensively that 'love is holy' and retire into falsehood once again: 'And my integrity ne'er knew the crafts / That you do charge men with' (33-5).

I have already noted that the threat posed by Parolles is an individualistic one which sets itself up against different embodiments of traditional natural order. One of the dominant ways that natural order is introduced into the play is through the idea of succession, which I discussed at the beginning of this chapter. It is interesting to note that both Parolles and Bertram pervert this idea, at least in its sexual reference, with their arguments against virginity ('And now you should be as your mother was / When your sweet self was got'). Furthermore, we have seen Bertram's failure to inherit his father's moral qualities as they are described by the Countess and the King. One of the most significant of these is the natural quality of his father's words and, by implication, their connection with genuine meaning: 'His plausive words / He scattered not in ears, but grafted them / To grow there and to bear ...' (i.ii.53-5). The image of natural growth contrasts rather pointedly with the artificial rhetoric of, say, Bertram's wooing speeches. Also, an intimate connection between words and moral action is suggested, especially if we extend the image with the biblical metaphor, 'By their fruits ye shall know them' (Matthew 7:16) or with the following passage from the Book of Common Prayer: 'Grant, we beseech thee ... that the words which we have heard this day with our outward ears may ... be so grafted inwardly in our hearts, that they may bring forth in us the fruit of good living.'[16] The ideas of succession and the connection between words and moral meanings are thus brought together.

In the scene with Diana, Bertram's ring provides another instance of succession as an aspect of natural order. According to plan, Diana requests and finally gets his ring. In the source, the ring has quite a different meaning from that which Shakespeare gives it: 'He greatly loved that ring and kepte it very carefully and never toke it from his finger, for a certaine vertue that he knew it had.'[17] For Bertram, however, the ring is a family heirloom: 'It is an honour 'longing to our house, / Bequeathed down from many ancestors, / Which were the greatest obloquy i'th'world / In me to lose' (iv.ii.42-5). He does not long hesitate to commit this obloquy, however, and gives over the ring. This action is a repudiation of succession and natural order and yet, ironically, it is an instrument of his redemption since it plays a role in his eventual confrontation with himself. There is a parallel irony in the fact that Bertram, who has so much trouble distinguishing appearance from reality, is deceived by false appearance (just as Parolles is deceived by false words) and thereby led back to himself. Bertram does not understand the complex morality implied by this kind of irony, though such complexity is at the heart of the play's moral vision.

Diana, in contrast, shows acute moral consciousness; aware of the duplicity of her actions and of the bed trick, she can nonetheless say with some truth: 'Only in this disguise, I think't no sin / To cozen him that would unjustly win' (iv.ii. 75-6). She can also split up words and meanings, though with a further, richer meaning in mind: after the arrangements with Bertram have been made, she says to him: 'You have won / A wife of me ...' (64-5). Such equivocation derives more from Helena than Parolles. Diana is aware of the apparent meaning and the real meaning and her purpose is to make Bertram eventually see the split, both in this particular instance and in general. Her equivocation differs from Bertram's in that it is directed at, and hints of, an ordered comic end. It fights fire with fire, setting off a process of unblinding similar to the lords' unmasking of Parolles. When Bertram can see both meanings and accept the connection between the word 'wife' and the fact 'wife' with the moral implications that involves, then Diana's work is done.

In this scene, as in other plays we have looked at, illusion is being used to bring a person face to face with reality. Diana is conducting a 'scene' which will be instrumental in creating the comic resolution. The major difference, however, between this play and *As You Like It*, for example, or *A Midsummer Night's Dream*, is that the *process* of role-playing (or being involved in the scene) does not in itself lead to understanding and fulfillment. Events are external and have no internal correlative; Bertram is acted upon; he does not act out the process of achieving identity. The reason for this change is that here, as in *Hamlet* and *Troilus and Cressida*, illusion has become a threat. False appearances, far from being benign, stunt growth and hinder awareness, which is why, to adjust slightly what I said in the preceding paragraph, the duplicity of even the innocent Diana seems a little shady. It cannot *fully* work, given the negative power of deception in the play generally. At the end, then, there is a neat resolution of the comic plot (with attendant ironies) but little sense of comic process and fulfillment.

Helena is the focus of the tension in the play between the romantic, fairy-tale elements and the realistic, cynical ones. Perhaps the best example of this is her attitude towards the bed trick, an element which derives from folklore. Critics have been divided over the morality of this trick, but Shakespeare seems to have regarded it as highly ambiguous (as might be indicated by the strong divergence of critical opinion).[18] He uses the device only twice, here and in *Measure for Measure*, and in both plays he places it in a context of ambiguous morality and complicated verbal analysis. Helena has no compunction about using the trick, but in two different speeches, one just before the sallies against Parolles and Bertram and one just after, she takes a penetrating look at what she is doing. In the first of these, she introduces the problem of appearance and reality directly into the moral sphere, and characteristically emerges with paradox:

> Let us assay our plot, which, if it speed,
> Is wicked meaning in a lawful deed,
> And lawful meaning in a lawful act,
> Where both not sin, and yet a sinful fact.[19]
>
> (III.vii.44-7)

The problem is expressed in terms of a split between law and morality suggestive of *Measure for Measure*. There, however, acts which are unlawful are said to be in a higher way moral whereas here, Bertram will be immoral while unknowingly remaining within the confines of the law. Such a speech gives us a sense of

Helena's moral perceptiveness and her ironic attitude towards the very means of her rebirth; she recognizes it as ambiguous and equivocal, sees its dangers, and yet makes use of it. This distinguishes her from Bertram, who has no sense of the moral ambiguity of his actions; nor can he take a detached view of himself in a personal situation. He takes himself too seriously, is incapable of mature self-judgement and unable to control himself or his situation. He thus becomes a traitor to himself and a liar to others.

After the trick has succeeded and Parolles has been stripped of his pretensions, Helena has another even more penetrating speech, this time concentrating on the feelings more than the intellect, and on debasement rather than unlawfulness:

> But, O strange men!
> That can such sweet use make of what they hate,
> When saucy trusting of the cozen'd thoughts
> Defiles the pitchy night; so lust doth play
> With what it loathes for that which is away. (IV.iv.21-5)

Once again we have the language of paradox and the accompanying sense of incongruity. Here too, perhaps more than anywhere in the play, we have a sense of deep ironical awareness, a perceptiveness about human relations which goes beyond the reaches of the ordinary sensibility. A.P. Rossiter comments acutely: 'These terrible lines purport to be about what only Helena can know ... The woman is left feeling prostituted (a thing lent for gain, not for love of the man), knowing that the man can only take her on debasing, defiling terms.'[20] He goes on, however, to suggest that such a disturbing note of ambiguity seems out of place in a play like this, which he finds not basically 'unpleasant.' What I have been trying to show is that it is very much *in* place and that such awareness is very much a part of what Helena is and must be. The passage itself deals with the morality of deception in strongly personal terms; Helena realizes that such deception is a way of meeting Bertram's single-minded lust but not of transforming it. Her cozening and his trusting defile the night. She is acutely aware not only of the impersonal generalized quality of lust and its susceptibility to deception, but also of the ambiguity of her own involvement.[21]

In her next speech, Helena reverts to her role as romantic heroine, an indication that Shakespeare did not blend the romantic and realistic features of the play as successfully as he could have (and as he did in *King Lear* or *The Winter's Tale*):

> But with the word, the time will bring on summer,
> When briars shall have leaves as well as thorns,

> And be as sweet as sharp. We must away;
> Our wagon is prepared, and time revives us.
> All's well that ends well ... (IV.iv.31-5)

Here we have a belief in the power of time itself to transform and revive, the kind of feeling that pervades *The Winter's Tale*. In *All's Well that Ends Well*, however, there is no real context provided to give weight to such a statement. It is hard to imagine how a woman who had just spoken the earlier lines on lust and deception could, with the next breath, ignore their import so completely and, seemingly, so unconsciously. This is the difficulty with *All's Well that Ends Well*; moral and psychological perceptions overpower the possibilities of the plot and the assertion of the plot undercuts the power of these perceptions.

Like the last plays, *All's Well that Ends Well* is an attempt to place evil within a total, comic view of experience. It employs many of the same devices – magic, 'resurrection' of the heroine, emphasis (as in this passage) on regeneration, and an extensive, highly complicated dénouement. But somehow the central role of Helena does not possess the power to draw the disparate elements together. None of the romances has a manipulating heroine; furthermore, the romance heroines – Marina, Imogen, Perdita, Miranda – are either protected from evil (the latter two) or oblivious to it (the former two). Nor is the complex moral awareness arising from the romances a product primarily of the heroines or their insight; they are more agents of grace than anything. It is the men, like Leontes and Prospero, who must face and control evil, either in themselves or in the external world. Helena's problem in *All's Well that Ends Well* is that she can be neither a Rosalind nor an Imogen, but only a much more equivocal figure than either.

G.K. Hunter develops an argument for the continuity of problem plays and romances on the basis of the handling of the final scene.[22] The last scene of *All's Well that Ends Well*, which has been both attacked for its clumsiness and praised for its theatrical effectiveness, is, according to Hunter, an attempt to go beyond a personal to a spiritual reconciliation involving 'the ransom of wickedness by the overflowing power of mercy.'[23] Shakespeare's failure in this view is essentially a poetic one, a failure to find a stylistic mode proper to the material he is dealing with. The subtle psychological probing calls for personal reconciliation, while the romance plot and the complexity of the final scene seem to push beyond the merely personal. By the time Shakespeare wrote the romances, he was able to harmonize 'the jarring elements' of *All's Well* through 'the power of a new poetic vision,' as in the recognition scene in *Pericles*. This is an attractive theory, but I think the problem runs far deeper. As I have been trying to argue, the difficulty consists to a large extent in Shakespeare marrying a theme and a structure that are very uncomfortable bedfellows.

In the source, the dénouement is handled neatly and simply. Giletta returns with her twins during a feast, presents herself to her husband, tells her story, and is accepted with sympathy and love. Shakespeare complicates this enormously, adding an extra ring, and therefore an extra strand of complication, 'blackening' Bertram's character,[24] introducing Lafew's convenient daughter (first mentioned in IV.v) to mire Bertram even more deeply, bringing in Diana as riddling stage manager, presenting Helena as a theatrical coup, and, finally, dismissing Bertram to happiness, to adapt Johnson's acute phrase. Why, beyond sheer love of elaboration, does he do it? The whole scene is consciously engineered by Helena as a play within a play, while remaining part of the main action, much the way Portia manages the trial scene in *The Merchant of Venice*. Is it meant to provide the same kind of awareness and self-knowledge that are the products of such manipulations in earlier comedies? This is not really its effect; for the theatricality of, say, the last scene of *As You Like It* is the culmination of a process operating throughout that play and its strictly theatrical virtues depend on what has gone before.

In *All's Well that Ends Well*, on the other hand, there is no such purpose discernible in the rest of the play. We have already seen how playing scenes, manipulation effected through role-playing and the like, are not accompanied by any corresponding inner development. The two realms of the play, the magical and the realistic, each demand their own characteristic response, each generate a unique kind of awareness, but they never fully combine in one subtly modulated point of view. At the same time, it seems unlikely that Shakespeare intended to invest the final scene with quite the universal regenerative effect that Hunter talks about. The wholesale blackening of Bertram's character *during* the scene and the tentative nature of the actual resolution (which should, even in Hunter's terms, be a symbol for larger reconciliations) seems to argue against putting too much weight on that explanation. Shakespeare's very uncertainty of intent is of course the source of our unsureness. In contrast both to the late plays and to the earlier plays (even *Hamlet*) that we have looked at, we have in *All's Well that Ends Well* an *assertion* of theatricality on the part of author and heroine, calculated to mortify Bertram and force him to learn the hard way. Such shock tactics may indeed be necessary given the degree of self-deception and duplicity of which Bertram is capable. They do not, however, provide the audience with the subtly ironic point of view typical of the earlier comedies.

Shakespeare seems equally if not more interested in stressing the kind of divisiveness and tension so common in the rest of the play. The use of the comic framework thus works as an ironic counterpoint to what is actually going on. What is typical of this finale, as of the whole play, is not resolution but paradox. The play is organized around many sets of opposites (eg, youth-age, providence-human effort, magic-realism, word-thing) most of which have to do with modes of perception, especially faulty ones. The confusion and lies that dominate the first half of the last scene underline the difficulties inherent in true perception. These difficulties are reinforced by the note of paradox which is introduced, significantly, by Parolles and which dominates the last part of the scene. 'He lov'd her, sir, and lov'd her not' (v.iii.248), says Parolles. To which the King replies, 'As thou art a knave, and no knave.' There follows Diana's riddling equivocation over the ring, which culminates in more paradox: 'Because he's guilty and he is not guilty. / He knows I am no maid, and he'll swear to't: / I'll swear I am a maid and he knows not' (290-2). The paradox of being both guilty and not guilty recalls Helena's earlier awareness of a 'wicked meaning in a lawful deed' and suggests that the complex point of view she then manifested is being required here. The play seems to be asking for a darkening of what Bertram and the rest *know*, what they see, and a subsequent questioning of their perception; a quizzical or detached attitude towards what one perceives is hence a prerequisite for an adequate understanding of appearance and reality.

The paradoxes here might recall those at the end of *Twelfth Night* or *Troilus and Cressida*, but the tone and purpose differ from play to play. In the 'happy' comedy, opposites dissolve like a trick of illusion. 'What is' and 'what is not' cease to be opposite and become complementary; in *Troilus and Cressida*, on the other hand, the paradox ('This is and is not Cressid') is a torture, a split in nature and in the mind. *All's Well that Ends Well* lies somewhere between these two. Opposites can and do co-exist, but there is none of the sense of merging and harmony typical of *Twelfth Night*; rather, we are left with a feeling of division and unresolved tension which, though less pervasive than in *Troilus and Cressida*, persists despite Shakespeare's apparent efforts to the contrary.

The final paradox is: 'He knows himself my bed he hath defiled, / And at that time he got his wife with child. / Dead though she be, she feels her young one kick. / So there's my riddle: one that's dead is quick' (v.iii.301-4). Helena is both dead and alive; lifeless, yet she 'feels her young one kick.' The solution to all these puzzles is of course Helena herself; she *is* the meaning, as Diana says: 'And now, behold the meaning.' But even this meaning is paradoxical; her first words, spoken in response to the King's incredulous question 'Is't real I see?' express her perception of the ambiguous relation between appearance and reality, between language and object; she can at this point only see herself in terms of an appearance, a word, since Bertram has done nothing to realize her existence: 'No, my good lord, / 'Tis but the *shadow* of a wife you see, / The name and not the thing.' Acceptance of her requires acceptance of the miraculous, irrational, and paradoxical (as it did for the King earlier) and involves some kind of insight into the relation between name and thing. Bertram's response seems an attempt to heal the breach between word and thing, and hence to repudiate

Parolles and turn to Helena: 'Both, both! O, pardon!' But the irrational and miraculous present more difficulty for him. His demand for clarity of explanation and his use of conditionals in his next and final speech do much to account for the sense of inconclusiveness we feel about this resolution: '*If* she, my liege, can make me know this clearly, / I'll love her dearly – ever, ever, dearly.' We get the idea that at least part of his 'conversion' is due more to sudden remorse than to a solid and lasting sense of his own personal and social identity. The King's final speech also leaves us with a feeling of tentativeness: '*If* thou be'st yet a fresh uncropped flower ... All yet *seems* well, and *if* it end so meet ...'

I would like to emphasize one other aspect of Diana's phrase, 'behold the meaning.' This is a cue for Helena's entrance and her appearance is a kind of *gestalt*, a visual phenomenon of great importance as a theatrical (for the other characters and for the audience) and as a 'real' event. The theatrical and the real here merge in one image, an image which is the culmination of the plot. As such it is related to similar manifestations in other Shakespearean plays where a major character is resurrected and presented to the rest of the characters: Claudio in *Measure for Measure*, Thaisa in *Pericles*, Hermione in *The Winter's Tale*, Ferdinand and Miranda in *The Tempest*. The device is essentially one of romance and Shakespeare, by putting each of these events into a theatrical setting *within* the play, is able to deepen the reality of such events even as he places them as unreal, as a part of romance. In *All's Well that Ends Well*, the emphasis on the ideal continuity but actual discontinuity between appearance and reality surrounds Helena's manifestation and is quite naturally related to the theatrical context. Helena is presented as an image of the ideal. Shakespeare uses jewel imagery to suggest this ideality. The King says, 'We lost a jewel of her, and our esteem / Was made much poorer by it' (v.iii.1-2). This sense of Helena as priceless jewel runs through the last part of the play and is complicated by Diana's reference to her as the 'jeweler' (295) who owns the token-like ring. She is, then, both jewel and jeweler, both image and magician, and as such she commands a much wider realm of understanding and experience than anyone else. The significance and value of this understanding is what is being presented to the court and to us through Helena's appearance. The problem, however, is that even this powerful symbolism can only accentuate the unresolved conflict between such magic and the bitter psychological probing which Shakespeare neither abandons nor successfully integrates.

All's Well that Ends Well, in contrast to the earlier comedies, leaves behind the more manageable problems of romantic love and turns to complicated moral questioning. The achievement of romantic love typical of *As You Like It* – sane, moderate, ironic, and charming though it was – is no longer a real interest. Such love cannot be an effective instrument for dealing with complicated moral problems. Of the many polarities in the play, there is one, as I have mentioned, between fate, or providence, and individual will. Related to this is a tension between constraint, both heavenly and human, and love; this affects Bertram especially, who says to Diana, 'I was compell'd to her [Helena], but I love thee / By love's own sweet constraint ...' (IV.ii.15-16). The confusion of constraints manifested here and the misunderstanding of heavenly and earthly priorities is in sharp contrast to Helena's conciliating role in both these areas. The play is examining the nature of the different freedoms involved in the actions of these people and is distinguishing between enlightened and false freedoms. At the same time, it is criticizing the view of love (anarchic and aggressive) that derives from the conception of freedom embodied in Bertram. An aberrant view would only have been mocked and/or clarified in earlier comedy. Here, however, the hero's attitude is a threat to the delicate balance of the play's world. Furthermore, a special flavour permeates this play precisely because the education of Bertram is so difficult and, ultimately, so unsuccessful. Despite the neatness of the resolution, we are not left with a firm sense of the value of the playing which has brought it about. The ending of the play, especially, makes us question the structural assumptions on which it is built. Perhaps, in creating Duke Vincentio, Shakespeare hoped that an older, more mature man, faced with similar issues of freedom and constraint, would be able to exert a psychological control unavailable to an innocent young woman. Or, on the other hand, perhaps he realized that the old skins he had prepared were unfit for such new and acid wine.

6

Measure for Measure

The conflict between restraint and liberty is a major theme in *Measure for Measure* as it is in *All's Well that Ends Well*. Again we are faced with a set of false freedoms, especially sexual ones; but the later play goes further by adding a set of false restraints as well. Angelo's restraint, for example, his snowy coldness, is falser than Mistress Overdone's liberty; the restraint imposed upon Claudio, the physical one of prison, is a false way of dealing with 'too much liberty'; Isabella's desire for 'a more strict restraint' (I.iv.4), we later learn, derives from a misunderstanding of herself and human passion generally. Such false conceptions of liberty and restriction are the result of a failure to perceive truly and to judge correctly. From the misjudgements (and consequent misrule) of the Duke before the play begins to the highly theatrical misjudgements of the final scene, the play is riddled with misconceptions and errors of perception.

The Duke, I think, sees as his task the elimination of various misperceptions, or at least the ferreting out of 'seemers.' But because of his own mistakes of judgement and his own 'seeming,' the results are highly ambiguous. From the point of view of the audience, the comic structure that arises out of the Duke's role creates a certain set of expectations which are not really met as the play unfolds. This heightens our sense of ambiguity and may make us uneasy. We expect the Duke and his disguise to have an effect parallel to that described in connection with the earlier comedies. At the same time, different expectations are created by the tone of the play, which is predominantly urban and ironic, and by the brilliant psychological analysis typical of the first two acts. The audience is thus led in two directions at once and ends up a little bewildered and unsatisfied. Misjudgement and misperception actually become a feature of the audience response, as they are of the characters' reactions to events within the play. It seems unlikely to me that Shakespeare was fully in control of the resulting ambiguities, partly because the play is split so cleanly down the middle, though he was surely aware of the unsettling effect of the play's construction, and may even have intended the ironic thrust of the play to undermine its comic structure. Be that as it may, I intend to approach the problem as the play does, by confronting first the power of its psychological insight and then by considering the strengths and weaknesses of the Duke's manipulation.

Isabella and Angelo are both moral tyrants; both are cold and rigid; both make crucial decisions during the play but, as Philip Edwards remarks, the responsibility for these decisions is taken out of their hands and put into the Duke's.[1] In the case of each, we are set up to expect a recognition, which could come in either a tragic or a comic way, but which seems both necessary and imminent. Through a series of twists in the plot, tragic anagnorisis is neatly and artfully avoided. When Shakespeare changes his tragic notes to comic, he provides a formal structure which could, in a different context, lead through illusion to recognition. But the involvement of both Isabella and Angelo in roles and illusion does not seem to have that effect. This is at least partly the result of the problems they encounter and the general bitterness of the play. Shakespeare seems to be suggesting that typically comic techniques are inadequate in the face of the actual and severe pressures of moral evil.

Isabella begins as an absolutist, sure of her virtue, calling for more strict restraint on the daughters of St Clare. However, she also has her pragmatic side and is quite willing to accept practical solutions without moral condemnation. Her initial reply to Lucio's story about Claudio and Juliet, 'O let him marry her' (I.iv.49), is an indication of this. There is nothing in this scene with Lucio that indicates any moral repugnance on her part. As the play proceeds, we get the impression that her chastity is more a way of avoiding her own sexuality than it is a moral conviction. This is the reason she wishes a stricter restraint: because she is afraid of her own passion and the possibility of its getting out of hand. She seeks external curbs because she cannot trust her own internal ones. (It is worth noting that in making her a nun, Shakespeare was departing from all his sources.) Only once during the play does the full force of her passion get away from her, but from this instance we can appreciate its power, and her apprehension. It is not sexual passion but anger, anger at her brother for wanting to stay alive at her expense. The hysterical rage which bursts from her at that point manifests the sort of passion that she is bottling up inside herself. It is significant, too, that the outburst is occasioned by Claudio's suggestion that she sleep with someone; a great part of the anger is sexual. Secondarily, of course, her chastity *is* a moral conviction, but one which arises from deep in her personality. Her revealing lines to Angelo, 'There is a vice that most I do abhor / And most desire should meet the blow of justice' (II.ii,29-30), from an ethical standpoint are unacceptable, since in strictly Christian terms fornication between a betrothed couple is one of the least abhorrent of vices. In addition, the fact that sexuality cannot and ought not be regulated by law is already becoming apparent in the context of the very case she is arguing. But for her the law is one more restraint to be set on the runaway passions which she fears so deeply. There is perhaps some reason for her to be apprehensive. Her sexuality, like her anger, is very close to the surface; Lucio recognizes this and so, in his perverse way, does Angelo. Lucio's method of egging her on during her first interview with Angelo expresses his perception of her sexuality. Through his commentary, the whole contest takes on sexual overtones. In production, such aspects should be clear, though subtle, just as they are in the text. Lucio interprets the action for us by his comments: 'You are too cold ... To him, I say' (ii.ii.45-7) 'Ay touch him! There's the vein' (70); 'O to him, to him, wench! he will relent; / He's coming' (123-4).

As I said, Isabella can be coolly pragmatic as well as moralistic, shrewd as well as passionate. Her quick jump to attempted blackmail once she learns Angelo's intentions in ii.iv indicates her readiness to let the pragmatic outweigh the ethical; so too does her acceptance of the Duke's plan to trap Angelo and thus place Mariana in the same 'vice' for which Claudio and Juliet were condemned and which she professes to abhor. She is ignorant of the role her personality plays in her morality; and she must become much more self-aware if the full comic process is to be effected. Isabella's only soliloquy, immediately following her second scene with Angelo, reveals nothing in the way of developing self-knowledge under pressure of adversity. It contains a bitter and observant condemnation of Angelo, a statement of confidence in her brother's virtue, and another declaration of her own rigidity: 'Then, Isabel, live chaste; and, brother, die! / More than our brother is our chastity' (ii.iv.184-5). The pompous and imperial 'we' of this last line, and the cold-hearted matter-of-factness of the first, underscore the moral absolutism and corresponding failure of self-knowledge typical of Isabella.

These lines also provide an extreme example of the general tendency among the main characters to place abstraction before humanity. Not only Isabella's chastity, but Angelo's justice and even the Duke's ethic of deceit and manipulation are all too abstract, divorced from human bodies and human experience. This tendency is reflected in the language of the play, where a recurrent use of the abstract instead of the concrete creates a sense of disembodiment, of dissociation of mind and body, feeling and action. The Duke speaks this way more than anyone else: 'I thought your marriage fit. Else imputation, / For that he knew you, might reproach your life, / And choke your good to come' (v.i.425-7). 'Imputation' is personified and the human element in the action is excluded. Again, 'Love talks with better knowledge and knowledge with better love' or 'Mortality and mercy in Vienna / Live in thy tongue and heart' (i.i.45-6). The tone created by such language is crucial to an understanding of the whole play and the implicit criticism of certain 'virtuous' modes of action, including the Duke's. Angelo, too, uses the same disembodied language: 'What's open made to justice, / That justice seizes' (ii.i.21-2), or 'It is the law, not I, condemn your brother' (ii.ii.80). The law is pictured as something absolute and mechanical, with no connection to individual thought or emotion. Such modes of speech are merely a gloss on Angelo's actions, which themselves express a fanatic loyalty to a false ideal caught in a web of circumstance which makes it criminally dangerous.

After the Duke's intervention, Isabella (to return to her) ceases to be such an interesting character. Her role becomes passive; she is an actress in the Duke's comedy.[2] As such, she follows her instructions right to the end, although she allows herself one passionate outburst when the Duke tells her that Claudio has been executed despite their trick. His telling her this, he claims to the audience, is 'to make her heavenly comforts of despair / When it is least expected' (iv.iii. 114-15). What good this will do her is not clear. However, she does pass the test, as her plea for Angelo in Act v indicates. She gains compassion and an insight into legal modes of argumentation. She seems able to forgive Angelo: 'I partly think / A due sincerity governed his deeds / Till he did look on me' (v.i.450-2), though it is worth remembering Dr Johnson's cynical, anti-feminist comment on this passage.* Her legal distinctions are even more questionable:

> My brother had but justice
> In that he did the thing for which he died.
> For Angelo
> His act did not o'ertake his bad intent
> And must be buried but as an intent,
> That perished by the way. (v.i.453-8)

Angelo's act may not have been as bad as his intent but he did end up doing precisely what Claudio had done – a fact which Isabella ignores – and with a more vicious intent. Thus, he should be liable to the same punishment, if such punishment is 'but justice.' J.W. Lever observes that her pleading here, unlike that for Claudio earlier, takes into account extenuating circumstances which materially alter the case. He goes on to argue that this indicates that she has learned something important about the foundations of secular justice and the difference be-

---

* 'I am afraid our varlet poet intended to inculcate that women think ill of nothing that raises the credit of their beauty, and are ready, however virtuous, to pardon any act which they think incited by their own charms.'

tween public legal justice and individual ethical justice.³ But the fact that her argument does not stand up *legally*, as well as the implicit criticism of a merely legal justice which the whole play provides, indicates that such a lesson is not worth learning. The failure of legal processes to take the most basic issues into account is implicit in the final lines of Isabella's speech: 'Thoughts are no subjects, / Intents but merely thoughts' (458-9). This general principle that she derives from the case at hand ignores the fact that the question of intention is often a very important factor in legal judgements. In addition, it pinpoints an inadequacy in merely legal proceedings – that they must deal with acts rather than attitudes. The trial of Angelo is clearly not just a legal matter: it is meant to establish certain ethical values as well, and whether Isabella has realized this is not at all clear.

If she has learned anything through the Duke's manipulation, is it something valuable? Does it add up to a genuine recognition? As I mentioned above, the most important blocks in her personality are her inability to accept the passionate, sexual side of her nature, and her blindness about the make-up of her moral nature. The plea for Angelo's life does not get close to these problems. Her self-protective shell is not, after all, threatened by Angelo's release. To plead for him, it is not necessary that she face the peculiar combination of sexiness and frigidity which informs her personality. On this score, it seems to me significant that she has no answer for the Duke and his proposal of marriage. But perhaps she realizes that she need not fear too much since he is neither young nor passionate. As such he is a mate both unsuited and unchallenging to her, partially because their coming together does not demand full self-awareness on her part. He is the sort of suitor who is forced on unwilling young heroines at the beginning of more conventional comedies and subsequently outwitted. I think we can conclude, then, that although Isabel does change, this change is by no means a full self-recognition and acceptance of the sort typified by the term 'identity' as I have used it earlier. The change may be an attempt on Shakespeare's part to justify the comic pattern but, remaining true to his unfaltering sense of human character, he was unwilling or unable to wrench her into a mould completely consistent with that pattern. Perhaps this is the reason that the proposed marriage with the Duke is so half-hearted; it is an artificial addendum which does not fit the human facts of the play (as such, it is a miniature of the last scene, the artifice of which conflicts with, instead of fulfilling, the view of human experience the play presents).

Angelo, like Isabella, begins in absolutism and ends with somewhat more flexibility, able to admit his crime and plead for death. But, again, any gain in self-knowledge that he may have achieved seems both incongruent with the intense insight he exhibits early in the play and independent of the Duke's eager manipulation. Knowing Shakespeare's use of comic form, we expect some growth associated with it, but to claim that this is what we get is to let our expectations blur our perceptions.*

Let us look at Angelo for a moment. He has exhibited a good deal of self-knowledge during his two soliloquies in Act II; they come as close as any others in Shakespeare to the sort of self-scrutiny typical of Hamlet. They reveal him as a man made suddenly, passionately aware of his inner nature, not through the Duke's tricks but through Isabella's 'virtue.' He begins the first soliloquy with a hypersensitive response to her parting pleasantry, a response which reveals his bristling inner state: 'ISABELLA Save your honour. ANGELO From thee: even from thy virtue' (II.ii.162). The irony, of course, arises from the fact that Isabella's attempt to *use* her virtue results only in his lust for her. His sudden temptation makes it clear to him that his 'honour' – both his title and his chastity – are threatened by that virtue. He continues with a brilliant image of corruption through which he consciously places himself in the context of the general social corruption of Vienna: 'It is I / That, lying by the violet in the sun, / Do as the carrion does, not as the flow'r, / Corrupt with virtuous season' (II.ii.165-8).[4] It is the perversity of immorality stemming from such goodness that stops him short and impels him inward; and it is this to which he returns again and again in the speech; it kindles his imagination and occasions some of his most dazzling poetry: 'Having waste ground enough, / Shall we desire to raze the sanctuary, / And pitch our evils there' (170-2). We have, too, the intriguing lines, 'O cunning enemy, that, to catch a saint, / With saints dost bait thy hook' (180-1), lines that lead us to suspect Angelo of a blindness to the evil in himself. But in the very act of saying it, he is reassessing his conception of himself as a saint; he begins to face the sort of evil he is susceptible to. The last lines of the soliloquy reveal the same mental process: 'Ever till now, / When men were fond, I smiled, and wond'red how' (186-7). At this very moment he is discovering that his seeming invulnerability to love and desire has been a deception, and this forces introspection. This 'invulnerability' may remind us of the Duke, who says confidently of himself, 'Believe not that the dribbling dart of love / Can pierce a complete bosom' (I.iii.2-3). Both men are deceived about themselves, but Angelo learns more quickly and violently how he has misjudged himself. The Duke's reversal comes later and in a decidedly more comic way, structurally.

---

* In saying this I am in no way arguing that Shakespeare *should* have provided such a change in Angelo, or in Isabella. We must approach the plays as they are, and certainly *Measure for Measure* is more interesting as it is than it would be as a rehash, say, of *Much Ado about Nothing* or *Twelfth Night*. I am interested in this chapter, as in those on the other 'problem' plays, in analyzing what has happened to those techniques used in a happier way in the earlier comedies.

Angelo, in the midst of his self-examination, touches the crucial question: 'O, let her brother live! / Thieves for their robbery have authority / When judges steal themselves' (II.ii.175-7). This is a common sentiment in the play, but nowhere else is it stated with such personal questioning and agony. It probes deeply to a fault with justice as an ideal, a fault which Angelo had not recognized earlier but which he now sees clearly enough. Before his confrontation with Isabella, he had lectured Escalus: 'The jury, passing on the prisoner's life, / May in the sworn twelve have a thief or two / Guiltier than him they try. What's open made to justice, / That justice seizes' (II.i.19-22). His statement penetrates to the heart of the problem, though Angelo does not realize this until he is facing himself in a parallel situation. The fact that justice seizes only what is 'open made' to it reveals the failure of justice as an ideal, since human justice is always fallible. There will always be a discrepancy between the concept of justice and its human realization. Failure to take into account such a discrepancy is vicious, precisely because it is an absolutist position in a world where certain knowledge is impossible.

This moral problem that the judge must face is continually being presented to Angelo, perhaps never more forcefully than by Isabella earlier in the scene under discussion:

> Go to your bosom,
> Knock there, and ask your heart what it doth know
> That's like my brother's fault. If it confess
> A natural guiltiness such as is his,
> Let it not sound a thought upon your tongue
> Against my brother's life. (II.ii.136-41)

It is immediately after this speech that Angelo speaks his first aside, 'She speaks, and 'tis / Such sense that my sense breeds with it.' The irony is thick at such a moment, for this is the first verbal indication (though in production some gesture could previously have indicated something of his feeling to us) that Angelo's inner defences are crumbling. It is a typically Shakespearean stroke that this should follow Isabella's plea. The juxtaposition jolts us into a recognition of the moral and psychological problem that he now faces, a recognition that Angelo is also coming to, as we see moments later in his soliloquy. Hence both Angelo and audience are involved in the same mental process, a fact which helps to bring us closer to him.

The problem is that Angelo is right on one important count (as, in a certain way, Isabella is right about chastity). The law and judges must remain impersonal if the law is to survive at all. For a judge to let a thief go because the judge knows himself a thief is to destroy the law. The whole question of human authority hency involves a certain amount of injustice, a painful fact that King Lear expresses in his great speeches to Gloucester at Dover Beach. On the other hand, a judge who knows himself as guilty as the man he condemns must, if he is at all sensitive, suffer for it, because there is another law at work here, another kind of morality based on more far-reaching ethical principles. This leads us to the role of Christianity in the play: it is not really the ultimate solution so much as a moral system to set against the legal system and thereby show the latter inadequate. Here again, as with Isabella's speeches in the last scene, we are faced with a distinction between law and morality. To say that Angelo does not recognize this problem, or to claim that he is merely a 'seemer,' is to miss the emotional import of the scenes under discussion when, it seems to me, we are very much *with* him. It is only when he becomes viciously cruel, when he orders Claudio killed and his head brought up for inspection, that our sympathies are repulsed. But even this action, I believe, can be mitigated if we realize what Angelo is going through – the guilt and the fear of being detected. It is this fear which most of all drives him to do what he does, a fear which can only bring relief when he is finally exposed. G. Wilson Knight comments: 'To Angelo, exposure seems to come as a relief: the horror of self-deception is at an end.'5 I would amend this slightly: I do not think Angelo is self-deceived; that is precisely why he is relieved to be found out. The horror of trying to deceive others is at an end.

Angelo's second soliloquy again provides violent and incisive instances of his growing, painful awareness. As in the similar moment in *Hamlet*, when we are suddenly brought close to Claudius and allowed to see his inner suffering, Angelo, though trying to pray, finds that all his thoughts remain below. Angelo's problem, however, is unlike Claudius's, since guilt is not yet the issue, but temptation. The intensity of his feeling inspires a violent and highly compressed poetry, poetry more charged than any in the play:

> Heaven hath my empty words,
> Whilst my invention, hearing not my tongue,
> Anchors on Isabel. Heaven in my mouth,
> As if I did but only chew his name,
> And in my heart the strong and swelling evil
> Of my conception! The state, whereon I studied,
> Is, like a good thing being often read,
> Grown sere and tedious. Yea, my gravity,
> Wherein (let no man hear me) I take pride,
> Could I, with boot, change for an idle plume
> Which the air beats for vain. O place, O form,

> How often dost thou with thy case, thy habit,
> Wrench awe from fools, and tie the wiser souls
> To thy false seeming! Blood, thou art blood.
> Let's write 'good angel' on the devil's horn,
> 'Tis not the devil's crest. (II.iv.2-17)

The first part of the passage moves from the dialectic of heart and tongue which is so common in this play (and in *All's Well that Ends Well*) to an astonishing image for it. 'Heaven in my mouth, / As if I did but only chew his name' suggests some sacrilegious communion service, a physicalizing of something essentially spiritual. This polarity carries over into the next lines where the physical sexual act of 'conception' provides the metaphor for Angelo's mental process, which is, of course, appropriate since his conception is encircled with sexual desire. Equivocation over the intellectual and sexual meanings of the word 'know' is common throughout the play, especially in the final scene, where it results in paradoxes and theatrical misconceptions. But here the relationship is felt and realized. The connection in Angelo seems inescapable and absolute. The elaboration of the metaphor ('strong and swelling evil') underlines this connection, since it recalls the many actual pregnancies in the play and connects with the general theme of 'creation.'[6] But again, the relationship is anything but abstract; it is an inner actuality and, moreover, an evil and destructive growth, not a creative one. This, then, is a moment of fusion, where the externals of the play reveal their internal dimension.

As he continues, Angelo pulls back a little from this intensity and becomes more reflective. He feels that the whole carefully built structure of his public personality, which he seems never before to have questioned or thought of as fraudulent, is crumbling around him: his gravity, he could 'with boot, change for an idle plume.' The parenthetical 'let no man hear me' is a master stroke. It indicates Angelo's fear of being detected as well as his 'false seeming,' but most of all it shows us how aware of himself and his mask he is quickly becoming. His state, which he has studied to adopt, has now 'grown sere and tedious' but he cannot back out of his position of prominence and authority. He can only deprecate it on the basis of his new-found knowledge. This is the motive for his attack on 'place' and 'form,' and the violence that their 'false seeming' effects in the world.[7] Suddenly, blood intrudes on his meditations. Blood is the antithesis of Angelo's studied deceit. It is irreducibly actual and can't be disguised. It is linked throughout the play with sexuality and is opposed to reason and judgement. Angelo's blood 'is very snow-broth' (I.iv.58), says Lucio; but now he is falling, like Claudio, 'by prompture of the blood' (II.iv.178). He is discovering that his blood is palpable and warm.

His soliloquy over, Angelo is immediately thrown into turmoil by the servant's announcement of Isabella's arrival. As he waits for her, he develops an elaborate simile comparing the rush of blood to his heart to the crowding of subjects around a king and to the pressure of onlookers around 'one that swounds.' The clever artifice and full articulation of this passage contrasts with the hurried and intense tone of what he has just said. It tends to distance us and hence prepares us for what follows. As the scene with Isabella progresses, he gets more and more desperate and his cruelty mounts with his frustration and guilt. Despite the high pitch of his desire, he nonetheless regains thorough control of himself as his sensuality develops into sadism: 'I have begun, / And now I give my sensual race the rein' (ii.iv.159-60), he tells her at the end – and we believe him. It is fascinating to watch this change in Angelo and to feel our sympathies waning. His sadism is the chief cause of this effect and itself arises as a consequence of his sudden intense preoccupation with physicality: if Isabella does not yield, Claudio 'must not only die the death, / But thy unkindness shall his death draw out / To ling'ring sufferance' (165-7).

We now have a clearer picture of how Shakespeare has manipulated our feelings towards Angelo. At the outset, we accept him as an upright and almost self-effacing substitute. Shakespeare soon begins to suggest his iciness and rigidity and then shows him in action as the inflexible, almost inhuman judge. But soon after, he begins to evoke our sympathy for Angelo. We get closer to him than to any other character in the play. Then Shakespeare again starts moving him away and we become more and more repulsed. After the scene just discussed, we do not see him again until iv.iv, although all the interim action revolves around him. What he does during this period – sleeping with Isabella / Mariana, rushing instead of repealing the order for Claudio's execution, and demanding to see the head – reveals him at his most despicable, and we are kept carefully at a distance from him so that his actions are not in the least extenuated. Whether this shift should be termed a failure or a change of intention (or neither) is a moot question. It is, however, an indication of what Tillyard characterizes as the shift from the poetic to the prosaic that takes place in the middle of the play.[8] Angelo's final soliloquy (in iv.iv) illustrates this shift. There is none of the intense feeling and supercharged poetry that we saw in the first two. Rather, we remain distanced from him as we watch his self-protective impulses at work. He admits to the same fault as before – that of the guilty judge – but this time in depersonalized language that dries up any intensity of feeling: 'A deflower'd maid! / And by an eminent body that enforced the law against it!' (iv.iv.23-5). This is the kind of language typical of Angelo before his scenes with Isabella, when, in contrast to the Provost's human and personal 'groaning Juliet,' he could call her a 'fornicatress' (ii.ii.23). Such phrases as 'eminent body' and 'deflower'd maid' suggest a similarly detached and superior attitude. The rest of the soliloquy describes how his 'authority bears so credent bulk' and thus can override anything that Isabella might claim, and explains why he had Claudio put to death – in order to protect himself. Only at the end do we get some sense of what he must be feeling: 'Would yet he had liv'd! / Alack, when once our grace we have forgot, / Nothing goes right! we would, and we would not' (iv.iv.34-6). This expresses simply and acutely what Angelo has been enduring: the feeling of miring himself deeper and deeper into a morass which he cannot avoid without exposing himself; the desire to free Claudio coupled with the desire to get rid of incriminating evidence; the increase of guilt at every turn.

We may return now to the question, what does Angelo really learn from the Duke's manipulation and exposure? He is intensely relieved and pleads for death in accordance with the strict justice he had upheld at the beginning of the play: 'When I that censure him do so offend, / Let mine own judgement pattern out my death' (ii.i.29-30). (In strictest justice, as he himself knows, his principle demands death even before exposure; his awareness of this was part of his agony.) He is penitent and apparently humble. But has he really achieved some new self-knowledge, or developed a more flexible and complex moral sense? I do not think so. Such a view is derived from an expectation of how the play should work if it followed certain structural patterns typical of Shakespearean comedy. My point is that it does not. Again here, though it takes a different form from *All's Well that Ends Well*, we have a comic pattern without comic process; the comic pattern does not comprehend the kinds of experiences, like those of Angelo and Isabella, at the emotional centre of the play. Rather, it forces them into moulds which do not quite fit. Hence the morality of the play is ambiguous, since it is derived partly from the comic frame and partly from those things which are repressed or excluded by that frame.

The Duke, more than anyone else, is the builder of the comic structure, the ambiguous figure who stands at the intersection of illusion and reality. In contrast to the earlier comic heroines' or even Helena's, his role, though it informs the structure of the play, is rather abstractly conceived. W.W. Lawrence makes the point that his character springs from the demands of the plot rather than vice versa.[9] Why does the Duke adopt a disguise in the first place? Not really to *use* illusion (unlike, then, Portia, Rosalind, Hamlet, Helena), but simply to watch. He recognizes the corruption of his city but deputes Angelo to do the cleaning up, contenting himself with the role of observer. He is, then, making use of Angelo in order to shirk his own responsibility. He wants, too, to find out 'If power change purpose, what our seemers be' (i.iii.54). His purpose is therefore threefold: to get the city cleaned up, to avoid doing it himself (and thereby lose the affection of his subjects), and to test Angelo the seemer. He does not seem to realize that being a seemer himself in such a situation is a little equivocal. Thus, though we appreciate the fact that he sees things and people clearly (his knowledge of his own role in causing the city's corruption is acute), we are made a little uneasy about his methods. This kind of ambivalence is typical of our reaction to the Duke throughout the play and explains some of the sharp disagreement among critics over his role. To see him as an embodiment of divine providence[10] is to ignore not only certain facts of his character and the play (his abdication and his misjudgement of Angelo are only the beginning), but to turn one's back on important tonal qualities such as the ambivalence I am discussing. On the other hand, to see him as a vicious and amoral schemer would be an even more obvious misreading.

The Duke's failure to manage Barnardine according to his designs is a minor, but characteristic source of the ambivalence we are led to feel towards his role and the control be begins to exert through it. Barnardine's stoic, unyielding resistance, his simple-minded, sleepy determination, is the lowest common denominator of the sort of heroism available to characters in the play. He is 'unaccommodated man' with an unswerving, animal-like instinct for survival and as such he is admirable; on one, limited, level, more admirable than almost any other character in the play. The Duke's inability to move him is an instance of the inadequacy of his manipulative skill in a basic human matter, that of life or death, a central antinomy with immediate significance for nearly every person on the stage. Critics have claimed that Barnardine's 'creator came to love him so much that he had not the heart to decapitate him, although Barnardine was only created to be decapitated,'[11] which I think is romantic nonsense. There is no evidence whatever that Shakespeare intended to kill him off; from his very first words, Barnardine refuses to be executed and the Duke looks helpless and rather silly in the face of such absolutism. The whole scene, in fact, smacks of farce with the Duke as butt:

> BARNARDINE I will not consent to die this day, that's certain.
> DUKE O sir, you must! and therefore I beseech you.
> Look forward on the journey you shall go.
> BARNARDINE I swear I will not die today for any man's persuasion.
> DUKE [He's stammering now.] But hear you –
> BARNARDINE Not a word. If you have anything to say to me,
> come to my ward: for thence will not I today. (IV.iii.58-63)

The Duke's pious clichés do not have any effect here, as they do with Juliet in II.iii; instead, they bounce back at him and make him look foolish. We are allowed to see the inadequacy of the disguise, to see the Duke playing friar rather poorly and at the same time feeling frustrated, since without the disguise he could exert more effective control (on this score he is the direct opposite of figures like Portia or Rosalind). This is an example of the inversions which are so typical of this play; a ruler is forced to plead with a common criminal, is rejected, and ends by looking meaner than the criminal himself.[12]

Shakespeare created Barnardine, not to be decapitated, but for very much better reasons. Barnardine is the exemplar of the only kind of absolutism left uncriticized in the play – the insistence on the absolute value of life itself. He has nothing else to recommend him beyond his refusal to die; but this stolid virtue is enough to gain him his proper reward in the end – life. Shakespeare emphasizes the emptiness of his life to make the point even clearer. Thus Barnardine is continually either drunk or asleep or both; his sleepiness, in fact, is his most distinctive quality. His jailers spend a good part of their time awakening him and trying to prepare him for death, but to no avail. He is totally unaware of any spiritual or moral values; his hold on life is essentially animal-like, but there is a peculiar nobility in it. J.W. Lever makes a related point: 'The basic need for Barnardine's existence on the stage was surely that he might assert the major truth, that no man's life was so worthless as to be sacrificed for another's convenience.'[13]

Another indication that the Duke's manipulative control is anything but god-like arises from the mistakes he makes. The most serious of these is his misjudgement of Angelo, both initially and, even more seriously, at the point of Claudio's expected reprieve. But for a gratuitous circumstance, Claudio would have been executed. The Duke is convinced that Angelo will honour his promise:

> This is his pardon, purchas'd by such sin
> For which the pardoner himself is in.
> Hence hath offense his quick celerity,
> When it is borne in high authority.
> When vice makes mercy, mercy's so extended,
> That for the fault's love is th' offender friended.
> (IV.ii.111-16)

The rhymed couplets, the confident tone, the sententious morality all combine to create a secure, proverbial mood which is immediately undercut by the Provost's reading of Angelo's letter. Never has the Duke been more mistaken. We are made aware not only of the Duke's fallibility, but also of the extent of the evil and the inadequacy of the Duke's sententious morality in the face of such evil.

Other of his actions require explanation. Why, for example, does he tell Claudio that he has no hope to live when he has just devised the plan to save him? Presumably to educate him; to prepare him for death, which is a prerequisite, it seems, of preparing him for life. Claudio seems ready for death, or so he says in his next speech: 'I am so out of love with life, that I will sue to be rid of it' (III.i.174-5). But since he makes only one brief appearance before his unveiling in Act V and speaks but three lines after this speech in the whole rest of the play, such an interpretation is difficult to establish. Perhaps it is best to say that the Duke wants to reconcile brother and sister and this seems the best way of doing it. This latter interpretation is consistent with the Duke's most treasured general principle, a sort of moral pragmatism, or, essentially, that the end justifies the means. This at least is how he justifies the use of the bed trick (which is handled more abstractly, with less self-awareness than in *All's Well that Ends Well*) and the elaborate duping that follows. He explains to Isabella that 'the doubleness of the benefit defends the deceit from reproof' (III.i.267-9). This is a problematic statement. Does it hold in life as it does in comedy? Throughout this chapter, I have been insisting on the fact that this play takes place in the real world and explores issues resulting from the confrontation of human beings with each other in tense social and private situations. We are no longer in the self-contained world of comedy *per se*, the land of Illyria, for example, or the Forest of Arden. The intensively urban flavour of the play, the feeling of the pressures of city life, the presence of the institutions of the city (prisons, law courts, bawdy houses, nunneries), all combine to underscore the sense of the real world which the play, I think, is designed to foster. Such statements as the Duke's or that of Polonius on 'indirection,' are acceptable within a comic world but problematic in plays like *Measure for Measure* or *Hamlet* where the ethical struggles involve issues we must face daily outside the theatre. In *Measure for Measure*, comic processes make us uneasy, as do statements like the Duke's, because they roll too easily over the moral difficulties involved in their assertion. In *Hamlet*, the language of shady ends and means is put into the mouth of a scheming courtier, not the main character; the latter must and does face the moral ambiguity associated with the uses of illusion and consequently abandons his attempt at 'comic' manipulation.

The bland self-assurance of the Duke, with regard especially to the bed trick, contrasts pointedly with Helena's intense self-scrutiny in *All's Well that Ends Well*. Helena's integrity and motives are never called into question, partially because of her awareness; whereas in *Measure for Measure* we are kept constantly uncertain about the Duke and his machinations.[14] We might expect an older, more mature, male figure to be more effective in the elimination of evil and the nurturing of illumination than Helena; but though he exhibits a greater control over event, the Duke seems unable to transform the astringent realities raised by the Angelo-Isabella plot; in this he is as helpless as Helena. The play as a whole, then, seems to set comic structure in opposition to the extremities of human experience, with the result that the play is divided against itself.

In the final scene, the Duke manages and directs an elaborate play-within which is, at the same time, an important part of the main action.[15] Unlike the last scene of *All's Well that Ends Well*, where only a part of the confusion and ultimate clarification is a result of Helena's manipulation, virtually everything that happens in this part of *Measure for Measure* is the direct result of the Duke's fine theatrical sense. There is another important difference from *All's Well that Ends Well*. This time the judge, rather than the plaintiff, is the manipulator. Moreover, the true identity of the director is hidden from the actors. Hence Mariana and Isabella, unknowingly, are trying to convince a judge who is already convinced. Their ignorance is what gives them their passion. And yet, they too are playing roles, though somewhat against their wills. Isabella tells Mariana, in an interesting short scene immediately preceding the dénouement:

> To speak so indirectly I am loath:
> I would say the truth: but to accuse him so,
> That is your part. Yet I am advis'd to do it,
> He says, to veil full purpose. (IV.vi.1-4)

The recognition of the theatricality of the ensuing action is implicit not only in the word 'part' but in their whole manner of speaking of what they plan to do. Isabella, since she is not going to be telling the whole truth, is feeling somewhat guilty. In all the sources, the wronged woman simply presents her case to the ruler-judge and is recompensed. The fact that Shakespeare devised such a theatrical finale, and created a manipulative Duke chiefly for this purpose, argues some thematic relevance beyond the simple desire for dramatic effect, if only because thematic issues have been brought to the surface and examined, while in the sources they lay hidden and unattended.

Most of the show is produced for Angelo's benefit, but he does not seem to profit from it. He wriggles out of every tight squeeze by lying, much in the manner of Bertram in *All's Well that Ends Well*. As Bertram had accused Diana, 'My lord, she was a common gamester to the camp,' so Angelo claims of Mariana that 'her reputation was disvalued / In levity' (v.i.221-2). He keeps claiming ignorance of the unfolding events although, as the scene progresses, he realizes more and more clearly that he has been duped. Still, until it is suddenly made clear by the unmasking of the friar duke, he denies everything. He then switches with relief to penitent confession and exaggerated comparisons of the Duke to some 'Power divine.'[16]

What is happening in the whole scene is more complicated than what is happening to Angelo alone. Take, for example, the Duke's reply to Isabella's first cry for justice: 'Relate your wrongs. In what? By whom? Be brief. / Here is Lord Angelo shall give you justice; / Reveal yourself to him' (26-8). Let us take stock of the various responses to this statement. The Duke and we recognize a conscious irony in it; Angelo and Isabella see an unconscious irony of which the former must feign ignorance and which the latter will immediately expose. Escalus and Lucio see no irony at all. The whole problem of reliable knowledge is thus revealed. Shakespeare seems to be teaching *us* something about the varied masks of illusion and the difficulties of penetrating them, while reminding us of the unreliability of forms of human justice. The fact that what follows is the most extensive discussion of 'seeming' in the play is no coincidence. It is, as both the Duke and Isabella repeat, very 'strange' (the word echoes ambiguously through the end of so many of Shakespeare's comedies). But Isabella warns:

> Make not impossible
> That which but seems unlike. 'Tis not impossible
> But one, the wicked'st caitiff on the ground,
> May seem as shy, as grave, as just, as absolute
> As Angelo. Even so may Angelo,
> In all his dressings, characts, titles, forms
> Be an arch-villain. (V.i.51-7)

A man, as Hamlet says, may smile and smile and be a villain. Isabella's language reiterates the imagery of falseness used throughout the play, particularly in Angelo's earlier soliloquies.[17] She continues with her plea to the Duke, a plea which is an admonishment to us and a kind of epigraph to the whole play: 'But let your reason serve / To make the truth appear where it seems hid, / And hide the false seems true' (65-7). But this is essentially a naïve view since it fails to take into account the difficulty of achieving such an ideal. Reason is a weak instrument easily overrun by the powerful emotions which the play, especially the first half, presents. The Duke ironically alludes to this (and manages a dig at Angelo at the same time) when he refuses to believe Isabella and has her marched off to prison because her story 'imports no reason.'

Soon after, we are reminded of the weakness of reason when Mariana appears and poses two related riddles to the baffled judges: 'I have known my husband: yet my husband knows not / That ever he knew me' (186-7). Further on, she explains that her husband is 'Angelo, / Who thinks he knows that he ne'er knew my body, / But knows he thinks that he knows Isabel's' (202-4). The deliberate bafflement may remind us of Diana in *All's Well that Ends Well*; but if there the emphasis was on the truth of paradox, here it is on Angelo's inability to perceive at the deepest level. His uncertainties are the basis of her playing; and her playing makes us aware of his confusion as an instance of a more general misperception. The presentation of this little play is designed to enact precisely this theme. It becomes clear that Angelo, like King Lear, will only appreciate the very significant difficulties involved in judgement when he is aware of the fallibility of human knowledge. But if, in *King Lear*, the whole force of events is directed towards inculcating this kind of consciousness, in *Measure for Measure* it is by no means certain that Angelo achieves anything like it.

Although the playing and illusions do provide insight for us, there are ways in which our awareness is also curtailed rather than extended. Consistent with the imposition of comic form on anti-comic material, the ending of the play, its final vision, is in some ways repressive and inhibiting rather than inclusive and expansive. To consider the ending in this light leads us back to the low-life characters and their role. On one level, they embody the sexual vice which plagues the city. Sex, to them, is a commodity to be bought and sold, a material transaction. At the same time, however, they stand for a fundamental view of sex which is ignored (the Duke) or twisted (Angelo and Isabella) by the more 'idealistic' members of society:

POMPEY Does your worship mean to geld and splay all the youth of the city?
ESCALUS No, Pompey.
POMPEY Truly sir, in my poor opinion, they will to 't then. (II.i.242-4)

The assertion of sexuality as a vital force is part of the comic rhythm.[18] Hence it is not surprising that vice and vitality, as in the case of Falstaff, have their source in the same group of characters. Again like Falstaff, these characters are not included in the final reconciliation: Mistress Overdone is left to rot in prison, Pompey to earn his keep as assistant executioner, a 'mystery' even more abhorrent than his former one since it deals death rather than life. Their vitality is shut out with their vice, with the result that the point of view expressed by the end of the play is not comically balanced and rich, as it is in *As You Like It*, for example. Jaques' self-imposed exile does not represent the repression of important truths posed in the play· rather, his viewpoint leads us to adjust our own, to become partly sceptical and detached. In *Measure for Measure*, on the other hand, we have a situation like the rejection of Falstaff in *Henry IV*, Part II, where attitudes that pervade the world of the play and are essential to its reality, instead of being included, are simply shut out.[19]

Neither the presence of Lucio nor the pattern of marriages in the last scene compensates for this feeling of repressiveness. Lucio is introduced to us in the second scene, exchanging puns with two of the wormiest Gentlemen in all Shakespeare. His view of sex turns out to be debased and mechanical, as emphasized by the way he talks. He would be sorry, he says, that Claudio's life 'should be thus foolishly lost at a game of tick-tack' (I.ii.194-5); the Duke would accost a 'beggar of fifty and his use was to put a ducat in her clack-dish' (III.ii.132-4); or again, he says of Claudio that he is condemned 'For filling a bottle with a tundish' (III.ii.182). Given his apparent attitude, it is hard not to see his fertility speech to Isabella ('... her plenteous womb / Expresseth his full tilth and husbandry.' I.iv.43-4), as gently mocking and ironic, especially considering its grandiose, highly oratorical style. G. Wilson Knight comments on Lucio that 'his false – because fantastic and shallow – pursuit of sex, is the result of a false fantastic denial of sex in his world.' He can exist only in 'a society of smug propriety and self-deception.'[20] Unlike Pompey and Overdone, then, his sexuality is not fundamental and vital, but obsessed and parasitical. He is the sort who can ferret out a sexual meaning from the most innocent statements. During the final scene, Escalus says of Isabella, 'Give me leave to question. You shall see how I'll handle her.' Lucio is quick to reply, 'Not better than he, by her own report.' Escalus doesn't understand, 'Say you?' So Lucio elaborates, 'Marry, sir, I think, if you handled her privately, she would sooner confess; perchance, publicly, she'll be ashamed' (v.i.276-8). Such obsessive sexual awareness is typical of Lucio and, as Knight says, derives from the false view of sex prevalent in the society.

This repressive-obsessive kind of sexuality is not really tempered by the Duke's illusion-making or the forced marriages. It is important that Lucio is the one character the Duke cannot control during the scene and that his marriage is thrust upon him as a *punishment*. His marriage is a parody of Angelo and Mariana's; both are commanded by the Duke for legitimizing purposes, both are the result of sexual misdemeanour, both arise out of the tension between repression and obsession. The result is that another marriage (Lucio's) does not add to the festivity (as Touchstone's does, for instance). Instead, it adds to our sense of the legalism of the whole affair. Lucio's role in the final scene, then, actually increases our sense of the psychological inadequacy of the reconciliation and its essentially anti-comic nature, set though it is in comic form.

The legalism of the scene is not confined to the marriages alone. In general, the Duke advocates a strictly legalistic kind of justice. For him, 'The very mercy of the law cries out ... An Angelo for Claudio, death for death ... Like doth quit like, and Measure still for Measure' (v.i.412-16). What does not seem to have been recognized is that the Duke *means* this. But he has the luxury of equivocation available to him: 'We do condemn thee to the very block / Where Claudio stooped to death, and with like haste.' Angelo will get, according to this kind of justice, exactly what Claudio got. Everyone else on stage thinks this means death; the Duke knows, and we know, that it means that he will be snatched from death at the last minute by the providential hands of none other than the Duke himself.

Isabella's plea for Angelo's life (discussed above) provides another instance of legalism. In it, she makes distinctions which are legal rather than ethical, and in so doing, she unconsciously points to a serious division between morality and legality: 'His act did not o'ertake his bad intent ... Thoughts are no subjects, / Intents but merely thoughts' (456-9). But it can hardly be denied that what Angelo has done is immoral, even if it can be ingeniously pleaded that it is not illegal. This legalistic strain creates a tone that is essentially non-comic. Throughout the play, the law has been opposed to sexuality; this invocation of the law in the final moments of the play, especially with regard to the forced marriages – together with the exclusion of Pompey and Overdone – creates a final viewpoint which is exclusive rather than inclusive, confined rather than liberating, repressive rather than vitalizing.[21]

The Duke, in using irony and creating plays within, is intent upon bringing his own conception of justice to bear on the situation. Hence he holds back the one thing that makes this concept of justice possible to inculcate – the fact that no harm has been done, that Claudio is still alive. This is what keeps his justice from being merely a bitter mockery. The unveiling of Claudio is an important visual moment, related to the 'rebirth' of Helena or Hermione, but much less satisfying than either. It seems a theatrical coup, but not an organic fulfillment, it is in conflict with the dominant elements of the scene just discussed, and seems detached and inessential. The Duke's conception of justice and his means of asserting it seem out of touch with the world of the play as a whole. Comedy has its own kind of justice, involving for example the abrogation of arbitrary laws as in *A Midsummer Night's Dream*, or the overthrowing of false justice as in *The Merchant of Venice*; both these features are present, though in restricted form, in *Measure for Measure*. Comic justice can even include the banishing of the spoilsport, as in *Twelfth Night*. All of these events can occur under the aegis of a kind of justice peculiar to comedy but which, if practised in our world, might seem wildly unjust. Perhaps the best examples are rogue comedies like *The Alchemist*, where the clever criminals escape scot-free (Face is even commended) and yet we wholeheartedly approve. This is the world where the 'doubleness of the benefit' (and part of such benefit is surely the audience's delight) *can* defend 'the deceit from reproof.' However, Shakespeare makes it clear that this is not the world of *Measure for Measure*. The urban reality of this play and its searching analysis of character tend to sour the comic devices which we savour so readily in other comedies and in different comic contexts. The final vision is a world of complex and ambiguous moral feeling where the relative easiness of such a statement as the Duke's, and the comic patterns it suggests, conflicts with our profound sense of the difficulties and pressures of actual human experience.

7

King Lear, Antony and Cleopatra, and *The Winter's Tale*

Shakespeare, confronted by the apparent ineffectiveness, in the face of complex moral problems, of comic forms which he had developed earlier in his career, seems temporarily to have abandoned them as structural principles. But the deeper question of the uses of illusion as an instrument of illumination seems to have occupied him all the more. In the plays discussed in this chapter, we see him extending the range of the theme to reach the most fundamental tragic insights and the heights of tragic affirmation. In the first two plays, *King Lear* and *Antony and Cleopatra*, tragedy finally crushes the comic effort. In *The Winter's Tale*, the tragic movement is contained within a comic form, the framework of romance, which revives and redefines the earlier comic structure. Again, as in the early plays, it is the power of the illusory, of art (as if affects characters and audience), which finally brings about the necessary personal and social transformations.

In these plays, then, it is no longer a case of form colliding with subject matter, as in *All's Weil that Ends Well* and *Measure for Measure*. Rather, Shakespeare has learned to transcend the formal difficulties of the 'problem plays,' and to use the techniques discussed earlier to stretch our awareness without blurring the tragic design. And in the romance form, he finds a way of combining his interest in the mythical, schematic, and emblematic with his interest in the illusions of art and the theatre, to foster an awareness which can face tragic problems and, finally, assert a comic vision.

The method by which reality is projected in *King Lear* implies a recognition that drama is by its nature schematic and emblematic (even at its most realistic; just as even the most realistic painting involves some distortion), in that it is a distillation of human life into a created, artificial form. This play extends and makes explicit such a general recognition and actually deepens its meaning by doing so.

The chief vehicle for this extended meaning is the primitivism in the play, a quality which has been observed by a number of critics and which informs not only the setting and imagery but the dramaturgy as well. The eighteenth century misunderstood this primitivism, thinking it crude and unnatural, and thus preferred Nahum Tate's notorious version to Shakespeare's own.

In speaking of 'primitivism,' I am thinking of both the 'improbability' of events which Coleridge saw as merely the background, 'the canvas to the characters and passions,'[1] and of the 'abstract' nature of many of the characters mentioned by Bradley, who speaks of the periodic tendency of Shakespeare's imagination 'to analyze and abstract, to decompose human nature into its constituent factors and then to construct beings in whom one or more of these factors is absent.' As Bradley was aware, this is 'a tendency which produces symbols, allegories, personifications ...'[2] To a greater extent than Bradley would admit, *King Lear* presents its vision of reality schematically, almost paradigmatically. To the naturalistic mind it is thoroughly incredible – not only the emblematic first scene and the undue credulity of Gloucester and Edgar in Scene ii (which set the two plots in motion), but the definition of character and motivation throughout, the romance elements (eg, Kent's mysterious knowledge of Cordelia and hers of him), the bizarre and richly symbolic image of human reality depicted in the storm scenes (complete with Yeatsian visionaries – madman, beggar, fool), the incredible events, especially Gloucester's leap, the allegorical roles of Edgar; one could go on indefinitely. In its defiance of the canons of credibility, Shakespeare's play is persistently emblematic (though it is intensely actual as well).

The beginning of the play introduces us to the issues with which it will be concerned and, simultaneously, to a way of seeing the action – how we, as an audience, are meant to view the play. In many of his mature plays, Shakespeare shows great skill in such introductions, where the issues of the play are inextricably woven together with the manner of presentation. This will become clear if we contrast the opening of *King Lear* with that of *Othello*. *King Lear* opens slowly and deliberately. We are introduced to three characters, two of them by name, and told definite things about three others ('the King,' Albany, and Cornwall). Everything is very definite and explicit: in the first twenty-five lines, we learn that the King is dividing his kingdom and taking pains to divide it into equal moieties; we hear the older man tell us of the circumstances by which the handsome young man at his side was illegitimately conceived, and tell us in passing of another, legitimate, son who is yet 'no dearer' in his 'account.' In *Othello*, on the other hand, two men (one called 'Iago,' we soon learn) come on the stage engrossed in a heated conversation. They are in the middle of their talk and begin immediately to make references to 'this's,' 'such's,' and 'him's' of which we can have no knowledge:

RODERIGO Tush, never tell me! I take it much unkindly
That thou, Iago, who hast had my purse
As if the strings were thine, shouldst know of this.
IAGO 'Sblood, but you'll not hear me!
If ever I did dream of such a matter,
Abhor me.
RODERIGO Thou told'st me, thou didst hold him in thy hate.
IAGO Despise me if I do not. Three great ones of the city,
In personal suit to make me his lieutenant,
Off-capp'd to him; and, by the faith of man,
I know my price, I am worth no worse a place. (I.i.1-11)

This passage contrasts markedly with the opening of *King Lear*, where we feel as though the Gloucester-Kent conversation is 'staged' for our benefit, to give us a full background for what follows. In *Othello*, the audience is ignored. We have to eavesdrop; and we have to set our minds working at once in order to figure out what's going on. Uncertainty, bewilderment, a sense of rush and rage; these are the prevailing qualities of our response, and we spend the rest of the scene trying to piece the puzzle together. This opening is particularly appropriate because the audience, like Othello later in the play, is put into a state of uncertainty and encouraged to judge, to round out the story from the fragments of evidence which Iago and Roderigo let fall. Thus one of the great themes of the play, the problem of judging, of ascertaining the truth, is at the outset brought to life in the minds of the audience.

Returning to the first scene of *King Lear*, we note that a number of dominant themes of the play are, within a few lines, naturally and explicitly presented. We are introduced immediately to the idea of affection and the rather fuzzy relationship between such 'valuing' and its material manifestation:

KENT I thought the King had more affected the Duke of Albany than Cornwall.
GLOUCESTER It did always seem so to us; but now, in the division of the kingdom, it appears not which of the Dukes he values most, for equalities are so weigh'd that curiosity in neither can make choice of either's moiety. (I.i.1-7)

The same conflation of economic and familial valuing is manifested by Gloucester when he says that his legitimate son 'is no dearer in his account' than the illegitimate. As the plot develops, the demand that spiritual values be manifested materially becomes more and more sinister. The other major theme introduced in these lines, the idea of legitimacy, of 'natural' order within both the state and the family, is clearly related to that of value. Misvaluing is a threat to the natural order; it is a way of spawning illegitimacy. Furthermore, valuing in the play is presented as a way of *seeing*, spiritual blindness being identified with misvaluing, especially within the family, in the cases of both Lear and Gloucester. The pervasive imagery of sight (which has often been noticed),[3] the physical blinding of Gloucester and his subsequent gain in insight (marked first by his almost immediate revaluation of Edgar – 'Then Edgar was abused. Kind gods, forgive me that, and prosper him') – all drive home this connection between seeing and value. It is established in the first scene with Goneril's claim that she loves her father 'dearer than eyesight' and Kent's loyal admonition, 'see better, Lear,' that is, value Cordelia truly.

As I said above, the opening scene introduces us to a way of seeing (and valuing) the action of the play as a whole. It is a thoroughly emblematic scene, the King on his throne demanding formal declarations of love from his heirs, as he ceremoniously slices his kingdom into pieces. But the ritual is illegitimate and its values topsy turvy. Its fruits are disorder in the kingdom and in the mind. Thus the ritual is in some ways divided against itself and a tension develops between what is suggested by the manner of presentation and what is actually presented. For the emblematic form is easily associated with the old-fashioned and traditional, and hence with the values which the play offers as vital to the old-fashioned, ordered world, values which are being vigorously undermined by the 'new' men and women like Edmund, Cornwall, Goneril, and Regan. Hospitality, a sense of community and mutual concern, a nurturing femininity, together with a clearly defined and balanced sense of order – these are some of the values likely to be associated with old-fashioned 'primitive' or 'romantic' techniques. But the opening scene almost immediately establishes a tension between technique and subject matter, a tension which establishes the play's central conflict of values in dramaturgical terms. As an audience, then, we are taught to 'see better' in the sense that we are encouraged to view the action as emblematic and at the same time to see the value of the emblematic as a rich and complex means of projecting meaning. For us, as for Lear, 'seeing better' will mean, finally, recognizing the congruence of emblematic form and true value.

This tendency to value the emblematic and symbolical is encouraged as the play unfolds. We recognize that the most profound truths arise from just this manner of organizing events. The storm scenes are the fullest expression of this process. The storm itself is an emblem, and Lear is symbolically identified with it.[4] His insight, and our own, derive from his confrontation with the symbolic storm and, further, with a symbolic madman who is, in reality, not a madman at all, but a disguised nobleman. It is Edgar's disguise that brings Lear to his deepest insights, especially his sympathy for, and identification with, 'unaccommodated man.' His belief that Poor Tom is a philosopher also has its point – the fact that truth is obscured by the accretions of falsehood, and nakedness is truth's genuine condition. The mock trial scene, perhaps the maddest in the play, is also emblematic in that it focusses the play's intense concern with justice in one mocking, questioning image. It is the real 'handy-dandy' of the justice in the play, a mad trial which expresses true feeling and true value, as opposed to the 'sane' acts of 'justice' referred to and enacted in other parts of the play, which are based on misvaluation, or worse, on cruelty and expediency. This truth-in-madness is brilliantly emphasized in the juxtaposition of the trial scene with the following one, which presents a *real* travesty of justice:

> Though well we may not pass upon his life
> Without the form of justice, yet our power
> Shall do a court'sy to our wrath, which men
> May blame, but not control. (III.vii.24-7)

Thus Cornwall, who then proceeds to pluck out Gloucester's eyes, mocking him as he does so. The extreme brutality of this act makes it hard to watch, harder still to believe in. It takes place in a context of political realism and ambitious manipulation which, reminding us of *Hamlet*, gathers resonance from its relation to important historical and cultural shifts involving the ideology of the 'new' men. In fact, we have a sense of a palpable society behind most of the action of the play (a sense which derives partly from a strong feeling of geographical locale and partly from the highly particular, 'local' language). But the plucking out of Gloucester's eyes is almost more than we can endure; we are forced into taking it as an emblem, even as we are appalled and shocked by the felt actuality of it ('Out, vile jelly!'); even, that is, as we avert our eyes, we must remind ourselves that it is 'only' a play. This is an act, then, that knits together the symbolic and realistic strands that weave through the play.

We come now to Act IV, Scene vi, the richest scene in the play from the point of view of the uses of illusion.[5] Gloucester's leap from the 'cliff' is the most extreme emblem in the play, the action which most strains our belief but which at the same time demands to be accepted. The scene begins with Edgar's famous speech from the top of the cliff, a superb example of the blending of the deliberately fictive and the vividly actual. Vertiginous poetry at its most dizzying, it is a real *tour de force*, and all the more because it comes from one who has just claimed to be poor mad Tom still:

> How fearful
> And dizzy 'tis to cast one's eyes so low!
> The crows and choughs that wing the midway air

> Show scarce so gross as beetles. Half way down
> Hangs one that gathers sampire – dreadful trade!
> Methinks he seems no bigger than his head.
> The fishermen that walk upon the beach
> Appear like mice; and yond tall anchoring bark,
> Diminish'd to her cock; her cock, a buoy
> Almost too small for sight. The murmuring surge
> That on th' unnumb'red idle pebble chafes
> Cannot be heard so high. (IV.vi.11-22)

One of the most striking things about this speech is its command of the actual, the precisely observed quality of it. The other striking fact about the speech is that it is imaginary, its actualities are all made up, and, indeed, might even be said to arise from the imaginary context. As such, it can be viewed as an image for dramatic poetry and the process which brings it into being; all dramatic poetry presents us with fabricated actuality, but here the fabrication is deliberately and self-consciously effected by a character in the play, with the result that the actuality is doubly imaginary. Edgar is like the dramatic poet, staring at an open field and recreating for Gloucester and for us the cliffs of Dover.

In the final sentence quoted, the irony gets more involved: the sea, which Gloucester thinks is there but Edgar and we know is not, is said to be murmuring, though the murmur is inaudible. A little later, in a different role, the disguised Edgar sounds the same note; to Gloucester's question, 'But have I fallen or no?' he replies:

> From the dread summit of this chalky bourn;
> Look up a-height; the shrill-gorg'd lark so far
> Cannot be seen or heard. (IV.vi.57-9)

In both cases, Edgar affirms the real existence of things which cannot be perceived, but which *are* there (within, that is, the play he is constructing though, of course, they are not 'really' there at all). Besides highlighting the fictiveness of Edgar's enterprise, such language has a further point, and that is to derange Gloucester's senses, to undermine his trust in them so that he can 'see' beyond them. (Appropriate retribution, I suppose, for the sensual man.) This process is set in motion at the beginning of the scene, when all the evidence of Gloucester's senses is systematically refuted by Edgar:

GLOUCESTER When shall I come to th' top of that same hill?
EDGAR You do climb up it now. Look how we labour.

GLOUCESTER Methinks the ground is even.
EDGAR   Horrible steep.
Hark, do you hear the sea?
GLOUCESTER No, truly.
EDGAR Why then, your other senses grow imperfect
By your eyes' anguish.
GLOUCESTER   So may it be indeed.
Methinks thy voice is alter'd, and thou speak'st
In better phrase and matter than thou didst.
EDGAR Y' are much deceived. In nothing am I chang'd
But in my garments. (IV.vi.1-10)

Not only sight, but hearing and even touch, must be disregarded or denied in order for Gloucester to achieve a full measure of self-understanding and true patience. He is like a walking exemplum of Christ's statement to Thomas, 'Blessed are they who have not seen, and yet have believed.' Gloucester's belief in an illusion, in defiance of his senses, leads to his 'redemption' (to use Bradley's word), or, at least, to a new acceptance and a richer understanding. In Lear's great speeches later in the scene, we again see how a confusion of the senses, a purposeful synesthesia, can lead to insight: 'A man may see how this world goes with no eyes. Look with thine ears; see how yond justice rails upon yond simple thief' (152-4). In fact, Lear's madness is another illusion which illuminates as it deludes. Its juxtaposition in this scene with Gloucester's despair and ultimate achievement of patience brings home the fact that what is being enacted physically and shown theatrically in the Gloucester plot is being played out within the soul of King Lear.

Furthermore, Gloucester's belief in an illusion is an image within the play, related to Edgar's imaginary actuality discussed above, for the audience's necessary acceptance of the 'unbelievable' in the play as a whole. Just as Gloucester suspends his disbelief in a situation in which it is not easy to do so, so must we. Gloucester's leap is a symbolic event which he must accept as real in order to redeem himself. And his acceptance, far from making him a fool, leads us to the same place. Moreover, it gains for him a deeper insight; so with us, acceptance of the allegorical and schematic as a way of projecting experience opens up the full significance of the play as a whole. And our understanding, like Gloucester's, is enriched.

The disguised Edgar is the agent of Gloucester's change and the 'scene' he must play demands two roles in quick succession. In both plots, in fact, Edgar's roles are the instrument of increased awareness (which may be why Shakespeare made him Lear's godson), though in the main plot, the range and depth of Lear's response to his disguise seem outside his control. Edgar's manipulation of Gloucester's spiritual senses through disguise is reminiscent of the similar process in *As You Like It*; for Gloucester, as for Orlando, accepting illusion is the most important way of penetrating one's own illusions and delusions about the moral life. The crucial difference between them is that Orlando is only asked to accept the game as game; Gloucester must go further and accept illusion as actuality.

No one in Shakespeare has as many disguises as Edgar, no one plays so many roles. In iv.vi alone he has three, Poor Tom (but a very different Poor Tom), the well-spoken, sympathetic young man on the 'beach,' and the boisterous peasant who sends the mean and ambitious Oswald to a well-deserved grave. In the second of these roles, he witnesses the extraordinary spectacle of madman preaching to blind man about the pervasive bitterness and hypocrisy of life in the world. Soon after, he can answer Gloucester's question, 'what are you?' by saying, most truthfully,

> A most poor man, made tame to fortune's blows;
> Who, by the art of known and feeling sorrows,
> Am pregnant to good pity. (iv.vi.224-6)

Not the least of these sorrows is the scene he has just witnessed. His disguise has not only helped Gloucester and Lear, but has changed him too. He is no longer the naïve boy of the early scenes, but a man who has seen, experienced, and learned from extreme suffering. His multiplicity of roles seems partly a response to such suffering – both an escape from it and a way of confronting it – and partly an expression of the pure delight he derives from them (as in the Oswald duel). He can, of course, also recognize them as effective tools of beneficent manipulation. He seems to have a plan by which to rescue not only his father but the kingdom as well; but, as we eventually come to see, his view is finally too limited.

By the time we reach the end of iv.vi, we have come a great distance from the placidity, almost smugness, of the first scenes. In both plots, the thoughtless disorders of two fathers and the treachery of their children have wrought profound consequences of both suffering and revelation. The disordering of nature that we witness in the division of the kingdom, the banishing of Cordelia, the eclipses, the ambitions of Edmund, the cruel inhospitality of Goneril and Regan, all has resulted in a sundering of nature itself (both human and inanimate), blinding Gloucester and maddening Lear. At the same time, those with the remorselessly materialistic, self-interested view of nature, especially Edmund, have been succeeding extraordinarily well, from the point of view of the world.

We, the audience, are not fooled by this success, however. We are aware of the values involved in the insights which accompany Lear's madness, especially the acid criticism of 'society,' and of the 'nature' that Edmund invokes in his first soliloquy and then exemplifies in his behaviour. The breakdown in natural order thus leads in the long run to a far deeper perception of true nature, the realities of life in the world, and human needs and sufferings – 'we come crying hither.' This is a paradox like that of the 'happy fall' and is related to the paradoxical dramaturgy of the play, the fact that the most profound truths in both plots are revealed through emblems and deceptions, especially those created by Edgar.

Act IV, Scene vi, presents us with the *bottom* and the suggestion of an upswing in both plots: Gloucester's attempted suicide and his subsequent resolution, 'Henceforth I'll bear affliction till it do cry out itself "Enough, enough," and die'; Lear's deep but perceptive madness and the intervention of Cordelia. She it is 'Who redeems nature from the general curse' and her redemption of nature, as so often in romance, is associated with curative fertility: 'All blest secrets, / All you unpublish'd virtues of the earth, / Spring with my tears!' (IV. iv.15-17).

As we move into the last act, Edgar, with his schemes and his scurrying, begins more and more to dominate the action. In v.ii, he again braves out a wave of paternal depression with his famous 'Ripeness is all'; but, as we shall see, this is not a fully adequate statement, and in the last scene, Edgar finally succumbs to the implacability of events. This last scene presents us with a fully elaborated, rather drawn-out dénouement; it is a highly theatrical, 'stagey' scene. There is, for one thing, the chivalric challenges, trumpets, and fight; there is Goneril's consciousness that the triangular intrigue and Albany's ironic attitude towards it make up 'An interlude' (90); more importantly, there is Edgar's role as the disguised hero who will come to the rescue of the forces of good. But Shakespeare's unrelenting perception is that this kind of comic-romantic disguise does not solve tragic problems, does not make the world any less tragic, even though the attitude it fosters may allow a man to see more deeply into things. For a while it proceeds exactly as we want it to: Edmund gets squashed, Regan killed, Goneril insulted and humiliated (which leads her to suicide); all of which is self-consciously melodramatic. For a while, we forget Edmund's order given to the cold-blooded Captain at the beginning of the scene; then Shakespeare twice reminds us of it, both times obliquely (at line 165, and again at 202), building suspense as he lets Edgar tell his story leisurely and fully. (As I argued in the chapter on *The Merchant of Venice*, this kind of suspense is normally a comic device, a prelude to a comic conclusion.) We are, from the general movement and tone of the scene, set up to expect a reprieve. The suspense is drawn out. We learn finally what Edmund's orders were and Albany breathes, 'The gods defend her'; but as he says it, in one of the cruellest ironies in drama, Lear enters with Cordelia in his arms. The comic 'theatrical' order is utterly overwhelmed by such a profoundly tragic perception, which is why, it seems to me, Edgar's sententious attempts at summing up, 'ripeness is all' or 'the gods are just ...' are not fully adequate statements of the play's meaning. They fall short of its vision, exactly as Gloucester's despair does. The full significance of the play is lodged squarely on the shoulders of the tragic hero, and for him that vision is finally inarticulate.

As in *Hamlet*, the final summary (again it is Edgar's), and the society which is established, move back from the experience of the tragic hero. All that extraordinary weight of pain and understanding is somehow beyond the scope of ordinary society to comprehend. We are left with the sense that retrenchment and relative stability will follow, but a stability unable to perceive what the chaos and disorder that preceded it could ultimately reveal.

Throughout *Antony and Cleopatra*, the characters manifest a consciousness of *story*, an awareness that they are playing a part in a significant action. Octavius wants to 'see his nobleness well acted' (v.ii.45), Enobarbus hopes that his 'allegiance' will earn him 'a place in the story' (iii.xiii.45), and hero and heroine are at all times conscious of the dazzling effect their shows will have upon their various audiences – 'the nobleness of life is to do thus' (i.i.36-7). The magnificence of Cleopatra's first show at Cydnus, 'The barge she sat in, like a burnish'd throne, / Burned on the water ...,' and the tragic devotion of her second metaphorical one, 'I am again for Cydnus to meet Mark Antony' (v.ii.228-9), manifest a similar awareness. Much of what is acted in the play includes, on the part of the actors, a consciousness of audience, an audience within the play and outside it as well.

To pursue this theme, I want to focus attention on two scenes, that in which Antony tries to kill himself (iv.14), and the final scene, that of Cleopatra's triumph through death. The first thing to notice about both scenes is that they are full of what ought to be comic devices. In iv.xiv, we begin with a bad joke on the part of Cleopatra (the false news that she is dead), pass by Eros's little trick of killing himself behind Antony's back, then come to Antony's absurd muffing of his own suicide, and finally to the entrance of Diomedes, the messenger with the true story, who arrives just a moment too late. In most contexts, such a confluence of device would make a scene unacceptable or ludicrous, but here it does not. Why?

In order to answer, I want to return to my point that, in this scene and in what follows, both Antony and Cleopatra are defined in terms of *acting*. Even after death, they will be putting on a show:

Where souls do couch on flowers, we'll hand in hand,
And with our sprightly port make the ghosts gaze.
Dido and her Aeneas shall want troops,
And all the haunt be ours. (IV.xiv.51-4)

Or again, after Eros's suicide, Antony speaks of how his 'Queen and Eros / Have by their brave instruction got upon me / A nobleness in record' (97-8), a noble place in the story. On the other hand, there is a different kind of show, demanding a different kind of acting, and this is at all costs to be avoided:

Eros,
Wouldst thou be window'd in great Rome and see
Thy master thus with pleach'd arms, bending down
His corrigible neck, his face subdu'd
To penetrative shame, whilst the wheel'd seat
Of fortunate Caesar, drawn before him, branded
His baseness that ensued? (IV.xiv.71-7)

To be played, rather than to play, to have a false and base identity thrust upon one, this is what Antony (and later Cleopatra) cannot accept.

I think that it is this definition in terms of appearance and role that allows us not only to accept the 'comic' devices, but to welcome them as adding to the tragic effect. For tragedy, like comedy, is essentially fictive, though a self-conscious awareness of fictiveness is more typical of comedy. For us to be made aware of the fictional quality of events here at the end, far from vitiating the tragic power, tends to increase it by bringing us closer to the 'story' and its mythic protagonists. We do not feel so far away from Antony and Cleopatra as we do from Lear, Macbeth, or Othello. The comic elements make for a different sort of tragedy, one which, to borrow a term from C.L. Barber, can best be described as 'festive.'[6]

Act IV, scene xiv begins with Antony's great speech about the pageantry of clouds which, besides telling us a good deal about Antony's shifting identity, is also a focal point for an important strain of imagery:

Sometime we see a cloud that's dragonish;
A vapor sometime like a bear or lion,
A towered citadel, a pendent rock,
A forked mountain, or blue promontory
With trees upon 't that nod unto the world
And mock our eyes with air. Thou hast seen these signs;

> They are black vesper's pageants ...
> That which is now a horse, even with a thought
> The rack dislimns and makes it indistinct
> As water is in water ...
> My good knave Eros, now thy Captain is
> Even such a body. Here I am Antony;
> Yet cannot hold this visible shape, my knave. (IV.xiv.2-14)

Personal shape is as momentary, shifting, and uncertain as that of clouds. As in *The Tempest*, the clouds speak of the illusory nature of solidity and of reality. Personal identity and the great globe itself – both are part of the 'insubstantial pageant.' Antony is abandoning himself to the pageant, to the inevitable show of which he is the hero, even in defeat, and the irony is that such is the only way he will finally become himself.

The speech's imagery of melting and 'discandying' is common in the play and often implies a kind of solidity and worldly power to which it stands in opposition: 'Let Rome in Tiber melt, and the wide arch / Of the ranged empire fall!' As the play depicts it, melting and liquidity are Egyptian; solidity, power, and authority, Roman. When, for example, Antony says 'Authority melts from me,' he is expressing a slide from his Roman to his Egyptian self, as well as simply bemoaning the loss of lackey-kings. The continuous shifting and fast fading from one role to another manifested by both characters, especially Cleopatra, also seems typically Egyptian, contrasting with Roman deliberateness, seriousness, and politic hypocrisy, and gives concrete meaning to the imagery. Thus, when Antony talks about being unable to hold a 'visible shape,' he is describing a personal shifting not unlike that required for the many roles that he and Cleopatra play.

In the scene under discussion, the movement towards becoming himself begins as he rids himself of his armour, the last emblem of his solidity, his Romanness: 'O cleave, my sides! / Heart, once be stronger than thy continent, / Crack thy frail case! Apace, Eros, apace. / No more a soldier ...' (39-42). It is as though he is removing the very bands that are holding him together. The tragicomic irony of this, however, is that the process thus begun is a result of a lie, an illusion, a trick on the part of Cleopatra. It is precisely this trick that allows him to see the truth, that Cleopatra has *not* 'packed cards with Caesar.'

The revelatory quality of illusion and 'pageant' thus adds dimension to the tragic effect. But the chief part of that effect comes from the intensity of what is being shown, the love that reaches to fullness as it approaches death: 'But I will be / A bridegroom in my death, and run into 't / As to a lover's bed' (99-101). Despite, then, the near farce of his bungled suicide (together with the other elements I have been discussing), and even partly because of it, Antony emerges from the scene larger, more *human*, than ever. His magnanimity towards Cleopatra, never questioning her motives or actions, goes beyond wrangling and beyond even the amorous bravado of the earlier scenes. He wishes, now, only to be with her: 'Bear me, good friends, where Cleopatra bides; / 'Tis the last service that I shall command you.'

When he is brought to her, there is again a comic edge. Cleopatra's venal concern for her own safety (which keeps alive our ambivalence) is easily outfaced by her proud determination not to be a 'brooch' to Caesar's 'imperious show,' and by her powerful desire to have him by her. There is comedy in the spectacle of the women trying desperately to heave him aloft, Cleopatra meanwhile chattering an accompaniment, then pulling herself up short with graceful and precise self-irony: 'wishers were ever fools.' And there is comedy in Antony's attempts to deliver his death speech and Cleopatra's repeated interruptions. But the total effect is grand, the show both noble and moving.

Throughout the play, as many critics have observed, there is a sharp division between Rome and Egypt, between duty and pleasure, pragmatism and sensuality, moderation and abandon. Rome, we notice, despises Egypt, while Egypt accepts Rome. Why do the Romans object so vigorously to Antony's 'dotage?' Not just because it is impractical or intemperate, surely. The very vehemence of the objections seems to indicate a deeper reason. They recognize in what they call 'dotage' an allegiance to a different, subversive set of values, which constitute a threat to the stability of Roman society, a threat to law and order itself. Roman ambition, Roman authority, Roman repression (according to Freud the fundamental mortar of society), are all implicitly or explicitly called into question by Antony's behaviour. Freud developed the idea that a strong fear or sense of being threatened usually covers up a wish, a forbidden wish. This seems applicable here since underneath the Roman rejection we can sense a hidden desire to be like Egypt, to let things go, to seek pleasure. This is subtly expressed in the scene in which Maecenas and Agrippa hang on to Enobarbus's every word, as he describes in detail the luxurious pleasures of Egypt. But the Romans embody the realization that to seek such pleasure, to organize life around it, is to abandon their civilization, their Empire; and so, they drastically rein in their emotions. Those that don't, like Dolabella, end up betraying their master.

As I said above, Roman civilization is depicted in the play in powerful images of architecture, stability, and solidity. Shakespeare seems to recognize Freud's point that civilization, city-building, necessarily requires and absorbs much of the erotic energy that might otherwise go into sexual relationships;[7] thus his use of strong architectural images in connection with Rome is psychologically very appropriate. 'Let Rome in Tiber melt and the wide arch of the ranged empire fall' expresses the recognition that Antony's redirection of energy towards Cleopatra does indeed undermine the actual city he has helped to build. Conversely, as the Romans see it, his 'dotage' is the spiritual equivalent of the wide arches of Rome melting into Tiber.

Throughout the play, of course, Antony is profoundly ambivalent about where his choice should ultimately reside, ambivalent about the total commitment that Egypt and Cleopatra require. It is only in defeat and death that he can make this commitment without flinching and so finally achieve heroic, almost mythic, stature. After the battle of Actium, though, it becomes clear that this is where he is headed. In an extraordinary scene (iii.xi), which also has a comic side to it, imploring attendants shove the two glum lovers at each other and into a reconciliation (significantly, Cleopatra is for once almost totally silent). The result is Antony's most extreme statement in the play of the conflict of values, the worthlessness of the 'world' when weighed against the transcendent value of Cleopatra and what she represents: 'Fall not a tear, I say. One of them rates / All that is won and lost. Give me a kiss. / Even this repays me' (69-71). This is a quiet and intense moment in the play, one of the few before the end when the lovers are truly and fully together, and it gives us a sense of the potential wholeness of their union. They do, I think, achieve some kind of transcendence, but the wonder is that it results from a crazy mixture of the everyday, the comic, the ludicrous, and the profound.

The last scene presents what I can best describe as a conflict between two would-be playwrights, between the plays that each is trying to script. Each of them, in fact, wants to write the script for the other. The two are, of course, Cleopatra and Octavius, and their battle of wit and will assumes the dominant interest after the death of Antony. Octavius would like to 'let the world see / His nobleness well acted' (v.ii.44-5), that is, he wants to *show* himself to the world by making Cleopatra part of his act. Ultimately, he wants to dramatize his victory by 'showing' Cleopatra in his triumphal pageant, by making her into an emblem of his power. (This same tendency to manipulate people like objects is manifest in the Roman treatment of Octavia, whose body and spirit are bartered for the sake of 'peace.')

Cleopatra, for her part, is determined not to be an actress in Octavius's play. She insists, as Antony had earlier, on avoiding that disgrace: 'Shall they hoist me up / And show me to the shouting varletry / Of censuring Rome?' (v.ii.55-7). The worst kind of opprobrium is not only to be denied the freedom of playing oneself but, worse, to be played (and played falsely) by someone else:

> The quick comedians
> Extemporally will stage us, and present
> Our Alexandrian revels. Antony

Shall be brought drunken forth, and I shall see
Some squeaking Cleopatra boy my greatness
I' th' posture of a whore. (v.ii.216-21)

She will let no one else make her play.

The play that Cleopatra does want to write and direct is of a thoroughly different sort. Its first aim is not to show off her own noble qualities (though that element is certainly there) but rather to exhibit Antony's heroism, to give him, in fact, the status and the stature of a mythic hero:

His face was as the heav'ns, and therein stuck
A sun and moon, which kept their course and lighted
The little O, th' earth ...
His legs bestrid the ocean: his rear'd arm
Crested the world ...
Think you there was or might be such a man
As this I dreamt of?
DOLABELLA   Gentle madam, no.
CLEOPATRA You lie, up to the hearing of the gods!
But, if there be nor ever were one such,
It's past the size of dreaming ... (v.ii.79-83, 93-7)

His sheer size, his humanity, and his godlike association with the great forces of nature – all are emphasized and seen as part of a continuing harmony, a beneficent power that never tires or congeals. (The fact that this affirmation also has a partly comic setting – Cleopatra's passionate insistence undercut somewhat by Dolabella's polite unbelief – once again does not invalidate the claim she is making. The slight irony tends to support that claim since we let Dolabella's scepticism substitute for our own, making it easier for us to suspend our disbelief.) Antony emerges as a figure of imagination and dream, but he is a reality too: 'yet t'imagine / An Antony were nature's piece 'gainst fancy.'[8] He is, in short, a myth.

The purpose of Cleopatra's play, then, is to give Antony an identity after death; she is attempting to create his mythic identity. We have already alluded to Antony's rather uncertain sense of himself, his feeling that he lacks a 'visible shape,' his definition of himself in terms of pageant and story. From the start, we have references to his not being Antony (eg, i.i.57), which culminate after Actium in the degrading image of the 'doting mallard / Leaving the fight in heighth' and flying after Cleopatra (iii.x.19-20). For a great hero, Antony is throughout surprisingly inactive and passive, which of course is consistent with the shakiness of his Roman self and the gradual dissolving of that individual positive identity in his union with Cleopatra. This process is strongly emphasized at the end both in his death scene and in the final scene, where he is made into himself by Cleopatra. It is, finally, only the play itself, and Cleopatra's play within it, that can give Antony his identity in the fullest sense. The earlier shifts, the role-playing, the lack of self-definition, all culminate in the fictive solidity of his final heroic identity, which is at the same time both made up, and yet as real as anything the theatre can offer us.

The first scene in the actual conflict between Cleopatra and Octavius is comic. The brief business with Seleucus provides us with a conventional comic moment and device – the unmasking of the con artist (similar, though in a minor way, to the unmasking of figures like Volpone and Subtle in Jonson's comedies). Seleucus's revelation that Cleopatra has kept back money and goods 'Enough to purchase what you have made known' puts her on the defensive and she is forced into two long, apologetic speeches (with an occasional lash at her treasurer) in an attempt to redeem herself. But this bit of conventional comedy is embedded in a subtle framework. It seems likely that Cleopatra has staged the whole scene with Seleucus, with or without his knowledge, in order to mislead Caesar into believing that she intends to live. Octavius, thinking that he has bettered her, takes the opportunity to act out his nobleness by 'forgiving' her: 'Caesar's no merchant, to make prize with you / Of things that merchants sold' (v.ii.183-4). But it soon becomes clear that his 'acting' is indeed only an act, that it is hollow and hypocritical, that his promise 'to dispose you as / Yourself shall give us counsel' is simply false.

It is evident that Octavius wants to keep Cleopatra alive in order to have her grace his triumph. This is exactly what is faulty about his 'play' – it is a lie which is staged for his own aggrandizement. Cleopatra has a more transcendent end in view, an expression of the *unity* between herself and Antony, an external representation of inner reality. Cleopatra, of course, is far from perfect; she lies to save herself just as Octavius lies in order to gain power over her. But her lies protect an inner truth which she must express; Octavius is defined purely in terms of cool, external power and adulation. The comedy of the unmasking helps to place the tragedy of her death in a context which changes the quality of the tragedy (making it a little bit commonplace and a trifle mocking), without reducing its power.

After Octavius leaves, Cleopatra expresses her awareness both of his hypocrisy and of her own mission: 'He words me, girls, he words me, that I should not / Be noble to myself' (v.ii.191-2). She *does* know how to act out her 'nobleness' (her use of the Roman word is significant; she slides towards Rome as Antony had towards Egypt), and that nobleness is intrinsic; it does not depend on outward applause or vindication. Iras responds with a kind of prologue to her death: 'Finish, good lady, the bright day is done, / And we are for the dark,' a motif that links the ensuing scene with the death of Antony, who had said to Eros, 'The long day's task is done and we must sleep' (IV.xiv.35-6).[9] The metaphorical connection is strengthened by a symmetry of action as well – the fact that both hero and heroine are preceded in death by a true servant whose death in a sense upbraids them.

After Iras's little prologue, we have Cleopatra's rejection of the role that Caesar would impose upon her (quoted above) and her subsequent preparation for her final, very different, show:

> Now, Charmian!
> Show me, my women, like a queen: Go fetch
> My best attires. I am again for Cydnus,
> To meet Mark Antony. (v.ii.226-9)

She will put on her costume, the attire of queenliness, and adopt a regal bearing. (Conversely, Antony had divested himself of his Roman costume.) In a move reminiscent of the liberation at the end of traditional comedy, she frees her servants (as Prospero does Ariel at the end of *The Tempest*): 'When thou has done this chare, I'll give thee leave / To play till doomsday.' She is almost ready. But before all is complete, she must play one more scene; another comic moment interposes just as we near the catastrophe. The interlude with the clown is unique in Shakespeare's tragedies, coming as it does between the death of hero and heroine; its uniqueness might best be appreciated if we were to try to imagine such a scene coming between the deaths of Romeo and Juliet, Desdemona and Othello, or Cordelia and Lear.[10] The clown, mysterious and visionary, as well as earthy and peasant-like, is a masterly creation. His reiterated, clownish but clairvoyant, 'I wish you joy o' the worm' echoes through the scene.

All the while, the play has been building toward its climactic show, and the stage is now set:

> Give me my robe, put on my crown, I have
> Immortal longings in me. Now no more
> The juice of Egypt's grape shall moist this lip.
> Yare, yare, good Iras; quick: Methinks I hear
> Antony call. I see him rouse himself
> To praise my noble act. I hear him mock
> The luck of Caesar, which the gods give men
> To excuse their after wrath. Husband, I come!

Now to that name my courage prove my title!
I am fire and air; my other elements
I give to baser life (v.ii.283-93)

Not only is her action noble, but her act, in the theatrical sense, expresses her nobility. It expresses more than that, however: a kind of exultant purge, a melting away of baser elements and a merging into a full unity with Antony, symbolized simply and powerfully in her use of the word 'husband' – mortality melting into immortality. The significance of this act within the play is parallel and analogous to the significance of the play in the theatre; the one leads to and upholds the other.

Shakespeare does not let go of the comic thread; he weaves it into even the death scene itself. As Cleopatra kisses Iras good-bye, the latter drops dead; and Cleopatra, surprised, asks, 'Have I the aspic in my lips?' Cleopatra to the last, she hurries to her death lest Iras first meet Antony and rob her of 'that kiss / Which is my heaven to have.' A comic edge is maintained throughout these final scenes and is, as I have argued, an important part of the total effect. It even touches Octavius and his role in Cleopatra's show, a role which he is unwilling to play but which, ironically, he is forced into. She addresses the asp and wishes that she 'might hear thee call great Caesar ass / Unpolicied.' Octavius, despite his power, ends the play as the comic butt, the 'ass unpolicied,' the Malvolio or Shylock of the piece. His 'luck,' because it is ultimately worthless, is therefore mocked. And Cleopatra ends, symmetrically, as the 'lass unparalleled' of Charmian's parting speech. Dolabella speaks of the final result of the conflict of plays in similar terms, thereby tying action and metaphor together in a short summary: 'Caesar ... thyself art coming / To see performed the dreaded act which thou / So sought'st to hinder.'

The final parts of the play, then, present us with, in Barber's phrase, an 'epiphany of the hero,'[11] a theatrical showing forth of hero and heroine, and of their unity. The comic elements are not specifically ironic; they are not there to diminish the main characters. Rather they lift the action out of the purely tragic mode, inducing us to see characters and action in a comic context, a context which places Antony and Cleopatra in a story, which provides them and us with an awareness of their theatrical existence and *consequent* mythic (for what is myth but story?) stature. The result is that, simultaneously, Antony and Cleopatra become more ordinarily human and more heroic than they would have been without such devices. Such scenes as Antony being lifted up to Cleopatra, his sheer weight and the difficulty it presents to her, emphasize his human side, but remind us of his heroic 'weight' as well. In many plays, Shakespeare makes brilliant use of the commonplace at moments of intensity, and what we get here is really a slight transformation of the kind of device used to such effect in *King Lear*, for example, where the ordinary adds immeasurably to the tragic ('Pray you undo this button').

The transcendence achieved by this mixing of the commonplace and the superhuman is fulfilling and enriching, but this does not mean that there is no tragic failure. Antony and Cleopatra must, and do, die. But their tragedy merges with the tragedy of society, a society which cannot accommodate the self-emptying and self-fulfillment of the central characters, a society which must, in fact, destroy that commitment in order to ensure its own survival. At the end, we are faced with a situation, like those in *Hamlet* and *King Lear* only more extreme, where the society that remains must deny, or has never understood, the vision of the tragic partners.

The Winter's Tale, in a way which brings together some of the issues raised by *King Lear* and *Antony and Cleopatra*, connects the art of seeing with the seeing of art, especially the magic art of the theatre. As in *King Lear*, seeing is a metaphor for valuing. Leontes' inability to *see* Hermione for what she is, his misperception of the quality of her relationship with Polixenes, expresses his distorted sense of her value. He insists on the moral truth of what he sees, and tries to thrust his vision on others ('Have you not seen, Camillo – / But that's past doubt, you have, or your eyeglass / Is thicker than a cuckold's horn ...'). For Leontes, 'seeing better' will mean repudiating such false sight and allowing what he sees to become congruent with what is. But, as with Gloucester in *King Lear*, gaining true sight is a product of involvement in falsehood, in the illusory magic of art. And in *The Winter's Tale*, unlike *King Lear*, the 'acts' of the younger generation can restore sight and life to the older generation, turning the mockeries of art into actuality. Love and social value are no longer in opposition (as they were in *Antony and Cleopatra*), but rather love, far from being isolated, can transform the social wasteland as well as the personal, so that the tragedy of society, as well as that of the individual, is averted.

Leontes' jealousy is based on acute misperception. And his misperception is associated with his failure to remember.[12] Shakespeare gives both Hermione and Polixenes opportunity to elaborate on their past relationship with Leontes, thereby unobtrusively suggesting the latter's failure of memory. In the trial scene, Hermione speaks of her past life with Leontes and appeals to his sight and his memory to vindicate her:

> You, my lord, best know
> (Who least will seem to do so) my past life
> Hath been as continent, as chaste, as true,

As I am now unhappy; which is more
Than history can pattern, though devis'd
And play'd to take spectators. For behold me,
A fellow of the royal bed ...
      here standing
To prate and talk for life and honour fore
Who please to come and hear. (III.ii.33-43)

Her truth and her unhappiness, like Hamlet's, go beyond what can be played or shown on a stage. She herself is a sight which expresses fully her grief and convinces us of its truth; similarly, at the end, the sight of her coming back to life is an *appearance*, a visual fact which convinces, though the story, if simply told would be a subject for derision: 'That she is living, / Were it but told you, should be hooted at / Like an old tale; but it appears she lives ...' At the end, Leontes can see her and is convinced; but at the trial, he is blind to her reality. He believes only in the show he has created, even to the extent of repudiating the true seer, the Oracle.

 Polixenes, when he recalls his friendship with Leontes, evokes a pastoral innocence, a prelapsarian paradise broken only by the intrusion of women into the male world:

We were as twinn'd lambs that did frisk i' th' sun ...
     we knew not
The doctrine of ill-doing, nor dream'd
That any did ...
Temptations have since then been born to 's; for
In those unfledg'd days was my wife a girl;
Your precious self had then not cross'd the eyes
Of my young playfellow. (I.ii.67-80)

Polixenes' words reveal a basic fear and distrust of women, an attitude that plagues both Leontes and himself, as the parallelism between Leontes' accusation of Hermione and Polixenes' later attack on Perdita indicates. Leontes, of course, allows the temptation of jealousy to poison his relationship with Polixenes as well as with Hermione, and by so doing confirms his friend's words and shows that he no longer remembers or values that past friendship. If Leontes is cut off from innocence, Polixenes seems stuck in it, or at least he has reverted to a boyhood view of women and sexuality (it is significant that his wife, like Lear's, is not in the picture). And such 'innocence' among grown men can be brutal and dangerous. It takes the experience of the pastoral on the part of the younger generation, with all its suggestions of a fertile male-female sexuality, to revive the innocence and free it from misogyny, and to reinstate the relationships between Leontes and Polixenes and, finally, between Leontes and Hermione.[13]

The play asks us to accept Leontes' jealousy; there is no observable motivation for it nor is there meant to be (productions which overdo the friendliness between Hermione and Polixenes and/or show Leontes jealous from the beginning – both temptations surely – miss the point). It is simply a *donné*, a necessary part of the scheme. As such it is abstract, almost allegorical. Even more than in *King Lear*, Shakespeare seems intent on presenting his story schematically, without great regard for credibility. Many critics have observed that the events of the play are often described by the characters as like 'an old tale' (see v.ii. and v.iii especially), which draws our attention to the artifice of the story even as it disarms a possible stock response. Beginning with Bethell, who described the 'antiquated technique' of the play and argued that its crudities deliberately distance us from the action and lead us to consider 'inner meanings,' critics have shown that the 'primitivism' of the play, its use of incredible events as well as its flouting of structural conventions, is a self-conscious technique designed to evoke the mystery of fabulous tales and, simultaneously, to put these tales in a sophisticated perspective. A 'double consciousness' is thus elicited.[14] Shakespeare's aim in the play, then, is to keep us aware of the artifice and open to the paradoxical power of that awareness.

But it is also true, again as in *King Lear*, that the schematic blends with a concrete grip on the actual in order to invoke a reality beyond the merely credible. The verse, for example, which expresses Leontes' allegorical passion is as actual as bodies: 'Too hot, too hot! / To mingle friendship far is mingling bloods ... But to be paddling palms and pinching fingers, / As now they are ... oh, that is entertainment / My bosom likes not, nor my brows' (I.ii.108-19). Everything is bitterly physical; even at his most abstract, Leontes uses violent physical language: 'Affection! Thy intention stabs the center.' There is an inordinate physical perceptiveness with no relaxed, thoughtful deliberation to balance it. Many people have noticed the difference between this language and that of Othello (who goes from grandiloquence to epileptic inarticulateness). One of the reasons for the contrast, leaving aside questions of character and Shakespeare's own development, is that the playwright needed to make us believe utterly and instantly in Leontes' passion, in spite of its seeming incredibility. He could not leave time, as he had in *Othello*, for a long build-up. In a production, then, the point would be to create the discrepancy that Shakespeare intended between what Leontes sees and what we see, and let the language of Leontes' jealousy convince us of its actuality.[15]

If the early parts of the play present us with a series of true acts which Leontes insists on seeing falsely, the great pastoral scene, like the play as a whole, presents a series of false (ie, played) acts which characters and audience must see as true, and which turn out to be true in fact. From the opening speeches of the scene, there is a consciousness of costume and role and the realization that this playing heightens love rather than falsifies it:

> These your unusual weeds to each part of you
> Do give a life – no shepherdess, but Flora,
> Peering in April's front! This your sheep-shearing
> Is as a meeting of the petty gods,
> And you the queen on 't. (IV.iv.1-5)

There is an equivocal truth to this act since Perdita really is a Queen and is associated with a reviving, spring-like power which has real effects in the play. This whole theme is elaborated later in the scene; speaking of the flowers of spring, Perdita says to her friends:

> O, these I lack
> To make you garlands of; and my sweet friend,
> To strew him o'er and o'er!

And Florizel, listening, interjects, 'What, like a corse?' 'No,' says Perdita,

> No, like a bank for Love to lie and play on;
> Not like a corse; or if – not to be buried,
> But quick, and in mine arms. Come, take your flow'rs;
> Methinks I play as I have seen them do
> In Whitsun pastorals. Sure this robe of mine
> Does change my disposition. (IV.iv.127-35)

Perdita finds her own talk about love a little extravagant. She catches herself playing her role too fully, and draws back to ascribe it to the sort of playing typical of Whitsun pastorals (festivals of spring with both pagan and Christian connotations). Her 'robe,' her role, changes her disposition, allowing her to say what as herself she could not say (as do those of figures like Rosalind and Portia). Also, both Florizel and Perdita, as a result of the roles they have adopted, are compared during the course of the scene to fertile gods and goddesses, Perdita with Flora and, obliquely, Proserpina; Florizel with Jupiter, Neptune, and Apollo (see ll.27-31). A sense of magical power, which is appropriate to their renewing and reviving roles in the final scenes, accrues to them through these associations.

In Florizel's great speech, we again have an appraisal of 'act' as something theatrical and at the same time fundamentally real:

> What you do
> Still betters what is done. When you speak, sweet,
> I'd have you do it ever. When you sing,
> I'd have you buy and sell so ....
> When you do dance, I wish you
> A wave o' th' sea, that you might ever do
> Nothing but that, move still, still so,
> And own no other function. Each your doing,
> So singular in each particular,
> Crowns what you are doing in the present deed,
> That all your acts are queens. (IV.iv.136-46)

This speech, coming on the heels of Perdita's remark about playing in Whitsun pastorals and in the midst of a scene which depends on disguise (those of Polixenes and Camillo as well as those of hero and heroine, and, to balance, that of Autolycus as ironic counterweight) leads us to the conclusion that Shakespeare is here alluding as much to the artistry of the actor as to the artlessness of the heroine.* The fact that Perdita is playing the role of a queen, plus the fact that even her most trivial acts ('buy and sell so') are part of an 'act' which expresses queenliness, both lead to the affirmation of her actual queenhood later; put in another way, her acting out of her metaphorical queenliness works to make her a queen in fact. Florizel speaks of her as imposing an order on all the acts of life. It is the order of art, of singing and dancing, which is identified with the order of acting, and being, a queen. The stately movement of the speech, its repetitions and balanced rhythms, combine also to suggest this careful ordering.

---

* G. Wilson Knight, in 'Great Creating Nature' (*Shakespeare: Modern Essays in Criticism*, ed. Leonard Dean, New York 1961), observes of Autolycus that initially he is 'spring incarnate' and that his ballads are 'burlesques of our main fertility myth, stuck in as gargoyles on a cathedral' (379-80). Later, he is used to 'elaborate the vein of court satire already suggested by Polixenes' behavior' and we notice that, as with Falstaff, social advancement tends to make his humour crueller and less delightful (388, 391). Many more recent critics, Joan Hartwig (*Shakespeare's Tragicomic Vision*, Baton Rouge 1972) and D.L. Peterson (*Time, Tide and Tempest*) especially, have seen Autolycus as a foil to, and burlesque of, major figures. We may develop such views further, I think, and argue that Autolycus's career is an extended parody of Perdita's. Like her in his association with spring and fertility (though on a scurrilous level), he is shoved into court clothes and into the pretence of higher status through the manipulation of Camillo, even as Perdita achieves such status through a lucky combination of coincidence and design. Again like Perdita, this higher status thrusts upon him a public role, though his venal use of it contrasts, of course, with her queenliness.

Perdita, both here and at the beginning of the scene, seems chary of disguises and playing ('But that our feasts / In every mess have folly ... I should blush / To see you so attired; swoon, I think, / To show myself a glass'), just as she is chary, too, of art interfering with nature ('There is an art which in their piedness shares / With great creating nature'). Her naïveté, like Miranda's, is charming but limited. It is still anchored in the pastoral world, out of which she, and the play, must move to fulfillment. Her discomfort with art, and with the art of playing, expresses a recoil from the assertion of human power over nature; but such an assertion is crucial not only to the vision of this play or *The Tempest*, not only to Shakespeare's work as a whole, but to the life of the artist itself. And if we think of art, as the Renaissance did, as power over nature, then we can see its relation to magic and understand more fully the magical associations of Perdita and Florizel and the analogies with magic both here and in *The Tempest*. The play goes further than this, however. Nature is more than the raw material of art, it is the final product as well. For just as Perdita's queenly act turns into a reality, so the art created by the play is transformed into nature, its structures penetrating and irradiating the imagination of the audience. The crowning symbol for this process is the transformation of the chiselled Hermione into a living, breathing reality, an event which is presented in a self-consciously theatrical context, calling attention to the artifice of the old tale even as it asserts its validity. This event, more than any other, goes a long way towards erasing the boundary between art and nature and affirming their fundamental identity.

When Polixenes interrupts the festivities of the sheep-shearing to scuttle the love he finds there, his action parallels Leontes' behaviour at the beginning. Leontes had seen illicit love where there was only the proper bond of affection; Polixenes cannot recognize genuine love and calls it illegitimate. Despite the tenets of his presumed philosophy about marrying 'a gentler scion to the wildest stock,' he cannot see the truth expressed through the acts of his son and the shepherdess. Florizel sees the truth in 'falsehood'; Polixenes, like Leontes earlier, sees falsehood in truth. We are, in a sense, half way through the movement the play traces on this theme. In the beginning we had radical misperception; here we have a complex interplay of true and false perception, real and illusory action. Through his long 'recreation,' Leontes eventually gains true sight, as indicated by the renewed memory which informs his regard: 'I thought of her [Hermione], / Even in these looks I made' (v.i.227-8). Fooled at first by the falsehood of the statue, his sight is at last trained to rest on the ultimate visual truth, the resurrected Hermione.

Polixenes, to return to iv.iv, can only see a sort of desperate magic in Perdita, rather than the goddess-like fertility and benevolent queenliness that Florizel sees. Like Brabantio's fear that Othello has bewitched his daughter, which is at bottom a fear of the sexual power of the black man, Polixenes' accusation of witchcraft springs from a fear of the sexuality of women. He calls Perdita an enchantress, a 'fresh piece / Of excellent witchcraft,' and sees her body as an agent and expression of such dark power: 'if ever henceforth thou / These rural latches to his entrance open, / Or hoop his body more with thy embraces, / I will devise a death as cruel for thee / As thou are tender to 't' (448-52). Such frankly sexual talk (the 'rural latches' line looks like an unconscious sexual metaphor) to a young maiden may seem unroyal, but Polixenes has, like Leontes, associated sexuality with dark, threatening power and fails to see the sunny and natural sex implicit in the love of Florizel and Perdita and typified by the openness of the whole festival. His fear erupts as violent aggression against her body, both in the threat of death that he holds out and in the desire he expresses to destroy her beauty: 'I'll have thy beauty scratched with briers and made / More homely than thy state' (436-7). Polixenes fails to see the true magic in the pageant, but our eyes are not so clouded.

The magic that guides the play is no black, sinister force but a beneficent art which, like that in *The Tempest*, bears a close resemblance to the art of the theatre. It is really an art of illusions and shows, wherein a seeming death will do as well as a real one, where a transformation of perception can result from belief in an illusion, and where the breaking of the spell of the illusion can solidify that new perception. Such is the process completed in the concluding scene, and Paulina is its priestess. (The fact that the final discoveries result from a sequence of lies and deceptions on the part of both Paulina and Camillo keeps before us the realization that deception is the bedrock of drama, and it seems appropriate that the two are married off when their work is done.) 'If this be magic,' says Leontes, 'let it be an art / Lawful as eating' (v.iii,110-11). Only such magic can bring the dead back to life, and only in such a way. The whole scene is a theatrical act par excellence, culminating in the bodying forth of Hermione, who steps down as Paulina directs her to 'be stone no more.' This act is similar to the 'resurrection' and presentation of Helena or Ferdinand and Miranda, only much more astounding because the audience is not made aware of the truth beforehand (the only example of Shakespeare withholding such an important fact from the audience), and must experience Leontes' wonder with him.

Paulina plays her part well; like Portia toying with Shylock, though to a very different end, she builds up suspense, makes her audience 'marvel' (as in *The Tempest*, a necessary part of dramatic response), and manipulates Leontes into a state of enraptured confusion. Paulina's function in the play is to force Leontes, in Kent's words, to 'see better,' although her habit of driving Leontes' thoughts back to himself more nearly parallels the Fool's role than Kent's; such is the purpose of her earlier roles as gadfly and nag, manipulator and counsellor (this last in v.i). Her role as priestess and stage manager here is the culmination of these other parts.[16] In the final scene, she moves to close the curtain and, as Leontes protests, she comments ironically, 'No longer shall you gaze on it, lest your fancy / May think anon it moves.' But this very act and the play as a whole are meant to foster precisely this sort of sight, the vision of the fancy which can merge with reality in true perception.

The wonderfully lifelike quality of the statue mocks them, as Leontes says, with art. This mockery transports him so far that Paulina, again pushing forward as she seems to pull back, comments, 'He'll think anon it lives.' Leontes' response describes a kind of delusion that is superior to sanity, a madness which, in contrast to his earlier, bitter delusion, sees into the truth of things:

> O sweet Paulina,
> Make me to think so twenty years together!
> No settled senses of the world can match
> The pleasure of that madness. (v.iii.70-3)

This belief in fancy's truth in the face of reason's doubts recalls Florizel's declaration of love in iv.iv. To Camillo's 'Be advised,' he answers:

> I am, and by my fancy. If my reason
> Will thereto be obedient, I have reason;
> If not, my senses, better pleased with madness,
> Do bid it welcome. (iv.iv.493-6)

Both men welcome a madness which, far from deranging their senses, makes them sharper; both accept a delusion which leads them to truth. Such is the mockery that Leontes speaks of; it is art creating nature.

As a preliminary to the final merging of art with nature, Paulina warns, 'It is required / You do awake your faith,' but the faith required (for us as for the characters) is as much theatrical as theological. This psychological awakening leads to the real awakening of Hermione, who moves as Paulina says 'Dear life redeems you.' Paulina tells us that the event, 'Were it but told you, should be hooted at / Like an old tale.' But we do not hoot, any more than Leontes does, because the play has shown her and her life to us, has taught us to see just as it has him. The art of the dramatist, like that of the illusory sculptor who chiselled even the breath of Hermione, is to transform nature into art and art into life again. It is the double process that makes us see better, just as Leontes, in order to redeem his vision, must awake his faith in the nature that art makes.[17]

In a final theatrical image, Leontes suggests that each of the characters be ready to tell of 'his part / Perform'd in this wide gap of time since first / We were dissever'd.' We are aware, as they go off, that Perdita and Florizel, having left the pastoral world, must now adopt a public role, must find fulfillment in a life which ties private care to public responsibility. Their pastoral experience has given them the insight to make their public life, like their private, fertile and redemptive. Leontes had welcomed them to Sicilia by saying, 'Welcome hither, / As is the spring to the earth' (v.i.151-2), and a moment later had prayed that 'The blessed gods / Purge all infection from our air whilst you / Do climate here.' The society established at the end has been purged of the infections of jealousy and diseased public relations through the actions of the young. The far-ranging awareness that the play develops is embodied in the new social order established at the end, in contrast to the tragedies where, as we saw, the political order established or left behind in plays like *Hamlet, King Lear,* or *Antony and Cleopatra*, retreats from or somehow fails to include the consciousness of the tragic heroes.

8

The Tempest

The Tempest makes the most complete statement about theatrical artifice of all Shakespeare's plays and Prospero is the ultimate disguised manipulator, the invisible magician who is the double of the playwright within the play. It resolves many of the problems posed by *Hamlet* by moving them into the realm of the imaginary, by making them subject to the transformations that can be effected by art. Prospero's art of illusion, like Shakespeare's, works to create attitudes in both characters and audience which can ease the tension between the demands of personal identity and those of social solidarity. The techniques of the earlier comedies are reinstated, but with the difference that they are now both more inclusive and more fleeting. Great changes are possible under the influence of art, but they need the more pedestrian work of reason and virtue to make them stick. The value of art, as in *The Winter's Tale* as well, emerges as something actual but limited; Prospero's magic can bring about a temporary illumination, but not a complete metamorphosis.

The chess game in Act v provides some initial insight into how play can transform reality into ordered artifice. Why, we may ask, are Ferdinand and Miranda discovered to us 'playing at chess'? What are the symbolic connections between this event and the rest of the play? These questions may serve as the starting point of our investigation. Chess is a game which transforms combat into ritual, which transposes the experience of war and conflict into play. It is characterized by elaborate and artificially created procedures of behaviour (all games have such 'rules' but chess reveals their character more clearly than most) which bind the players to a limited set of allowable moves. There is no way that a player can break a rule and still be playing chess.[1] Another way of making this last point is to say that the world of chess is utterly self-contained, there is no way of allowing 'reality' (eg, doing what you want instead of what the rules allow) to intrude into the game world.

If chess presents a way of harmlessly transforming destructive energies abroad in society, so does *The Tempest*, and in a far more complete way. Both show us the power of play in this transformation, *The Tempest* emphasizing the illusions that both characters and audience must accept (like the rules in chess) in order to participate in the process. Similarly, the world of *The Tempest*, like that of chess, is contained by the boundaries it itself sets and is characterized by elaborate and artificially created procedures of behaviour.[2] Ferdinand, Alonso, even Prospero, must play the game according to rules which, again like those of chess, are both arbitrary and inevitable, and which are directed towards a specific end, an end that has something in common with checkmating (the King, after all, is defeated), but moves well beyond (the King is also saved).

It is by now well known that *The Tempest* presents a vision of nature cultivated and civilized, and is sceptical about idealized, primitivistic views of nature like those of Gonzalo (or Montaigne, of whose 'Cannibales' Caliban is a sort of parody), or cynical, self-seeking views like those of Antonio.[3] Chess is a 'civilized' pursuit; it is an elegant and courtly game and the fact that Ferdinand and Miranda are playing it bespeaks their cultured and educated attitudes. It is a form of 'nurture' that sits well together with the charming and naïve 'nature' that Miranda elsewhere manifests ('O brave new world ...'). The chess game is thus a small example within the play of the civilizing of nature and, in its reduction of powerful destructive energies to game, a kind of enactment of it. We can see now, perhaps, how the deliberately illusory, artificial quality of the play's form is related to the theme of nature and nurture. The play as a whole, in accordance with certain rules, presents us with the containment and harnessing of destructive energies, and it does so in specifically theatrical terms, drawing our attention to the importance, even the necessity, of *play* as a way of bringing about such a transformation. Play is the richest form of nurture.

To go farther afield now, in an attempt to present another relevant form of elaborately ritualized and patterned behaviour, I would like to turn to Lévi-Strauss's account of the face and body painting of a Brazilian Indian tribe, the Caduveo.[4] These people 'manifested in their face-paintings that abhorrence of Nature which made them resort so freely to abortion and infanticide.' Art is an absolute rejection of nature: 'not to be painted was to be one with the brutes.' From an analysis of their highly ornamental, dualistic style and methods of composition, Lévi-Strauss derives an argument that the elaborate structure of their art is comparable to the actual social structure of two different neighbouring tribes, and that in a sense it compensates for their own self-destructive social structure. The Caduveo art appears as a sort of dream:

They were never lucky enough to resolve their contradictions ... On the social level the remedy was lacking ... but it never went completely out of their grasp. It was within them ... In fact, they dreamed of it ... The mysterious charm and (as it seems at first) gratuitous complication of Caduveo art may well be a phantasm created by a society whose object was *to give symbolical form to the institutions which it might have had in reality*, had interest and superstition not stood in the way.[5]

The italicized phrase describes, to me, what is the primary function of *The Tempest*, and, more cheerfully, we may note that in the play the relations implied by such potential institutions are, at least to a degree, realized. In the play, the conflict between art and nature is harmonized through a kind of illusionary 'soul-painting' which, far from rejecting nature, has real ramifications in the world. The play, it seems to me, comes up with a better, fuller solution to the same problems confronted by the Caduveo. Lévi-Strauss concludes by remarking, 'Great indeed is the fascination of this culture, whose dream-life was pictured on the faces of its queens, as if, in making themselves up, they figured a Golden Age that they would never know in reality.'[6] *The Tempest* does this too, but recognizes the impossibility of the dream, as well as the incompleteness of art, without losing sight of the power of that art to point the way back to social solutions.

The Tempest creates illusions and invites our participation in them. It seeks to make us aware of the power of these artificial creations in the face of the resistance of nature. How this works will be my main concern.

I have heard of productions of *The Tempest* in which the storm scene was presented with Prospero on the stage, watchful and benevolent. Though the impulse to show Prospero's control from the start is an understandable one, it seems to me misdirected. The storm should strike us as it does Miranda; it should be as real and as horrific as possible. There are, in effect, two storms, as D.G. James points out,[7] the one Miranda sees and the one Prospero creates. Prospero's first theatrical effort is a highly realistic one which convinces his daughter that 'a brave vessel' has been 'Dash'd all to pieces' (i.ii.6,8). It has to convince us in the same way. Of course, we are aware of it as a piece of theatre, and hence as an illusion, and Miranda is not. For her, it is immediate and real. She only becomes aware of it as an illusion when Prospero tells her 'There's no harm done' (15). His statement describes the classic pattern of romance, where apparent disaster is metamorphosed into serenity and reunion. This introduces Miranda to a 'romantic' way of looking at events that is reinforced in the story that Prospero goes on to tell her, of how their 'sea sorrow' was transformed into their present joy 'By providence divine.' Miranda thus begins to recognize herself as part of a fable even as she retains her reality. She is being introduced to the mode of romance, and so are we. For Prospero's assurance that 'There's no harm done,' and his subsequent explanation, ought to have an effect on us similar to that it has on Miranda. What we had seen as a 'real' event within a theatrical illusion is itself transformed into an illusion so that the effect of a play-within-a-play is created. To accept this transformation is, for us, tantamount to accepting the romantic mode of projecting human experience and hence the rest of the play (beginning with Prospero's romantic tale). One effect of this process is that the suspension of disbelief so necessary for romance (which I find difficult to allow in *Cymbeline*, for example) is here quite naturally elicited.

The fact that Miranda sees in the storm what she must see there in order to participate fully in the later events of the play illustrates a general pattern which works with other characters as well. What at first glance are inconsistencies (like the 'two' storms) become part of a pattern necessary for the development of particular characters and their plot. The fact that, for example, it is still storming in II.ii for Stephano and Trinculo, though earlier it had stopped for Ferdinand and the court party, is, realistically considered, an inconsistency. It is, however, an explicable and, what is more, an ingenious device by which Shakespeare indicates the *created* quality of the different series of events. For Stephano, Trinculo, and Caliban, the storm really does continue, whereas for the others it really does not. This indicates something about the world in which the events of the play are occurring. It is a world which reflects the omnipotent and arbitrary power of Prospero. If the storm must continue, even if only for the sake of the amusing and imaginative way Caliban is brought into the service of Stephano and Trinculo, it will continue. Prospero's magic is a plot-making power and his world is a play-world, where reality is encircled by illusion.

The way the various court characters see and react to the island supports this idea. If we were to take their varying accounts at face value, we would be confronted with a series of contradictions. The point is that the island *is* different for each of them. Their responses have a good deal to do with what kind of people they are and what will be necessary for them during the course of the play. Ferdinand is enthralled with what he sees, Gonzalo is delighted and waxes philosophical, Alonso seems to notice nothing external to himself, and Antonio and Sebastian are scornful. All these reactions require testing, tempering, or transforming. The action of the play forces these trials upon the characters, showing us that Prospero's plot has an internal, as well as an external, form. The validity of Gonzalo's moralizing is tested and proven flabby, and at the end he seems less pedantic; Alonso is brought into direct contact with his guilt through his exposure to the island's wonders, and Sebastian and Antonio's scorn is turned to awe by the banquet. For Antonio, this seems only a temporary change, but its effect on Sebastian seems more lasting. Ferdinand is set in contrast to the rest of the court party. For him the island must be, and therefore is, miraculous, in order to provide a fitting prologue for his meeting with Miranda, the 'goddess' on it, and to introduce him to a way of seeing that will allow him to see her properly. When he does come face to face with her, he associates her with the wonderful music he has been hearing: just as he claimed of the music, 'This is no mortal business, nor no sound / That the earth owes' (i.ii.406-7), he perceives Miranda as a goddess and addresses her, 'O you wonder' (426). But even this perception must be tried and strengthened, and it appears later that Ferdinand's attitude is at once too naïve and too worldly; he so easily embraces the world of romance that he has to endure a few doses of 'reality' before getting things straight.

Prospero arranges Miranda and Ferdinand's meeting, 'discovering' Ferdinand to her as part of a theatrical event (as the lovers are discovered to the court party at the end of the play). Prospero then takes a part in the little comedy that he is presenting, that of the *senex*, the irascible father determined to keep his daughter separated from her lover. The role is a conventional one; it goes back to Roman comedy and is common in the *commedia* as well as in several of Shakespeare's own plays. Egeus, in *A Midsummer Night's Dream*, Cymbeline, and in an extended way, Baptista in *The Taming of the Shrew* all provide examples. (Brabantio, in *Othello*, is an example of the type set into a tragedy.) Prospero's adopted role is only a role, he is quick to assure us; its effect, however, is to allow us to see events in a comic context and to allow the lovers to assume, more or less unwittingly, the conventional roles of the lovers in comedy. Hence Miranda, quite contrary to what we have seen of her character, disobeys her father and, so she thinks, hoodwinks him. This little plot provides another glimpse of the play as a piece of theatrical art in which a series of spectacles, both conventional and unconventional, are held together by the plot-making of the magician-playwright.

After the storm and the action that proceeds from it, the next striking spectacle is the banquet that Prospero fabricates for the benefit of the court party. The ostensible purpose of this show is to confront the usurpers with their guilt and direct them on the road to repentance. But why does such a purpose demand such an extravagant and seemingly irrelevant vehicle? Compared to the varied reactions to the island itself, the various responses to the banquet are remarkably similar. For all the courtiers, initial incredulity melts quickly into belief and acceptance:

> SEBASTIAN A living drollery. Now I will believe
> That there are unicorns; that in Arabia
> There is one tree, the phoenix' throne; one phoenix
> At this hour reigning there.
> ANTONIO   I'll believe both;

And what does else want credit, come to me,
And I'll be sworn 'tis true ...
GONZALO   If in Naples
I should report this now, would they believe me?

(III.iii.21-8)

All of these comments go beyond the wonder of the present moment (Alonso is the one who emphasizes that element) to a consideration of belief itself. The truth of this vision justifies the otherwise unbelievable reports of travellers. (It is interesting too that Sebastian chooses as his example the very symbol of regenerative power, suggesting, perhaps, a connection between this scene and the process of regeneration so important in this play, as in all the romances.) Belief in the irrational or in the fantastic, for these practical men of the world, depends on their confrontation with a vision. The vision itself is so overwhelming that it keeps Gonzalo from philosophizing and Sebastian and Antonio from debunking, as they would be likely to do in less extreme circumstances. They simply accept; and with their acceptance of the vision comes an acceptance of the irrational itself, of everything that defies common sense.

The play reveals that some such acceptance and wonder is a necessary prelude to any kind of regeneration. As in several of the other plays discussed, Shakespeare is asking the audience as well as the courtiers to accept as real what defies common sense. In going to the theatre, an audience proclaims its willingness to accept an illusion as a kind of reality. Here, however, Shakespeare is asking more. By presenting an illusion as if it were a reality, within a larger illusion, and by making the acceptance of this an important aspect of the regenerative plot, he is asking us to recognize the power of theatrical processes both within plays and within theatres.

The banquet scene is, for the court party, an introduction into the psychic life of the island, a deeper step into the play's world. By means of this experience, they enter what Prospero has designed as the psychological plot of the play he is presenting. Their earlier scene (II.i) had brought them to the island and introduced them to its physical aspects. They became aware of the setting though they were deluded about it, as both Gonzalo's utopianism and Antonio and Sebastian's cynicism make clear. Now they are confronted with a play-world which is for them both impossible and intensely real; this, as we have seen, changes their perceptions. Prospero's dominant position on the upper stage during this scene indicates his powerful role as controller of just these processes.

As I said, this is the beginning of a psychological process which is continued while the characters are off-stage under the tutelage of Ariel; it is finally completed in the last scene, most successfully with Gonzalo and Alonzo, only partially so with Sebastian and, seemingly, quite unsuccessfully with Antonio. Beginning with the wonder and acceptance already discussed, the process develops with the disappearance of the banquet. Ariel appears to the sound of 'thunder and lightning,' which reminds both courtiers and audience of the opening storm and hence is reminiscent of the disorder, both political and personal, which still dominates the minds of these men. The setting and Ariel's speech are highly theatrical, even contrived, and this quality contributes something to the effect they have. The most immediate effect is to involve the hearers completely. This is not the sort of playing that induces detachment and irony; it attacks the mind directly. In this regard, it is worth noting that only the three guilty ones hear Ariel and they hear him both as a mysterious natural voice and as a personage. A concomitant effect is that the courtiers are more decisively cut off from worldly consideration – questions of the politics of Naples or the like – than they had been by merely landing on the island. Instead, they are led back into themselves and a consideration of their own guilt. On this point, it is significant that we hear nothing more about the projected conspiracy of Sebastian and Antonio. What has happened has deflected them away from such concerns. This deflection is, of course, only temporary; it takes the final unveiling and Prospero's confronting them with their guilt to consolidate it fully. Nevertheless, the efficacy of Prospero's design is clear, and it is not just a matter of plot. The high passion with which these two men leave the stage at the end of this scene is the result of a sudden confrontation with themselves and an unavoidable flash of guilt.

Of course, this process most clearly affects Alonso, who responds to Ariel's demand for 'heart's sorrow' with a richly poetic speech indicative of a new level of awareness:

> O, it is monstrous, monstrous!
> Methought the billows spoke and told me of it;
> The winds did sing it to me; and the thunder,
> That deep and dreadful organ pipe, pronounc'd
> The name of Prosper. It did bass my trespass.
> Therefore my son i' th' ooze is bedded; and
> I'll seek him deeper than e'er plummet sounded
> And with him there lie mudded. (III.iii.95-102)

Ariel's proclamation of Destiny and the judgement of its powers has touched a resonant chord in Alonso, allowing him to recognize his guilt and, beyond that, to open himself to the full repentance that the play and its romantic form require for full regeneration. This is indicated by the structural positioning of the speech, by its sounding of both marine and psychological depths, and especially by its metaphorical resonance.[8]

This scene, then, is very important both as an initiation of the process of re-generation for the courtiers and as a consolidation of Prospero's control. This latter aspect is made clear by Prospero's speech immediately following Ariel's proclamation. Speaking from on high, a position which in itself proclaims his providential role, he says: 'My high charms work, / And these, mine enemies, are all knit up / In their distractions. They now are in my pow'r' (III.iii.88-91). Even before Alonso's speech, Prospero recognizes that his plan has taken hold; it is *working.* More important, he alludes to the primary place of this scene in effect-ing his control. Only 'now' are his enemies really in his power; such has been the effect of his pageant.

The third striking spectacle that Prospero offers is the masque, which comes – a significant juxtaposition – in the scene immediately following the banquet. The masque is the only one of these shows whose audience is aware of its illusory character. This is one of many points of analogy between it and the whole play. The most basic point of analogy is the fact that both masque and play are cre-ated by Prospero, this presentation being an image of the much more compli-cated question of the creation of the whole play. Both masque and play are enactments of his 'present fancies,' the one using spirits, the other men. The spirits are conscious actors, the men unconscious. But both are being directed by Prospero. What he calls his 'art' is the operative force in both; both, in being en-actments of his 'fancies,' are imaginative embodiments of important truths, the one entirely symbolic, the other both symbolic and real.

Images of acting occur throughout the play and emphasize the fact that these men are indeed taking part in a theatrical action, though without being aware of it.[9] An important example is Antonio's exhortation to Sebastian, which moves easily from the dominant sea metaphor to the theatrical one: 'she that from whom / We all were sea-swallow'd, though some *cast* again, / And, by that des-tiny, to perform an *act* / Whereof what's past is prologue ...' (II.i.254-7, my italics). Antonio misunderstands destiny, thinking it fortuitous, and resolves to direct the subsequent action, to write his own play as it were, failing to realize that he is already an actor.[10] The association of destiny with the theatrical meta-phor prefigures Ariel's judgement speech and indicates an important imaginative connection that the whole play makes, since Prospero, even as he presents his pageants, is directly associated with providence and destiny. More important than such images, of course, is the fact that so much of the play is being *pre-sented* by Prospero to other characters or for their benefit. There is, in fact, a sense that the whole play as we have it is a kind of play-within, though the narra-tive into which it is set is not enacted, only recounted in Prospero's exposition.

As I said, another important connection between masque and play is that both embody truths which Prospero is intent upon propagating. Perhaps the pri-mary one concerns the relation between nature and civilization, nature and nurture, that I mentioned at the outset. That the play presents a vision of nature ordered by human reason and art need hardly be argued here. My point now is that the masque, too, as Leo Marx points out,[11] emphasizes not primitive nature but cultivated nature, despite its role as a fertility rite. This comes through clearly in the rural, farmland association of almost all the speeches, especially the fertility song: 'Earth's increase, foison plenty; / Barns and garners never empty, / Vines with clust'ring bunches growing, / Plants with goodly burthen bowing' (iv.i.110-13). This view of the masque goes a long way toward explaining Prospero's seemingly over-zealous insistence on the necessity of premarital chastity. That cultivation is a matter of controlling nature is a principle which applies as well to human sexuality and the human soul as it does to agriculture.

As with the courtiers at the banquet and us at the play, the relationship between audience and spectacle is important during the masque. Ferdinand and Miranda are faced with a scene of pure fantasy within a world that to them is real. Their real world is to us, however, pure fantasy. By implication, what we term reality is called into question. Furthermore, what to them is fantasy nevertheless projects meaning and elicits feelings of wonder and harmony: 'This is a most majestic vision, and / Harmonious charmingly' (iv.i.118-19). The play is meant to move *us* to a similar, if more guarded, response. The masque also opens their eyes to the power of illusion to signify and hence to enlighten. Being drawn into an illusion provides a movement away from reality to allow for retrospection (as we saw also in connection with the courtiers); and such retrospection is fruitful for an understanding of the place of illusion in what has happened to them in what they call reality. Theatrical spectacle and illusion are like dreaming and sleeping. The distinction between dream and reality is consistently blurred for all the characters on the island, including Caliban. The reason for this is that Prospero, or Shakespeare, is intent upon stressing the importance of a transformation of perception,[12] the development of a visionary perspective of which wonder is an important ingredient and awareness an important result. The last act is the culmination of this process and will be discussed in some detail later on. For now, it is enough to stress the place of the masque in the process, both as it affects Ferdinand and Miranda and as it affects us.

At the same time, Prospero is aware of the *temporary* quality of the wonder which he generates. Fantasy becomes mere escapism if it does not point back to reality. We may feel, with Ferdinand, 'Let me live here ever! / So rare a wond'red father and a wise / Makes this place Paradise' (iv.i.122-4). But the masque and play show us that such a response is inadequate, that we are meant to see the proper relation of fantasy to reality. Ferdinand's response is false inasmuch as it identifies illusion as reality and attempts to assign a permanence to something which is essentially transitory. Prospero's recognition of this transitoriness allows him to halt the masque (and later abjure his magic) just as a similar recognition prompts him to end the play with the imminent movement away from the island. To complete the pattern, the masque is followed by his speech, 'Our revels now are ended,' which spells out the theme of transitoriness, just as the play is followed by the epilogue, which stands in the same relation to the play as the 'revels' speech does to the masque.

It is imaginatively right, then, that the masque is abruptly cut off and that Prospero's mood changes from benign to severely agitated. The end of the masque is accompanied by a 'strange, hollow, and confused noise,' the very opposite of the rich harmonies which precede it. The basest kind of reality – 'the foul conspiracy of the beast Caliban' – intrudes upon the vision. The word 'conspiracy' reminds us of Antonio's original conspiracy and Sebastian and Antonio's more recent one and hence makes us aware of the necessity of watchfulness as well as wonder. If the masque and its implications envision a rich potential, its abrupt end signals the difficulty, or even impossibility, of ever fully achieving such potential.

Much of what I have been saying is implicit in Prospero's great speech, which many critics have seen as the imaginative centre of the play:

> These our actors,
> As I foretold you, were all spirits and
> Are melted into air, into thin air;
> And like the baseless fabric of this vision,
> The cloud-capp'd towers, the gorgeous palaces,
> The solemn temples, the great globe itself,
> Yea, all which it inherit, shall dissolve,
> And, like this insubstantial pageant faded,
> Leave not a rack behind. We are such stuff
> As dreams are made on, and our little life
> Is rounded with a sleep. (IV.i.148-58)

Reuben Brower indicates how the various metaphorical 'continuities' of the play converge here to convey the dominant sense of 'sea-change' or metamorphosis,[13] especially psychological metamorphosis and the movement towards regeneration. G.W. Knight sees in the speech a 'repudiation ... of human fabrication at its grandest' maintaining at the same time that there is no real 'negation,' but rather that some 'supreme positive' is 'mysteriously defined.'[14] Knight's sense of the supreme positive is undoubtedly the result of the metaphorical nexus which the speech, as Brower shows, contains. The speech also gives full expression to Prospero's awareness of illusion and its relation to play and to reality. Human creation is inevitably transitory and there is no great difference between the illusion we call 'pageant' and the illusion we call 'reality.' The distinction between sleep and waking is a doubtful one at best, and, perhaps, as the rest of the play intimates, what we dream is truer than what we 'experience.' The clothes images in this passage connecting the visions of art and dream ('baseless fabric' and 'stuff') corroborate a sense we get from the whole play that the two, art and dream, are closely associated. What happens to the court party, for instance, is seen by them as dreamlike ('Whether this be / Or be not, I'll not swear.' v.i.122-3), while we have seen these events as part of a play-action being directed by Prospero. What arises from this is a sense of the importance of dramatic art – and especially romance, itself a highly ordered form of dream, which raises the question in the most naked way – as a mode of replaying reality and clarifying it. This is the impulse behind the whole play: it is what Prospero wants his 'actors' to see, it is what Shakespeare wants us to see. And as such, it is a culmination of a thematic and structural concern in Shakespeare's plays almost from the beginning of his career.

To conclude, let us now turn to a consideration of the last of Prospero's 'pageants,' the dénouement of both his project and, simultaneously, of the play itself. We are introduced to this last section by an odd passage which has excited a good deal of comment, Prospero's apparent decision to be merciful to his enemies (v.i.16-32). There are two basic interpretations of this passage, one which claims that Prospero actually is, under Ariel's influence, undergoing a conversion at this very moment, and another which claims that what we are being shown is a 're-enactment' of a process that has already taken place.[15] All the evidence seems to uphold the latter explanation; everything that I have been saying about Prospero's control – his use of the banquet scene to evoke 'heart's sorrow' and self-scrutiny, his foiling of Antonio's and Sebastian's conspiracy, his establishment of the relationship between Ferdinand and Miranda as part of a pattern, his use of the very storm itself in a *harmless* way – all point to a single unified intention from the start, not a sudden shift at the last moment. At the same time, it is worth noting that this scene comes on the heels of his extreme agitation at the conspiracy of Caliban and the others. By the beginning of v.i he has regained his composure and looks forward to the resolution: 'Now does my project gather to a head ...' However, the re-enactment that follows may be a reminder that Prospero, like anyone, does not find it easy to forgive.

Seeing this passage as a re-enactment allows us to see it as another of Prospero's 'pageants,' this time one that dramatizes his own mind in quasi-allegorical terms: 'Yet with my nobler reason 'gainst my fury / Do I take part. The rarer action is / In virtue than in vengeance' (v.i.26-8). The importance of this presentation lies partially in what it shows and partially in where it is placed. What it shows is that the progress of Prospero's mind has traced a romance pattern, a pattern which he then objectifies by designing events to follow it. The placing of the re-enactment is important since it serves as an introduction to the final phase of the action; it allows us a glimpse of the pattern in miniature just before it is established on a larger scale. We are hence in a better position to appreciate both the psychological meaning of, and the impulse behind, the larger romance movement.

There is a thematic element which this passage also brings up. In saying, 'Yet with my nobler reason 'gainst my fury / Do I take part,' Prospero is pointing to one of the central issues of the play: the role of reason in perfecting human life. Just as art must civilize nature, so reason must civilize fury. Prospero describes his own conflict in an almost allegorical way; but the same conflict in the courtiers is dramatized much more fully and is described in terms of the dominant metaphors of the play:

> The charm dissolves apace;
> And as the morning steals upon the night,
> Melting the darkness, so their rising senses
> Begin to chase the ignorant fumes that mantle
> Their clearer reason ...
> Their understanding
> Begins to swell, and the approaching tide
> Will shortly fill the reasonable shore,
> That now lies foul and muddy. (v.i.64-8, 79-82)

The sea imagery and the metaphor of dissolving and melting link this passage to the theme of change and transformation spelled out in similar terms throughout the play.[16] The 'foul and muddy' minds of the courtiers are related to their delusion that, as Alonso says, Ferdinand is 'mudded in [an] oozy bed' (v.i.151). The language here also recalls Alonso's realization that his 'trespass' is the cause that 'my son i' th' ooze is bedded' and his subsequent desire to 'with him there lie mudded' (iii.iii.100-2). Thus the beginning of the process of regeneration and its culmination are spoken of in the same terms. Their muddy or mantled minds (the word recalls the 'filthy, mantled pool' – iv.i.182 – where Caliban and his cohorts are subjected to similar treatment though on a purely physical level) are about to be transformed into the clear fountain of reason.

This clearing of their minds is put in another way by Alonso: 'since I saw thee, / Th' affliction of my mind amends, with which, / I fear, a madness held me' (v.i.114-16). Madness and emotional turbulence are dominant states for most of the men in the play, including, on occasion, Prospero himself.[17] Criticism's emphasis on regeneration, serenity, harmony, and the like is apt to make us forget this. Alonso passes from one emotional pitch to another and comes, as he says, perilously close to madness. This inner disturbance is related to the storm and arises in the same way, as a result of Prospero's management. It is both like and unlike the usual correspondence between inner turbulence and stormy weather in Shakespeare. There *is* a genuine correspondence, but since the storm and the inner state are both artificial, manufactured by Prospero, the correspondence is not the same as in *King Lear*, for example, where both storm and madness are 'real.' Here, neither storm nor emotion are 'real' in the same way, since both are contained by an illusion within the play, but they are nonetheless extremely meaningful to the participants, who feel them as real.*

What I have been discussing forms a prelude to the dénouement, a prelude in which we are given, through imagery and the re-enactment of the process in Prospero, a sense of the shape and meaning of the whole design. The actual dénouement only takes place after Prospero has promised to renounce his art as part of the necessary process of returning to society, where 'reason' and 'virtue' must take the place of magic. The limitations of art are here clearly enunciated: in a sense, Prospero can only create plays; his power in the real world is limited. (Surely the ambiguity of Antonio's conversion is meant to remind us of this.) But the usefulness of such projects as Prospero's experiments on the island or Shakespeare's *Tempest* is not thereby reduced. The evening in the theatre ends just as the day on the island ends, but we are left with something akin to the courtier's experience to bring away with us.

The knowledge that this is Prospero's last act lends a particularly poignant yet decisive character to what follows. It is in the fullest sense final. The courtiers are led into a magic circle ('*They all enter the circle which Prospero has made and there stand charmed*') and become unwitting participants in a show. This is emphasized by the fact that the magic circle they occupy is set up within a larger magic circle – the island (and, by implication, the theatre itself). Throughout the play they have been wandering from the periphery towards the *centre* which they now occupy, both to present and to discover. Prospero's speech (58-87), already quoted in part, serves as a prologue to this final pageant. It announces the process which is then acted out before us. We see Alonso as his madness evaporates and his mind amends. Identity is re-established through the very shape of romance. We recognize what is happening as a representation in little of what the whole play puts before us. First there is Gonzalo's statement of the strange and terrifying contraries of the island and the need for guidance: 'All torment, trou-

---

* The characters' relation to the storm and inner turmoil in *The Tempest* is thus like an unconscious version of the audience's relation to storm and turmoil in *King Lear*. Only at the dénouement, when they are made aware of the delusions under which they have laboured, do they become like actual, though retrospective, audience members.

ble, wonder, and amazement / Inhabits here. Some heavenly power guide us / Out of this fearful country' (104-6). Next we have Alonso's statement of his mental affliction already discussed, and his resignation of the dukedom. The charm dissolves enough to allow Gonzalo some comfort but he is still confused: 'Whether this be / Or be not, I'll not swear.' The 'subtleties o' th' isle,' the deliberate blurring of dream and actuality, are still in effect. In a moment, Alonso's repentance, which develops as he participates in this action, reaches its most profound level with his response to Prospero's tale of loss: 'A daughter? / O heaven, that they were living both in Naples, / The King and Queen there!' (148-50). Here his repentance reaches out into compassion and a willingness to sacrifice not only his position but his life: 'That they were, I wish / Myself were mudded in that oozy bed / Where my son lies' (150-2). What he does not yet realize is that all this salutary emotion, while real, is contained by an illusion and hence can produce those very effects he prays for but thinks unattainable. Prospero can now present his *coup de théâtre*: 'My dukedom since you have given me again, / I will require you with as good a thing, / At least bring forth a wonder to content ye / As much as me my dukedom' (168-71). The force of the word 'wonder' here as it focusses the responses to the various 'pageants' can hardly be overemphasized. '*Here Prospero discovers Ferdinand and Miranda playing at chess.*' As I suggested at the beginning, the chess game and its theatrical context focus the element of play which is vital to the transformations that these sophisticated people undergo. This act of discovery is the culmination of all the theatrical presentations of the play. Beyond that, it is the culmination of a whole series of such acts in Shakespeare's plays. People long thought dead, Hero, Helena, Claudio, Posthumus and Imogen, Hermione, are resurrected before our eyes. The only possible response is expressed by Sebastian (significantly, only Antonio is silent): 'A most high miracle' (177). The courtiers, in the midst of acting out their regeneration, have been presented with this spectacle as a culmination of the very action in which they have been involved. The spectacle is at the same time supremely real, closing the distance between illusion and reality so that reality takes the shape of romance.

Miranda's 'O wonder! ... How beauteous mankind is! O brave new world / That has such people in 't' (181-4) gives us a slightly different perspective. Her wonder is not excited by the miracle of restoration, the miracle of reality turning into romance, or romance turning into reality. Hers is the wonder of a child at new undiscovered beauties. But it is an incomplete response; as Prospero says, ''Tis new to thee.' Hers is not a transformation of perception and it takes no account of the evils in life. It is still innocent. It is thus like Ferdinand's response to the masque; that is, the play goes beyond it in that the play's vision moves out of the pastoral world, while still recognizing the importance and beauty of the pastoral view.

Thus, the final scene recapitulates the form of the play itself in its presentation of the movement from chaos to order, darkness to illumination. After all is restored, Gonzalo sums up:

> Was Milan thrust from Milan that his issue
> Should become kings of Naples? O, rejoice
> Beyond a common joy, and set it down
> With gold on lasting pillars: In one voyage
> Did Claribel her husband find at Tunis,
> And Ferdinand her brother found a wife
> Where he himself was lost; Prospero his dukedom
> In a poor isle; and all of us ourselves
> When no man was his own. (v.i.205-13)

The paradox of the romantic design, the pattern of loss and restoration, is nowhere more clearly stated. The madness and turbulent emotion that Alonso spoke of earlier have been associated with a loss of identity. Now the theme of lost and regained identity is proclaimed in quite specific terms. Prospero, too, recognizes this movement as part of the process initiated by his charms: 'My charms I'll break, their senses I'll restore, / And they shall be themselves' (v.i. 31-2). His intention is to lead them back to a sense of their own identity, but with the difference that they will be more truly themselves when his project is fully accomplished. Prospero's promise comes at the outset of this final presentation and Gonzalo's speech at the end, thereby indicating that this is indeed what the scene and the play accomplish, though the difficulty of the project and the need for watchfulness are kept before us by the apparent failure to reach Antonio.

The final movement of the play is, as I have said, away from the enchanted world back into the real, political world. It is announced by Prospero's promise of 'calm seas, auspicious gales.' The storm is quieted, the chaos has been ordered, the sea itself is transformed into a symbol of harmony. There is some hope that the illumination provided by the island may be effective in the public world, but it is now virtue and reason, not magic, that must be used.

Just as the courtiers and lovers leave the island, so we must leave the theatre. The analogy is developed in the epilogue which touches on many of the themes I have discussed even as it consciously dissolves the theatrical illusion. Prospero here, like Rosalind in her epilogue at the end of *As You Like It*, is both the character and the actor playing the part. This double role gives an interesting twist to such pleas as 'Let me not, / Since I have my dukedom got / And pardon'd the deceiver, dwell / In this bare island by your spell' (5-8). The audience is put into

a position vis-à-vis Prospero like that of Prospero vis-à-vis the courtiers: he released his spell over them, now the audience should 'free' him. The 'bare island'
is both the island of the play and the theatre, a collocation which has been implicit throughout the play but which is here specified. The power of the audience is
emphasized even more strongly in the lines that follow, where there is an analogy between Prospero's role in dissolving the illusion of the island and freeing
Ariel, and the role of the audience in dissolving the theatrical illusion while still
retaining vestiges of it: 'But release me from my bands / With the help of your
good hands. / Gentle breath of yours my sails / Must fill, or else my project
fails ...' The language of the play is still operative – 'release,' 'gentle,' 'sails,' 'project' – but is here used metaphorically to denote actions or things at one remove
from the play-world itself. Thus the 'real' sails that will take Prospero and the
others to Naples here become metaphorical sails, though they derive their force
from the play and thereby retain a sense of the theatrical illusion, despite the
fact that the audience is being addressed directly and being told to applaud. This
delicate balance is maintained throughout the epilogue. The appeal to the 'mercy'
of the audience, or the call for 'release,' are analogous to the play-situation
where Prospero is very deliberately and providentially merciful and hence releases his enemies and his servants. Similarly, his 'project' in the play – to confront his enemies with their guilt, induce repentance, and create harmony – here
becomes the 'project' of the playwright, 'Which was to please.' The effect of this
balance and of the sliding of play-reality into metaphor is a modulation of illusion into reality where the one is recognized as a model or figure for the other.
We leave the theatre with a sense of the limitations of theatrical illusion, aware
of it as a temporary illumination which must come to an end, like the masque or
the courtiers' three hours on the island. But we are aware too that the power of
play, which we, like the characters, have just experienced, may provide an image
of grace together with an enriched sense of reality and thus create a model or
focus for what we call real life.

Notes

INTRODUCTION

1 Michel Foucault, *The Order of Things* (New York 1971) Ch. 1, provides a subtle analysis of this painting from a similar point of view.
2 Frank Kermode, *The Sense of an Ending* (London 1968), passim. See especially the first two chapters.

CHAPTER 1: *The Merchant of Venice*

1 J. Middleton Murry, *Shakespeare* (London 1936) 189. See also H. Granville-Barker, *Prefaces to Shakespeare*, Second Series (London 1939) 67.
2 J.R. Brown, in his introduction to the Arden edition of *The Merchant of Venice* (Cambridge, MA 1955) xxix-xxx, summarizes the arguments against accepting *The Jew*, exempted by Gosson from his general attack on plays, as a genuine source.
3 E.E. Stoll, among other critics, denies the pathetic quality of this moment (in *Shakespeare Studies* [New York 1960]), but his argument is wholly unconvincing.
4 See, for example, E.M.W. Tillyard, 'The Trial Scene in *The Merchant of Venice*,' *REL* II 4 (1961) 51-60; Barbara Lewalski, 'Biblical Allusion and Allegory in *The Merchant of Venice*,' *SQ* XIII (1962) 327ff.; Nevill Coghill, 'The Basis of Shakespearean Comedy,' *Essays and Studies* III (1950) 1-28. Let Frank Kermode, in 'The Mature Comedies,' *Early Shakespeare*, ed. J.R. Brown and B. Harris (London 1961) 224, speak for all of these: for him, one must make a determined effort *not* to see the main theme of the play, which 'begins with usury and corrupt love' and 'ends with harmony and perfect love.' Even Derek Traversi, in *An Approach to Shakespeare*, rev. and

enl. ed. (London 1968), considers Shylock primarily as a villain (192) and sees 'Mercy' as the core of the play's meaning (196).

5 C.L. Barber, *Shakespeare's Festive Comedy* (Princeton 1959) 165

6 Northrop Frye, *Anatomy of Criticism* (Princeton 1957) 165

7 Stoll, *Shakespeare Studies* 299. Stoll's attack is two-pronged: first, it is historical; he attempts to show that the expectations of Shakespeare's audience demand that Shylock, being a moneylender and a Jew, be the villain and that he be treated harshly in the end. Second, he takes a structural view, arguing that Shylock is the traditional comic butt and claiming further that his actions and reactions conform to Bergsonian principles of comic behaviour; these characteristics prevent him from ever being in the least pathetic. Stoll insists, too, on the effect of the arrangement of scenes in forming our view of Shylock as villain. Traversi's interpretation (*An Approach to Shakespeare*) makes many of the same points.

8 Stoll, *Shakespeare Studies* 318

9 A.D. Moody, *Shakespeare: The Merchant of Venice* (London 1964). Moody argues that the Prince of Morocco, not Bassanio, is the most deserving suitor. Belmont is nothing more than a 'false pretence' (50) and Portia's 'mercy' is unchristian, more a manifestation of the old law than the new (42). Furthermore, Shylock is an outward manifestation of the inner corruption of the Christians, whose indifference towards the human person is masked by their pretence of goodness and kindness, and his banishment makes him a literal scapegoat by which the Christians attempt to dismiss their inner evil (27-32). Though it may sound extreme, Moody's interpretation is well argued and supported by textual reference.

10 Ralph Berry, *Shakespeare's Comedies* (Princeton 1972) 145 and passim. For him, the play poses the problems represented by the polar opposition of critics like Kermode and Moody, but leaves us without sufficient 'guidance' as to its final attitude towards them.

11 Berry, *Shakespeare's Comedies* 135-6. 'Stage melodrama, with its ogreish knife-sharpening,' is ill suited to communicating the truth of the metaphor of exacting a pound of flesh. My contention, however, is that the 'ogreish knife-sharpening' is part, though only part, of Shakespeare's dramatic point.

12 D.J. Palmer points out the magic of Portia's role: 'Her acquisition of the arts that she practises in [the trial] scene is as magical as Bassanio's choice of the right casket.' See '*The Merchant of Venice*, or the Importance of Being Earnest,' *Shakespearean Comedy* (London 1972) 115. Her magic thus overpowers the sorcery of Shylock, a fact indicated also by her apparently magical connection with the return of Antonio's ships at the end.

13 See I.i.62 and II.vii.25 for examples.

14 Antonio has been seen variously as a repressed homosexual (eg, John Wain,
   The Living World of Shakespeare [London 1964] 78-9), as a compulsive,
   'passive-feminine gambler' (Berry, *Shakespeare's Comedies* 132), and as an
   'endogenous depressive' (W.D. Scott, *Shakespeare's Melancholics* [London
   1962] 35-46; cited in Berry, *Shakespeare's Comedies* 132n). D.J. Palmer's
   corrective commentary seems especially helpful here. 'Critics,' he writes,
   'who try like Salerio and Solanio to discover the cause of this sadness are
   wilfully ignoring its dramatic point.' It exists primarily as a 'loss of inner
   equilibrium,' which fittingly introduces a 'sense of things drawing apart
   into opposite extremes' and 'sets in motion the forces of division ... which
   will take the play to the brink of tragedy' ('*The Merchant of Venice*, or
   The Importance of Being Earnest' 103-4).
15 See Geoffrey Bullough, *Narrative and Dramatic Sources of Shakespeare* I
   (London 1957) 460 and 514.
16 I am indebted to Barber, *Shakespeare's Festive Comedy* 182, for this point.
17 *Shakespeare's Comedies* 132

CHAPTER 2: *As You Like It*

1 In *Twelfth Night*, Viola's disguise is subordinate to the twin motif from
   which most of the confusion arises. Viola's unmasking before the entrance
   or marriage of Sebastian would not solve the comic problem as would a
   similar unmasking on the part of Rosalind.
2 Some recent critics have argued that the 'power struggle' in Act I is an
   important thematic motif throughout the play and have maintained that
   the events of that act must not be written off as external but necessary.
   See especially Ralph Berry, *Shakespeare's Comedies* (Princeton 1972)
   177-8, and also Thomas McFarland, *Shakespeare's Pastoral Comedy*
   (Chapel Hill 1972) 98-101. Although Berry in particular makes a good
   case, I do not find his argument convincing for the reasons adduced in the
   rest of this paragraph. Shakespeare seems too intent on making these opening situations unreal.
3 Both Harold Jenkins (in '*As You Like It*,' *Shakespeare Survey* VII (1955)
   40-51) and Helen Gardner (in '*As You Like It*,' *More Talking of Shakespeare*,
   ed. John Garrett [London 1959] 17-32) remark on the absence of plot in
   the play.
4 See Northrop Frye, *Anatomy of Criticism* (Princeton 1957) 116, and
   A Natural Perspective (New York 1965) 73-4, for a discussion of what he
   calls 'irrational laws' (though the term 'arbitrary' might be more appropriate)
   and their function in comedy.

5 This idea is implicit in David Young's examination of Shakespeare's treatment of the pastoral tradition in *As You Like It*. See *The Heart's Forest* (New Haven 1972) Ch. 2.

6 This is a feature of *As You Like It* that has been commented on at length by various critics, originally by Harold Jenkins in his excellent essay on the play (cited in note 3 above) and C.L. Barber (in *Shakespeare's Festive Comedy*); more recently by David Young, *The Heart's Forest* and Thomas McFarland, *Shakespeare's Pastoral Comedy*. I will therefore limit my own remarks.

7 The term is Barber's.

8 Nearly all critics have something to say about this aspect of their roles. See, for example, Frye's *Natural Perspective* 93-101, for a discussion of the *idiotes* and clown figures, who have an important structural function similar to that discussed here.

9 See John Dover Wilson, *Shakespeare's Happy Comedies* (London 1962) 158.

10 For McFarland, Jaques is 'the figure who does most to define the idiosyncratic strain of malaise' in the play, though his criticism is balanced and sometimes mocked by Touchstone (*Shakespeare's Pastoral Comedy* 106-7). For both Young and Berry, Jaques, in the words of the latter, 'finds himself caricatured by the moralizing fool' (*Shakespeare's Comedies* 182).

11 McFarland makes this same point (*Shakespeare's Pastoral Comedy* 109).

12 Both Frye, *Natural Perspective* 103-4, and Barber, *Festive Comedy* 227-9, 232, discuss this aspect of the role of such figures.

13 The word is used here in Barber's sense to refer to a restriction of awareness; see his discussion of the 'sentimentality' of the exclusion of Falstaff at the end of *Henry IV*, Pt II; *Shakespeare's Festive Comedy* 216-20.

14 Thomas Lodge, *Rosalynde: Euphues' Golden Legacy* in Bullough, *Narrative and Dramatic Sources of Shakespeare* II, 211

15 One example of this is the system of 'discrepant awareness' discussed by Bertrand Evans in *Shakespeare's Comedy* (London 1960).

16 Barber uses the term 'clarification' throughout his book. See especially his first chapter.

17 Philip Edwards, in *Shakespeare and the Confines of Art* (London 1968) 61, notes the social nature of Hymen's wedding song.

CHAPTER 3: *Hamlet*

1 *Henry IV* provides, perhaps, an earlier instance, but it can be argued that Hal's role-playing and manipulation are primarily a means of personal growth. In *Richard III* as well as in several pre-Shakespearian plays (one need not look

any farther than Marlowe or Kyd), the dominant figure of the manipulating Machiavel is very much in evidence. Looking back to the chronicles, at Tudor morality plays, at More's history of Richard III, we become aware that Shakespeare, in presenting Claudius and his cohorts, and to some extent Hamlet himself, as scheming and manipulative, was participating in a well-established tradition. In relating Hamlet's activity to the comic modes which Shakespeare had developed before writing this play, as I do in this chapter, I am not disputing the connection between Hamlet and his Machiavellian forebears. I am trying to establish another connection, however, one that places *Hamlet* in the context of Shakespeare's development and opens up the play to political and structural analysis.

2 Michael Walzer made this point in a lecture on *Hamlet* at Harvard University, in which he examined the view and role of the court in the play and Hamlet's reactions to the courtly style.

3 John Dover Wilson, *What Happens in Hamlet* (Cambridge 1935) Ch. 2

4 For Hamlet's switching of roles in this scene, see Nigel Alexander's *Poison, Play and Duel* (London 1971) 85-6, 115-16.

5 G. Wilson Knight calls it both 'ritual and symbol' and sees it as a manifestation of the 'insecure balance of opposites' in the play (*The Wheel of Fire* [NY 1965] 323). Nigel Alexander, *Poison, Play and Duel*, has organized his whole book around this, and two other important symbolic motifs, poison and play.

6 Cicero, *De Oratore*, ed. and trans. E.W. Sutton (Loeb Classical Library, London 1948) I.viii.33. Quoted in William Nelson, *The Poetry of Edmund Spenser* (NY 1963) 27-8

7 Samuel Daniel, *Musophilus*. First published in 1599, II.939-48. Also quoted in Nelson, *The Poetry of Edmund Spenser* 28

8 Maurice Charney, in *Style in Hamlet* (Princeton 1969), notes Claudius's use of a 'polished' and 'embellished' style which, he says, tends to suggest hypocrisy. He observes as well that this style often merges with a simple, direct style which suggests determination (221-2). In general, Charney's book provides a useful description of the various styles in the play.

9 L.C. Knights, in *An Approach to Hamlet* (London 1960), calls attention to the irony of Claudius mentioning the 'first corse.'

10 Francis Bacon, 'Of Discourse,' in *Selected Writings of Francis Bacon*, ed. H.G. Dick (NY 1955) 89

11 Walzer (see note 2) refers to this process, though in a different context, and argues that it marks the moment when the traditional view becomes an 'ideology.'

12 Henry V refers to the *responsibilities* of kingship and bemoans the fact that subjects lay such responsibilities:

> Upon the king, let us our lives, our souls,
> Our debts, our careful wives, our children
> And our sins, lay on the king: we must bear all ...
> And what have kings, that privates have not too,
> Save Ceremony, save general Ceremony? (IV.i.247-56)

13 Charney, *Style in Hamlet* 256-7

14 Charney calls this style 'passionate.' In addition, he describes a self-conscious and parodic style which Hamlet uses to deflate the styles of others and to attack the 'malevolent circumlocution of the court style.' In all, Charney sees Hamlet using four styles, the two just mentioned, the 'witty' (which I dealt with above), and the 'simple' (to which I will turn later).

15 See Brian Vickers, *The Artistry of Shakespeare's Prose* (London 1968) 254-5, for a perceptive rhetorical analysis of this speech which supports the point made here.

16 Both Charney and Vickers comment on the simple, direct nature of this language. Charney especially sees behind it a kind of 'tragic calm' and 'tranquil self-assurance,' which I agree is there, but much more precariously and ambiguously than he seems to believe (*Style in Hamlet* 311).

17 Jones's perceptive idea (in *Hamlet and Oedipus*, London 1949, Chs. 6 and 7) that Polonius represents one part of a tripartite father-figure – the 'senile babbler' – also helps to explain Hamlet's attack.

18 Cf. Maynard Mack, 'The World of Hamlet' in *Shakespeare: Modern Essays in Criticism*, ed. Leonard Dean (NY 1968) 242-62. Mack sees the play-within as 'the full extension of [the appearance and reality] theme' in that it dissolves 'the normal barrier between the fictive and the real' (253). But he does not extend the notion of this theatrical ambiguity (which is, as I have argued, typically comic) into the question of the moral status of illusion and illusion-making.

19 As Dover Wilson argues, I think persuasively, in *What Happens in Hamlet*, 105-7

20 See my chapters on these plays for a full discussion of the way the theatrical techniques employed by the play as a whole are utilized within the play in such a way as to elicit audience acceptance and belief.

21 Unless we are willing to take Hamlet's easy rationalization in III.iii at face value, the inability to kill Claudius and the ease in killing Polonius, whom Hamlet supposedly believes (or half believes) to be Claudius, is a contradiction which can, I think, best be resolved by the psychoanalytic idea that Polonius and Claudius (together with Hamlet senior) collectively represent a decomposed father-figure; the result being that the mixed feelings normally felt towards an actual father are directed in three different ways. Symbolically,

then, Hamlet can kill the 'senile babbler' part of his father but not the husband of his mother part, since with that latter part Hamlet has a strong identification. See Jones, Chs 6-7.

22 Wilson, *What Happens in Hamlet* 96-8

23 See Angus Fletcher, *Allegory: The Theory of a Symbolic Mode* (Ithaca 1964) Ch. 2, for a discussion of the emblematic nature of dress. Note also the first scene of *Julius Caesar*, in which the tribunes attack the commoners for walking about 'without the *sign*' of their 'profession.'

24 Michel Foucault, *Madness and Civilization* (NY 1967), Ch. 1

25 Foucault 38. In a later chapter, Foucault describes how theatrical illusion was used as a method of treatment and again makes a parallel point: 'the imagination must play its own game, voluntarily propose new images, espouse delirium for delirium's sake, and without opposition or confrontation, without even a visible dialectic, must, paradoxically, cure. Health must lay siege to madness and conquer it in the very nothingness in which the disease is imprisoned ... Illusion can cure the illusory ...' (154).

26 My ideas here overlap somewhat with those of Theodore Spencer in *Shakespeare and the Nature of Man* (NY 1951). He sees in Hamlet's consciousness a conflict between the 'light' and 'dark' views of man's nature which were in conflict in Renaissance culture, but he does not define Hamlet's problems in terms of the conflict he describes. See Hiram Haydn's *The Counter-Renaissance* (NY 1950) for a full treatment of the 'darker,' counter-humanist trends throughout the Renaissance.

27 It seems to me that it can refer as easily to Hamlet's love for Ophelia as to Gertrude's former love for Hamlet's father. Perhaps both meanings merge in his mind.

28 See Robert Altick, 'Symphonic Imagery in *Richard II*,' *PMLA* LXII (1947) 339-65, for a full discussion of this and other patterns of imagery in the play.

29 See my final chapter for a full discussion of this whole theme. My presentation of it here is necessarily rather sketchy.

30 Jan Kott, *Shakespeare Our Contemporary* (NY 1966) 62

31 Wilson, *What Happens in Hamlet* 261, points to the irony of 'thoughts' rather than deeds here. Such an irony adds to my point that the details of language in the speech work against the main theme.

32 See, for example, the work of some of the most eminent critics: Bradley, Spencer, Wilson, Mack, Levin. A few critics seem to recognize the split between a tranquil, resigned Hamlet and an impulsive, highly political, almost ruthless Hamlet with a flair for theatrical destruction. Virgil Whittaker, in *The Mirror up to Nature*, sees a division in the final scene between Christian and non-Christian material. L.C. Knights (*An Approach to Hamlet*) regards

the 'Readiness is all' speech as partly ironic, as a 'paradoxical recognition of a truth glimpsed in defeat' (89). Knights's discussion of the last scene seems to me the only adequate one, one that responds to everything that's there. I owe something to his reading but see the scene in a very different context and take a different approach to it.

33 Harley Granville-Barker, *Prefaces to Shakespeare*, Third Series (London 1937) 307, 316. Nigel Alexander, *Poison, Play and Duel* in a similar vein, argues that Hamlet 'wins at the odds' in his 'duel' with Claudius, because he has 'sufficient command of the necessary arts of actor, soldier, and politician' (198). But as I have argued, his command of these arts is ambiguous and his victory seems Pyrrhic.

34 Wilson, *What Happens in Hamlet* 217, 275

35 A.C. Bradley, *Shakespearean Tragedy* (London 1904) 420-1

CHAPTER 4: *A Midsummer Night's Dream, Twelfth Night, Troilus and Cressida*

1 In this chapter, and again in Chapter 7, I extend my theme over a range of plays which do not conform strictly to the disguise structure I have been discussing but which do exhibit some features of that structure and form some important thematic links with the other plays. I have selected one or two scenes from each play as a focus for discussion, the centre of a web which I try to trace, in at least some of its intricacies, as it extends to the rest of the play.

2 My approach here and throughout this section is similar to that of David Young in his book *Something of Great Constancy* (New Haven 1966). Some of our conclusions, too, corroborate each other.

3 These lines are especially appropriate to the mood of *Romeo and Juliet*, a kind of companion piece to *A Midsummer Night's Dream*. Juliet, in fact, is given a speech similar to Lysander's. See *R & J*, II.ii.119, and Barber, *Shakespeare's Festive Comedy* (Princeton 1959) 126.

4 A feature of the lovers' change emphasized by Barber, *Shakespeare's Festive Comedy* 129-30, and implied by Young, *Something of Great Constancy* 156.

5 See John Russell Brown, *Shakespeare and His Comedies* (London 1957) Ch. 4, passim. Later commentators such as Young and Stephen Fender (*Shakespeare: A Midsummer Night's Dream*, London 1968), also draw attention to this motif.

6 Enid Welsford makes this analogy in *The Court Masque* (Cambridge 1927) 331-2.

7 See my chapter on *The Tempest* for a full discussion and documentation of these relationships.

8 The term 'mature' is Frank Kermode's. Hallet Smith (*Shakespeare's Romances*, San Marino, CA 1972, Ch. 7), along with a number of other critics, sees significant connections between *A Midsummer Night's Dream* and *The Tempest*.

9 The association of main plot and comic subplot and the connections between the play within and the play as a whole are explored by a good many critics (eg, J.R. Brown, David Young, and Thomas McFarland to name a few) and I have therefore kept my remarks to a minimum. Ralph Berry, *Shakespeare's Comedies* (Princeton 1972) 106, describes one aspect of the relationship succinctly: 'The lovers declare illusion to be reality; the actors declare reality to be illusion.'

10 This element is stressed (overstressed, in fact) by Jan Kott in *Shakespeare Our Contemporary* (NY 1966) 225-7.

11 Young, *Something of Great Constancy* 91, 125, and 151, makes much of this epilogue, arguing that it draws a circle of theatrical artifice around the other 'concentric circles' of the play world; furthermore, it connects the ideas of dream and play and it bridges the gap between art and nature.

12 John Dover Wilson, *Shakespeare's Happy Comedies* (London 1962) 170

13 See Harold Jenkins, 'Shakespeare's *Twelfth Night*,' in K. Muir, ed., *Shakespeare: The Comedies* (Englewood Cliffs, NJ 1965) 84-6.

14 A key word in the play, as Barber points out, *Shakespeare's Festive Comedy* 242.

15 Bullough, *Narrative and Dramatic Sources*, II (London 1963) 353

16 Joseph Summers, 'The Masks of *Twelfth Night*,' in L. Dean, ed., *Shakespeare: Modern Essays in Criticism* (NY 1961) 134

17 See my chapters on these plays for a full discussion.

18 Wilson, *Shakespeare's Happy Comedies* 169, and Herschel Baker, introduction to Signet *Twelfth Night* (NY 1965) xxx. At moments during the play, Viola's disguise seems to be designed partly to educate, especially in the ironic wooing scene with Olivia and in the scene in which she tells Orsino her life story. But the ultimate success of such 'education' is a matter of debate; and it seems clear that Viola herself does not go through a learning process comparable to that of Rosalind, say. Jenkins, 'Shakespeare's *Twelfth Night*,' makes a good case for the point of view that Olivia and Orsino do learn something, but his argument does not seem to me to fully fit either the facts or the spirit of the play.

19 In later plays, especially *King Lear*, a refusal to admit the evidence of the senses leads to new vision; this seems to be part of the point of the Gloucester plot. See Chapter 7.

20 L.C. Knights, '*Troilus and Cressida* Again,' *Scrutiny* XVIII (1951) 156

21 See D.A. Traversi, *An Approach to Shakespeare* (NY 1956) 330-2, for a perceptive commentary on such language.

22 Ibid. 331

23 W. Nowottny (in 'Opinion and Value in *Troilus and Cressida*,' *Essays in Criticism* IV [1954] 282-96) makes a similar point but sees an opposition between Greek 'opinion' and genuine 'value' on the part of the Trojans.

24 Shakespeare, and probably most of his audience, would have known that in the traditional story Achilles eventually kills Troilus.

CHAPTER 5: *All's Well that Ends Well*

1 Anne Righter, *Shakespeare and the Idea of the Play* (London 1962) 176

2 Northrop Frye, in *Anatomy of Criticism* (Princeton 1957) 164ff., discusses the conventional role of 'blocking characters,' whose function is to impede the successful resolution of the hero's and/or heroine's desires and hence create the comic problem.

3 It is significant that Shakespeare has added both the Countess and Lafew, neither of whom appears in the source.

4 This touches the point that some critics have seen at the heart of the play, the Renaissance debate as to what constitutes true nobility, birth, or merit. See M.C. Bradbrook, *Shakespeare and Elizabethan Poetry* (London 1951) 162-70.

5 W.W. Lawrence (in *Shakespeare's Problem Comedies*, New York 1930) points out that her magical powers and the tasks she is put through are related to ancient folklore motifs. Both G.K. Hunter (in his introduction to the Arden edition, Cambridge, MA 1959, p xlii) and Northrop Frye (in *Natural Perspective*, New York 1965, p 64) argue a symbolic connection between her virginity and her power to heal.

6 Lawrence, *Shakespeare's Problem Comedies* 79, 119. Lawrence notes this process in *Measure for Measure* but not in *All's Well that Ends Well*.

7 The ensuing discussion of the relation of *All's Well that Ends Well* to its source assumes a knowledge of that source – a tale from Boccaccio's *Decameron*, the ninth novel of the third day. It was translated by William Painter and published as the thirty-eighth novel in his *Palace of Pleasure* (1566, 1569, 1575). Shakespeare probably used Painter's version, which has been reprinted in Geoffrey Bullough, *Narrative and Dramatic Sources of Shakespeare* II (London 1963) 389-96.

8 Bullough 391

9 Ibid. 392

10 See Lawrence, *Shakespeare's Problem Comedies* 39-54, for analogues and discussion of this motif.

11 For a full discussion of the whole issue, see Hunter, Arden edition, *All's Well that Ends Well* xvi-xxi.

12 E.M.W. Tillyard makes a similar point about this speech in *Shakespeare's Problem Plays* (London 1950) 101.

13 See Eric Partridge, *Shakespeare's Bawdy* (NY 1948) 78, 136.

14 See Hunter, Arden edition, *All's Well that Ends Well* 106n.

15 Ibid.

16 Cited ibid. 19n

17 Bullough, *Narrative and Dramatic Sources of Shakespeare* 392

18 As Lawrence shows (*Shakespeare's Problem Comedies* 34-7), older critics regarded it as evidence of Helena's moral degeneracy and the most obvious instance of the play's general disagreeableness. A more recent example of this view is Clifford Leech's discussion of Helena's 'ambition' and 'deceptiveness' in the context of the 'satiric background' of the play ('The Theme of Ambition in *All's Well*,' *ELH* XXI [1954] 17-29). Since Lawrence, many critics have seen the bed trick as an essential element of the deliberately archaic plot. Combining the two views, A.P. Rossiter presents Helena as primarily a fairy-tale heroine in a bitterly 'realistic' world; her solutions are thus 'in conflict with the realistic psychological exposure' in the depiction of Bertram, Parolles, etc. (*Angel with Horns*, London [1961] 100). Most recently, Howard Felperin (in *Shakespearean Romance*, Princeton 1972) describes the bed trick as a form of 'shock treatment' within the romantic context, and argues, as I do, that there is a taint in the art of both Helena and the Duke in *Measure for Measure* (92-3).

19 I here depart from the text I have been using throughout, that of G.L. Kittredge, and retain the Folio reading 'lawful meaning in a lawful act' in place of Kittredge's unnecessary emendation, '... wicked act.'

20 Rossiter, *Angel with Horns* 101-2

21 The kind of awareness evident in such speeches is what most distinguishes her from the heroines of Lawrence's analogues, who are totally devoid of an inner life or moral sensitivity. This is where Lawrence, or anyone who attempts to interpret the play merely in terms of the conventions it uses, gets into trouble. Shakespeare is very much aware of the conventional and essentially illusory quality of the stories he is using. His introduction of questioning, undercutting elements thus implies that he is interested in calling attention to the disparity between these stories and a full representation of reality. It is the inclusion of both types of elements and the resulting tension which make up his total statement.

22 Hunter, Arden edition, *All's Well that Ends Well* liv-lvi
23 Ibid, liv. For a full discussion of this theme, see R.G. Hunter, *Shakespeare and the Comedy of Forgiveness* (New York 1965).
24 See Lawrence, *Shakespeare's Problem Comedies* 35, 62-4.

CHAPTER 6: *Measure for Measure*

1 Philip Edwards, *Shakespeare and the Confines of Art* (London 1968) 117
2 Tillyard, *Shakespeare's Problem Plays* (London 1950) 128-9
3 J.W. Lever, introduction to the Arden edition of *Measure for Measure* (Cambridge, MA 1965) lxviii-lxxii
4 See ibid. 49n, for commentary on the two meanings of 'season' and the extended meaning of 'virtue.'
5 G. Wilson Knight, *The Wheel of Fire* (London 1949) 94
6 Discussed by Lever lxxxiii-xci
7 The speech ends with one of the frequent images of writing and engraving that occur in the play and that generally refer to problems of perception and knowledge. (The relation of such writing to sexual 'knowledge' is brought out by Claudio when he says that 'it chances / The stealth of our most mutual entertainment / With character too gross is writ on Juliet' I.ii.157-9). The Duke says to Angelo early in the play, 'There is a kind of character in thy life, / That to th' observer doth thy history / Fully unfold' (I.i.27-9), giving us both an example of the image and an instance of misreading, of mistaking the appearance for the reality. At the end, the Duke says again to Angelo, though this time with full ironic consciousness, 'O your desert speaks loud, and ... it deserves, with characters of brass, / A forted residence 'gainst the tooth of time / And razure of oblivion' (V.i.9-13). This time he is using the image in a double sense: as a mode of supposedly genuine praise and as an instance of what he knows would be a *false* perception on the part of the 'readers' of such characters. That is, to read (or rather misread) Angelo's virtue in such externalized characters is the metaphorical equivalent of reading (or misreading) his brow and finding virtue there. This is a kind of inversion of the metaphor. But it still points to the same thing – how difficult it is to know and hence to judge a person's 'character.'
8 Tillyard, *Problem Plays* 123-5
9 W.W. Lawrence, *Shakespeare's Problem Comedies* (New York 1930) 111
10 See Knight, *The Wheel of Fire*, Ch. 4; R.W. Battenhouse, '*Measure for Measure* and the Christian Doctrine of Atonement,' *PMLA* LXI (1946) 1029-59. Josephine Bennett, in *Measure for Measure as Royal Entertainment* (New York 1966), seems undecided whether the Duke is God or merely

James I. For an effective attack on such theological criticism, see D.L.
Stevenson, *The Achievement of Shakespeare's Measure for Measure*
(Ithaca, NY 1966) Ch. 4.

11 R.W. Chambers, '*Measure for Measure*,' in *Shakespeare: The Comedies*,
   ed. K. Muir (Englewood Cliffs, NJ 1965) 106

12 Anne Righter comments acutely on the Duke's 'managerial role': the
   'actions he contrives continually seem to escape from his control.' She
   mentions Barnardine as an example of this and argues that the Duke is
   'committed to the idea of life as a thing poised and susceptible to rule'
   whereas reality is too 'turbulent' for such regulation (*Shakespeare and the
   Idea of the Play* 178, 180).

13 Lever *Measure for Measure*, Arden edition, xc

14 Howard Felperin (in *Shakespearean Romance* 94-5) argues that there is a
   taint in the art of both the Duke and Helena, but I think his point applies
   more directly to the former, since he claims that part of the taint comes
   from a lack of awareness of the limitations of such 'art,' an awareness which
   Helena does exhibit.

15 The fact that the Duke makes a play out of the last scene (complete with
   its own five-act structure) has been noticed also by Josephine Bennett,
   Measure for Measure as Royal Entertainment 131-3. Such a correspondence
   between her view and my own should carry some weight since in almost
   every other respect I disagree with her conclusions, most especially her
   determination to whitewash the play, to see nothing the least bit unsettling
   or ambiguous in it.

16 Commentators who take Angelo's comparison as though it were the key to
   Shakespeare's intention – hence seeing the play as a Christian parable – fail
   to take into account Angelo's state of mind at this point and thus confuse a
   character's response with the author's statement of meaning.

17 The word 'characts,' for example, alludes to the imagery of distinctive mark-
   ings, especially written characters, which can be read, or so easily misread.
   See 7 above.

18 See Suzanne K. Langer, 'The Great Dramatic Forms: The Comic Rhythm,'
   in *Theories of Comedy*, ed. Paul Lauter (NY 1964) 497-522; also, Frye,
   Anatomy of Criticism 163ff.

19 See Barber 216ff., for a discussion of the meaning and effect of this problem
   in *Henry IV*.

20 Knight, *The Wheel of Fire* 90

21 My whole discussion of this final scene may seem to support an interesting
   argument made by Felperin (*Shakespearean Romance* 95-6), that Shakespeare's 'design' was to show the inadequacy of the 'designs within the

play.' I would argue that the way Shakespeare uses comic techniques in this play indicates his disaffection with them. But I do not think that he exhibits the sort of control over his material that Felperin's argument implies: there is too much strain without adequate resolution.

CHAPTER 7: *King Lear, Antony and Cleopatra, The Winter's Tale*

1 S.T. Coleridge, *Coleridge on Shakespeare*, ed. T. Hawkes, Penguin Shakespeare Library (Harmondsworth 1969) 201

2 A.C. Bradley, *Shakespearean Tragedy* 264

3 See Robert Heilman, *This Great Stage: Image and Structure in King Lear* (Baton Rouge 1948), for a full discussion of this, and other, pervasive patterns of imagery.

4 See H. Granville-Barker, *Prefaces to Shakespeare*, First Series (London 1940) 141-3, for some good comments on this. He refutes Lamb's and Bradley's contention that *King Lear* is 'too huge' for the stage.

5 This is the same scene that Harry Levin has analyzed in his essay, 'The Heights and the Depths: A Scene from *King Lear*,' in *More Talking of Shakespeare*, John Garret, ed. (NY 1959).

6 See *Shakespeare's Festive Comedy*. Barber has used the same term to refer to *Antony and Cleopatra*.

7 See *Civilization and Its Discontents*, passim.

8 David Young, in discussing the superior reality of dreams, comments acutely on this passage: 'All the conventional distinctions between fact and fantasy, shadow and substance, dreaming and waking, and art and nature are broken down here to make room in the historical imagination for Antony's greatness, exaggerated and insubstantial, but somehow more real than the living Caesar ... Cleopatra joins the long list of Shakespearean characters who lose their confidence in the easy dichotomies of the reasonable and practical world.' *Something of Great Constancy* (New Haven 1966) 122

9 Barbara Everett, in the introduction to the Signet edition of the play (New York 1964), xxxv, makes this connection.

10 *Hamlet* has a comic scene between Ophelia's death and Hamlet's, but the focus of interest is almost exclusively on Hamlet, making Ophelia's death more incidental than central.

11 Barber (see n6) used this term to describe the end of the play, but in quite a different context.

12 Douglas L. Peterson, in *Time, Tide and Tempest* (San Marino 1973), devotes a good deal of attention to the importance of memory and belief in the process of renewal.

13 Taking the lead from J.I.M. Stewart (*Character and Motive in Shakespeare*), C.L. Barber has argued that Leontes' jealousy is a result of repressed homosexual feelings toward Polixenes. Such feelings can, according to Freud, result in extreme jealousy, the dynamic being, 'I don't love him, she loves him.' Thus, for Barber, the relationship with Polixenes must be *legitimately* re-established prior to that with Hermione. The way this is done, of course, is through the children, whose heterosexual love is reconciling and life-giving.

14 See S.L. Bethell, *The Winter's Tale: A Study* (London 1947) 47ff. and David Young, *The Heart's Forest* (New Haven 1972) 106. Young goes on to describe the late plays as 'experiments in the fabulatory, investigations of the fictive' (108). See also Northrop Frye, 'Recognition in *The Winter's Tale*,' in *Fables of Identity* (New York 1963); and E.C. Pettet, *Shakespeare and the Romance Tradition* (London 1949) 178. D.L. Peterson, *Time, Tide and Tempest*, argues that there are no real crudities of technique, that elaborate, thematically significant parallelisms (involving especially Autolycus in IV.iv) account for such structuring.

15 Howard Felperin, in *Shakespearean Romance* (Princeton 1972), describes the 'romantic verisimilitude' of the play, stressing its 'combination of romantic design with mimetic fidelity to life as we know it' (216). The greater part of its power comes from this latter quality and Felperin examines carefully how Shakespeare achieves this effect. Young, *The Heart's Forest*, also emphasizes the actuality of the play, but tends to see it as one of two poles, the 'psychological' and 'emblematic,' between which the audience is shuttled back and forth.

16 See Joan Hartwig, *Shakespeare's Tragicomic Vision* (Baton Rouge 1972), for a full discussion of Paulina's roles and their relation to the roles Leontes adopts, especially in the earlier parts of the play (106-8). Her argument is in some ways complementary to my own.

17 My argument about art and nature is similar to those of David Young (*The Heart's Forest* 126-33) and Howard Felperin (*Shakespearean Romance* 239ff.), whose books I read only after completing a draft of this section, although both writers take their analyses in somewhat different directions. Felperin argues that, in the end, all art is repudiated; whereas it seems to me that the magic art of the theatre, which makes it all possible, is celebrated, not rejected.

CHAPTER 8: *The Tempest*

1 I am indebted for this idea to an unpublished essay on the function of rules in games and various aspects of the law by Stephen M. Wexler. This charac-

teristic of chess distinguishes it from many other games (like hockey, for example) where rules can be broken without nullifying the game; instead, other rules are often created as guides for dealing with infractions.

2 Howard Felperin, in *Shakespearean Romance* (Princeton 1972), speaks of the 'almost hermetic self-containment' (249) of *The Tempest*, though in quite a different context. He also draws on analogy between chess and romance (*The Tempest* in particular), but grounds it on the conflict between vices and virtues (282).

3 These themes are discussed fully and (for the most part) convincingly by Frank Kermode in his introduction to the Arden edition of *The Tempest* (Cambridge MA 1954) xxxiv-lix; Leo Marx, 'Shakespeare's American Fable,' *Massachusetts Review* II (Autumn 1960) 40-71; J. Middleton Murry, *Shakespeare* (London 1936) 396ff.; and Felperin, *Shakespearean Romance* 266-7.

4 Claude Lévi-Strauss, *Tristes Tropiques* (New York 1968) Ch. 17, pp. 160-80

5 Quotations, in order, are from pp 168, 170, 179-80 (italics added).

6 Ibid. 180. The idea of dream, which Lévi-Strauss stresses here, provides another link with the play. That *The Tempest* is a dream, or presents life as a dream, has often been argued, and we can at least say that the imagery of dream is pervasive in the play.

7 D.G. James, *The Dream of Prospero* (London 1967) Ch. 2

8 In his excellent essay on the metamorphical design of the play, Reuben Brower discusses Shakespeare's use of 'continuities' of images, the most important of which have to do with storm and sea, and music and noise; all of the continuities are related to the play's 'key metaphor,' that of 'sea-change.' He writes of the passage quoted: 'It is admittedly odd that the confused noise of the tempest should, in Alonso's soul, compose a harmony – however gloomy – but the paradox fits in perfectly with the developing structure of the play. Alonso has just been told by Ariel that the storm had a purpose as an instrument of Destiny. Since at this moment remorse first appears in the play and the inner clearing begins, it is exactly right that storm sounds should seem harmonious and so point forward to the events of the fourth and fifth acts.' *Fields of Light* (New York 1951) 117

9 Some of these are mentioned by Anne Righter in *Shakespeare and the Idea of the Play* (London 1964). Although she takes her argument in a very different direction, Righter makes some similar points to mine. She comments that 'in *The Tempest*, the condition of the actor and the man in the theatre have become identical' (204). As I shall indicate, I don't think this is strictly true since there are important distinctions between actor, character, and audience member; I don't agree that *The Tempest* blurs these distinctions and hence leads right into the Jacobean masque. But her point is a fruitful one nonetheless.

10 Felperin also raises this point, arguing that Antonio's 'art,' like that of Prospero's retirement, is devoid of 'ethical and social concern' and hence 'collapses into egocentricity' (*Shakespearean Romance* 269-70).

11 Marx, 'Shakespeare's American Fable' 64-5; see also Philip Brockbank, '*The Tempest:* Conventions of Art and Empire,' in *Later Shakespeare*, ed. J.R. Brown (London 1966) 195.

12 The phrase is from Robert Langbaum's introduction to the Signet edition of *The Tempest* (New York 1964) xxxiii. Langbaum develops a similar idea about the masque, though in a highly concentrated form.

13 Brower, *Fields of Light* 115-16

14 G. Wilson Knight, *The Crown of Life* (London 1961) 246

15 See, for example, John Dover Wilson, *The Meaning of The Tempest* (Newcastle 1936) 16-17, for the former view, and E.M.W. Tillyard, *Shakespeare's Last Plays* (London 1961) 50-1, for the latter.

16 Brower, *Fields of Light* 118-19, relates ll 64-8 directly to Prospero's 'revels' speech.

17 Leo Kirschbaum emphasizes this aspect in '*The Tempest* – Apologetics or Spectacle?' in *Two Lectures on Shakespeare* (London 1961) 29-40.

Index